Shadows of Flight

Shadows of Flight

RICHARD JENKINS

Library of Congress Control Number:		2016913902
ISBN:	Hardcover	978-1-5144-9834-7
	Softcover	978-1-5144-9405-9
	eBook	978-1-5144-9404-2

Print information available on the last page.

Rev. date: 09/06/2016

To order additional copies of this book, contact:
Xlibris
800-056-3182
www.Xlibrispublishing.co.uk
Orders@Xlibrispublishing.co.uk
734319

Contents

After eight years of short service commission in the Royal Navy, which ended flying the latest supersonic jet fighter from the deck of an aircraft carrier, the writer moved to a new challenge, that of starting a farm in the wilds of the African bush in northern Rhodesia, or the dreaded Black North. After nearly twenty years as a successful farmer, growing tobacco and maize whilst ranching cattle on an adjoining farm, he returned to the commercial flying world as a charter pilot. He ended his career as an airline training captain, flying BAC 1-11 aircraft around the sunny Mediterranean.

This is the story of an ordinary individual named Richard Jenkins, whose philosophy in life is that "with God's help, anyone can do anything." This philosophy stood him in good stead throughout his life, whether being catapulted from aircraft carriers, bracing against the "winds of change" blowing over the farming area of Mkushi in the newly independent African state of Zambia, or trekking up to eighteen thousand feet in the Himalayas.

This book, written in an easy descriptive style, takes the reader on a long, unusual, and fascinating story of his experiences, which have not ended yet.

Acknowledgements

When I started writing this book, I could not type. I called on several people to assist me. Sally my wife naturally came in for typing more than her fair share, at which time I was getting grammar corrections and suggestions from Betty Turner. I went further afield to Lynda Jones, who offered to help out when Sally could not spare time for typing, and I asked her to make constructive criticisms at the same time. She found my story to be interesting enough to ask for more and more information to be added, where I had thought to gloss over much of the present story and just concentrate on our years in Africa. As a result, I started again from the beginning, making the book the story of my life ... an autobiography. So I have Lynda to thank for the extended book with which I have ended up.

Finally, my sister Joan came up trumps and typed the manuscript on her computer for me, taking some ninety-four hours of steady typing.

Without the help of these four ladies this book would never have got off the ground, and I am extremely grateful to them all and hope they enjoy the final article in which they played their part.

Richard

Preface

Lania-Cyprus, July 1996

In the cool of the morning, sitting at a table in the courtyard of a village cottage in Lania, I set pen to paper, inspired to paint a verbal picture of some of the interesting events of my life and of some of the people I have been pleased to call my friends during the last sixty years.

I have two good reasons for doing this, although I know it will be hard work. Firstly, having spent thirty years in Africa, much of my story will be of that fascinating country, which was feeling the "winds of change" from colonial rule to that of a newly independent African state. At the time, I was young and energetic, as ignorant as youth can be but unaware of that ignorance, as confidence in myself and my ability took pride of place. I was newly married to an equally dynamic, intelligent, and lovely young woman, keen to see me working near home rather than flying away for days at a time with a large airline. So we bravely set out to make our lives in the raw African bush, starting a farm from a piece of Africa that had probably never been farmed before.

We made many friends there who have remained loving friends to this day, the sort with whom you are immediately at ease should you call on them unexpectedly after many years of absence. Many of those friends would like some small written record of what went on in our farming area of Mkushi, and as I have the information, gleaned from a box file of letters written to my parents over those years, and I have the time and inclination to attempt this story, what better reason could I have?

In fact, I have another reason, which may be better.

Family history is in the main confined to the compilation of family trees and tracing back through church registers to names of the long distant past. Unless you happen across a well-known name about whom some historical facts are known or a story has been written, nothing further is likely to be discovered about that person. My father was probably an interesting man in his own way, having been in Cambrai, France, in the First World War at the age of sixteen, whilst in the Second World War, he was at Imphal in Burma when it was cut off by the Japs. But my father was not a communicative man – a family trait I fear – and as I was on the threshold of my life, with little time to waste on past years, the result was that I learned little of interest of a salient part of my father's life. What of my grandfather, who used to take me as a child to see the Elephant and Castle line trains at Carpenders Park, where he then lived with my grandmother? Apart from the fact that he was a publican who moved around London and the Home counties every few years whilst raising four children, I know nothing of him or his way of life. I blame myself, although it is only now that I have retired that I really have time to think of those of the family who have gone before me. I would love to have a book telling of their hopes and fears and of how they enjoyed their lives. Were they successful? Did they encounter tragedy? What sort of friends did they have and where did they live?

For me, those questions will never be answered, but for my children, my children's children, and those in future generations, I shall endeavour to give a picture of my life and that of Sally, my wife, who has stuck by me through thick and thin.

If any of our descendants, on retirement or before, have any desire to know anything about that very ordinary individual named Hugh Richard Jenkins, then here it is. It was written for you and for our very many special friends who have shared our journey through life. It is dedicated to the one who has contributed most and participated fully over the last thirty-seven years since I married her, my wife, Sally Elizabeth.

Chapter 1
The Early Years

I arrived in this world on 29 November 1932. My father, Henry William Alfred, was what was known as a turf accountant (a term he much preferred to bookmaker). After she married my father, my mother, May, was a housewife; prior to her wedding day, she had been a shop assistant. My sister Audrey was born eighteen months before I was, and our sisters Joan and Margaret joined the family within four years after my birth.

Although I was born in a house in Church Road in Watford, I have no memory of it at all. It was a lovely new house at Berceau Walk near Cassiobury Park that stirs my earliest memories. It must have been a lovely house; nowadays, that little cul-de-sac has Mercedes and Porsches parked outside many of the residences. I remember my father's large Hillman car bumping over the unmade road to such an extent that Uncle Jack got out and walked. I remember when the road was first tarred; I can still smell the cauldron of hot tar boiling away at the end of the road. The new pavements made the roads ideal for my tricycle; I wandered far afield whenever I got the chance.

We had a large garden, where I helped my father split logs with axe and wedges. It was my job to hold the metal wedges as he hit them with a large sledgehammer. Perspiration dripped from his body whenever he undertook any manual work.

At the end of the garden lawn was a rockery into which I blindly ran one afternoon. I was searching the sky overhead to sight an aeroplane, an unusual occurrence before the war. I got some dents in my forehead from the rocks – as well as a desire to have something to do with flying.

My bedroom was at the top of a lovely carpeted staircase that folded around the entrance hall. From the top of the stairs, it was possible to drop a small cat onto my grandmother's head – fortunately hatted – without damage to either but a surprise to both (and I was rewarded with a few sharp words).

My room overlooked the garden, so for safety reasons, a dressing table with a large circular mirror was strategically placed to stop me falling from the window. One summer evening, after I had been tucked up in bed by my mother, I heard the noise of yet another aeroplane flying low overhead. Scrambling from my bed, I clambered onto the dressing table to get a good view from the window and accidentally smashed the mirror in the process. *Do broken mirrors bring seven years' bad luck?* I wondered. I believe it's possible. My bad luck started immediately with a few flat hands on my round backside, accompanied by numerous admonishments and threats. It continued a few weeks later when a dog (completely unprovoked, of course) rushed from a neighbour's garden and bit my left heel! The family doctor was called to bandage the wound whilst for a change I received a lot of favourable attention, in which I revelled.

I do not think that I was a bad child. After all, a boy raised with three sisters naturally had to have some spirit, or he would be overwhelmed. I used to like to take a few sips of my mother's 11.00 a.m. Guinness when she wasn't watching. On one occasion, I even managed to open a full bottle in the garden shed. But I would help Audrey with the washing up on the odd occasion that I was unable to escape. It always amazed me how wet the drying-up cloths could get and still be expected to dry things.

Yet, good deeds brought rewards. Dad, having to go to Southend on business with his brother Jack, decided to take me along to my maternal grandmother for the day (she of the cat hat). I don't remember much of my time with this dear, fat, white-haired old lady in the black dress with pretty lace trimmings. She had a smiling face with very soft cheeks and spent most of her time sitting in a rocking chair.

I do remember that when business was finished, Dad collected me, and we went to the enormous fairground nearby. I wasn't keen on the big dipper, which Dad loved, but the giant wheel and the boats which slipped down a large water chute into a pool at the bottom were both scary and thrilling at the same time.

For some reason, we also called in at Southend Airport on the way home. Dad made enquiries about a plane to take the three of us up for a joyride. We looked at several aircraft close by, but none was big enough to take us and the pilot too. Perhaps it was just as well; I may have been put off flying for the rest of my life. Instead, not being able to fly that day only generated a little more interest in a subject which was to play so great a part in my life.

I remember going on holiday on one occasion to a bungalow close to the beach at Bognor Regis and seeing a large airship pass slowly overhead. Dad was not with us (he had to keep his business going), but my mother had some help with my two younger sisters from a nanny who lived in. I did my share where I could, for instance by counting the sacks of coal emptied into the coal cellar by the black-faced coal man. Admittedly, there was more work involved in trying to get me clean afterwards, but the counting was correct.

Shortly before the war broke out in 1939, we took another holiday down in North Devon at the lovely little village of Brendon (or rather, on a farm nearby). Dad drove us all there in his Austin car with a two-wheeled trailer hitched behind and laden with the necessities for four young children for three weeks. We struggled up Porlock Hill (where I was carsick) and, not much later, wound down the equally steep hill into Brendon village.

It was a lovely holiday. The sun blazed, the grass was green, flowers were in bloom everywhere, and we had the freedom to roam around safely wherever we wanted. There were eggs to find under the hens in the yard and lots of creamy milk available from the farmer's wife, who provided us with enormous, delicious meals with plenty of fresh bread and thick Devonshire cream. We went for walks, went exploring, and had picnics by the streams. Dad took me rabbit shooting in the evenings along the edges of the meadows. I even went to school with the farmer's daughter. We walked what appeared to be several miles along winding footpaths to a little building on the top of a hill. I felt brave taking this enormous step voluntarily but had my doubts on my return when it appeared that the rest of the family had enjoyed a better time than I had.

Before we knew it, the memorable holiday was over, and we set off back to Watford. A few weeks later, we went for a picnic on a Sunday morning. As I sat on the grass, watching people fly their kites, we heard on the car radio the news that England and Germany were at war. The sirens wailed their chilling sound. Mum and Dad's faces became suddenly quite grim on what had moments earlier been a lovely day. They said very little by way of explanation, except that we would have shelters to go to if we heard the sirens again in the future. The sunlight had gone out of the day, but we finished our picnic before driving slowly home.

Several months passed before the war had any effect on my sisters or me. Obviously, plans were made and discussed between our parents and other nearby relatives, taking into account all the news of the war to date. All of a sudden, we were packing up, loading the trailer again, and once more heading for Brendon, where Dad had rented a cottage on a long-term basis. He wanted us away from any built-up areas, which could be targets for the German Luftwaffe. Also, he wanted to feel that we were safe so that he could join up, as he did a few weeks later, into the Royal Air Force.

After he left for the RAF, we all set about making our new home in a small cottage that had running water from just one tap outside the back door, a kerosene cooker, Aladdin lamps, no electricity, and a sawdust-and-bucket toilet round the corner. With four children aged nine, seven, four, and two, my poor mother was left to sort herself out and look after us. As a consolation, she was allowed Rose to help her. Rose was a placid girl in her early twenties with a slight humpback. She did not appear to have any life other than helping Mum to look after us, which she did with a will.

I do not know how my mother managed. It was a daunting task she undertook, made even more difficult when one or other of us caught the usual childhood diseases, which then naturally spread through the family. Mumps, measles, and colds: We had the lot! Although Mum complained at times, she had little time for that. She was always busy with the cooking, cleaning, sewing, dressing, and caring for her ungrateful brood.

Audrey and I would be packed off to walk to the school at the top of the hill first thing each morning, regardless of weather. We would each have our sandwich box containing our lunch tucked away in our small satchels. We would get milk at the school. We were taught the basics of reading, writing, and arithmetic and were disciplined by a ruler over the knuckles if we misbehaved. The teachers, who consisted of a mother and daughter, may have had some training, I don't know. They were certainly able to control about thirty children from about six to sixteen years of age without difficulty.

We had small garden plots at the school where we were encouraged to grow vegetables, part of a "Dig for Victory" campaign (on which our small village, fortunately, did not have to rely). We collected every scrap of silver paper that we could find, to help some part of the war effort. This always had to be flattened out for some reason, and I remember having my knuckles rapped for not doing so on one occasion, and one occasion was enough! For the war effort we collected sphagnum moss, from which we understood iodine would be extracted. It had to be nicely cleaned of the twigs and leaves amongst which it thrived before being sent off to some distant collection point. All this appeared to be part of our school curriculum – as was chasing swarms of bees with the school bell. The theory was that the music of the bell would attract a passing swarm of bees and bring them to a halt in an accessible spot. Then armed with her beekeeping outfit, the younger teacher could collect the lot for an empty hive by the school. I remember it worked once; on other occasions, the bees just kept going.

We were well away from the war during those summer months of 1940. It touched us on only a few occasions, when we saw and heard dogfights in the sky high above. I spent my spare time around the local farms, riding horses to the fields and watching them being shod by the local blacksmith, who was also the village barber. We would go picking wortle berries on the slopes of the hills, which fell sharply away to the sea, slopes covered with gorse, bracken, and these little berry bushes. Four of us would travel miles on the two bikes we had between us. I usually sat on the crossbars, an uncomfortable ride but not considered such at the time.

The winter months that year were harsh. The River Lynn, which ran close to our front door, was frozen over, and the hills covered with deep snow drifts. School was closed for several weeks. Well wrapped up against the cold, we were able to throw snow balls and sleigh down the many slopes. Tin trays were the usual order of the day, although one older boy had a proper sledge with steel runners. His sister invited me to go sledging with her one morning, which I accepted with alacrity – the attraction being the sledge and not her. We got to the top of a gentle slope with a hedge at the bottom. She asked me if I knew how to sledge and how to steer. Naturally, my answer had to be in the affirmative; after all, she was only a girl, I was a boy. A few minutes later, she managed to pull me, scratched and bleeding, out of the hedge. My pride was battered more than my body as we returned home for ointment, bandages, and soothing balm from my mother. It's a funny thing: I don't think I ever really liked sledging after that.

The snow changed to rain, a thaw set in, the ice melted, and the river flooded. One morning, Rose failed to return from the outside toilet on schedule, so Mum went investigating, head down and looking carefully to avoid the many puddles. She knocked on the door, calling, "Rose, Rose, are you all right?" to which Rose replied frantically, "Yes, but Madam, look out: There's a bull behind you." With only one way to go, my mother returned undaunted to the back door, which she secured firmly behind her before sending me across the road to alert the postmaster to Rose's predicament.

That night, we heard some German bombers passing over on their way to bomb Cardiff and Swansea. However much we might try to forget there was a war on, it would intrude in our lives when least expected, in some horrible, menacing way.

Very infrequently, Dad managed to get to Devon to see us. He was at that time a corporal based at Feltwell in Norfolk, where his large build – six feet two inches, broad shoulders, strong thick arms with hands twice the size of most men's and size twelve shoes – made him an ideal N.C.O. in charge of men. Very soon, he was promoted to sergeant, which pleased the family enormously. Not so the news that he was soon to be posted overseas to Singapore. In fact, Singapore fell whilst Dad was on the high seas, and his ship returned to India, where he spent the next four years. I'm sure my mother was distraught at the prospect of being left to manage completely alone, miles from her nearest friends and relations. So before sailing away to the Far East, he decided on another move for us, this time to Northchurch near Berkhamsted, into a larger house with electricity and running water, a village store, butchery, and large town nearby, with regular bus service, which was completely lacking in Devon. Dad's brother Jack (who was also in the RAF) and his family lived in Berkhamsted. His parents lived at Hemel Hempstead, as did one sister, Hilda, with her husband. So it must have seemed like a return from the wilderness for my mother, who was much happier but without Dad and without Rose. She still had her work cut out, feeding four growing children on the meagre rations that she was able to purchase in 1942. We had a large garden in which she grew potatoes and many other vegetables, with a little assistance from me and a handicapped man who lived nearby. We had some Khaki Campbell ducks at the bottom of the garden, which I looked after. Their eggs were a continual source of supply to the larder, in exchange for potato peelings mixed with bran. We liked the eggs much better than the dried egg powder which we had otherwise.

In spite of her many problems, Mum still found time to place us in better schools than the village school, even though that was more convenient. In my case, she managed to get me into Berkhamsted Prep school, with a smart blazer and "BS" embroidered in large letters on its pocket.

I was very average throughout my school career, although I must have been able to scrape up enough knowledge to pass the eleven plus examination to get me into Berkhamsted Junior School a year later. I was much more interested in the many other activities which went on in the playground or out of school: things like conkers, marbles, cigarette cards, train and aeroplane spotting, and trick cycling. The latter did not involve anything drastic and was done on the second-hand bicycle on which I journeyed to and from school each day. With my school chums at weekends, we would experiment sitting on the handlebars and riding backwards – not a difficult feat. Getting up speed and standing on the crossbar or saddle required a lot more skill. Girls were obviously coming into the picture at this age, as I remember trying to impress one tender beauty with the saddle trick, only to come a tremendous cropper on the tarmac road, which skinned the palms of my hands terribly. Girls naturally were around with my sisters, but in general, I ignored them as far as possible for another two or three years. My sisters gave me enough trouble, as it was, without having more.

The war continued, and we listened regularly to the one o'clock news to see how "we" were progressing. Mum had stuck two large maps on the wall of the kitchen, and we moved red pins on it to show the advances of the Allied forces, once the tide had turned. News from Burma and Imphal was not good, and Mum asked me to say a prayer for Dad on Sunday in the church where I was a choir boy.

I got occasional letters from Dad, exhorting me to do my best in school exams, look after the rest of the family until he got home, and help Mum as much as possible. I did occasionally help bring her heavy shopping up the hill in my home-made trolley made out of the now-disused pram. Careering down the hill was exciting and relatively safe, as there was not much traffic on the roads then. Pulling the load back up the hill was still a drag but a great help to my mother. Her only relief, apart from her Craven A cigarettes (which were also scarce), was a monthly visit from Aunt Hilda, who would come for afternoon tea equipped with a bag of cakes or sweets. She had a damaged leg which hindered her walk but did not appear to give her any pain. Her face and body were angular, her heart warm and loving. She had two sons away at the war: Dick in the RAF as a gunner and Douglas in the Tank Corps in North Africa.

Mum and Hilda got on well together, and I'm sure they were a great support to each other. Before catching the bus home, they would walk to the Old Grey Mare pub for a drink to round off the day, leaving me in charge of the three girls (a point naturally disputed by my elder sister).

We started to see more soldiers around, practising their manoeuvres on Northchurch common. Camouflaged army lorries sped up the hill, and Bren gun carriers left their caterpillar tracks all over the local countryside. Soldiers dug trenches over the entrance to the railway tunnel, where in exchange for a jug of tea (which I scrounged from Mum), I was able to sight through .303 rifle sights, handle blank bullets, and even hold a Bren gun. A damaged bomber crashed nearby on its return from a bombing raid over Germany. It burst into flames, killing its crew and setting off the remaining ammunition. Then the doodlebugs (V1s) started coming with their distinctive throbbing engines, which after cutting off allowed you ten seconds to take cover. The V2 rockets gave you no chance at all – the first you heard was the bang of their arrival. Fortunately, we had very few of either coming down near us. Since the morning, when we were awakened by hundreds of black and white striped aeroplanes, towing big gliders with similar markings passing overhead on their way to Normandy, the tide was definitely turning in our favour; the war was receding. We looked forward to the day that Dad would be back with us once more.

Time appeared to drag on until eventually VE Day arrived, with all its accompanying celebrations and street parties. VJ Day was still to come, as was my father. When he did arrive home, he was very much a stranger to us as we, a far more grown-up set of children, were to him. We had all been through experiences which had moulded us into different beings from those who had parted about three and half years before. Following his demob, with his issued suit and pork-pie hat, Dad appeared lost. He tried gardening but was not much good at it – not as good as Mum and I. He tried an evening class, learning to make shoes, at which we turned up our noses as only children can. Looking back now, I do not think he got much help from his offspring until he landed on the idea of farming. One of his prewar colleagues knew of a farm near Aldenham, where a partner and some money was required to establish a pedigree dairy herd. The farm was for lease together with a farmhouse, labourers' cottages, buildings, and two hundred and fifty acres of pasture and arable land.

We drove over there one Sunday to have a look, thrilled of course by the idea of living on a farm and all those trivialities which would have no bearing on whether the farm could be a profitable enterprise. There would be a bedroom each for Audrey and myself (mine with an access to a large loft). A lily lake which froze over in winter, a river, a private drive from the village a mile away, lots of barns and sheds in which to play hide-and-seek.

Over the next few weeks, Dad was away each day, discussing the business of leasing the farm with Jim Rouse, making the decision and then purchasing the necessary dairy equipment, farm implements, and of course the animals in the shape of thirty pedigree Jersey cows.

A few weeks later, when we moved on to Wall Hall Farm, the farm was just about complete. Two men and an eighteen-year-old girl from the village looked after most of the work, like milking and mucking out or ploughing and cultivating the mangel-wurzels and hay for winter fodder. Jim, the partner, spent his time in the office, looking after the accounts and wages, while Dad did his utmost to learn fast and work hard where he could.

I revelled in the farm, quickly learning how to milk the lovely cows, even to squirt the warm milk from their teats at my sisters, if they came within range. Tractor driving became second nature to me after learning to rake up the hay during hay-making. Clearing the muck from the yard became a regular holiday job for me and my friends, as the yard was also our evening cricket field, where everyone was roped in to play. We had many hundreds of chickens, whose eggs went off to some market each day, and about fifty turkeys, which all disappeared at Christmas time. On Sunday mornings, it was Dad's turn to do the milk round. It wasn't a big round, as the crates of bottles easily fitted into the back of the car. I would go with him on the five-mile trip which circled the farm, giving us an opportunity to see how everything was growing.

We did not grow very much, so I suppose it was not surprising that my father, who had operated a very successful business before the war, soon realised that the cows and chickens could not support two families and three farm assistants. The first assistant left a month later. Jim now had to take his turn with the milking. The second to leave was my father, who had I think rightly come to the conclusion that he was wasting his time on the farm when he could start up his old business again more profitably. While we continued to live on the farm, he journeyed to Watford each morning and soon had his business thriving in a way that the farm wasn't.

The initial move to the farm made the journey to Berkhamsted School a nightmare. I tried it for a couple of weeks, with Dad driving me to Watford Junction, where I then boarded a steam train to Berkhamsted. It meant getting up at some unearthly hour as well as returning home very late. Once I missed the train, making me late for school, where my form teacher was not impressed. I was lucky to get a transfer to the Watford Grammar School following an interview there with some of the teachers, who were interested in whether I knew anything. I did know that Uncle Jack had been a student there some years before but never found out whether that fact got me in.

I was by now fourteen years old and able to notice a few things, such as the difference in the schools. Berkhamsted was nice and gentlemanly, where you were left to do the work set as you wished. Watford Grammar was a rude awakening for me. I was expected to get on with the work immediately, to learn it thoroughly, and to be able to answer exam questions about it – or else! We were left in no doubt whatsoever that when the time came to write our school certificate exams, we were expected to pass.

About two years later, I did pass in six or seven subjects, maths and English being the best. I was always in the C stream, unable to shine in any subject; in fact, my art was obviously of such a questionable standard that I was moved to the woodwork class, where I actually won the woodwork prize. School lessons were of less interest to me than the many other activities that went to make up Watford Grammar. Cricket and rugby football I thoroughly enjoyed and might have done well in them, if I had understood more about the games. Instruction in them was either very limited or I did not pay sufficient attention to the teacher. The school cadets I found to be of great interest. I must have looked a complete shambles, unwanted and unloved, when I first pitched up to school in my oversized army cadet uniform with gaiters back to front, belt upside down and a huge beret like a pancake flopped over my ears. I was sorted out by all and sundry who knew better to such an extent that I eventually ended up as company sergeant major, with the shiniest pair of boots ever seen in Watford. School cadet camp, a drill course and a weapons course during summer holidays, had all contributed to knocking me into shape. I also belonged to our army cadet band where, not having enough puff to blow a bugle, I was given a side drum and drumsticks, which were much easier and just as much fun.

The school organised a holiday in Switzerland during the summer of 1948, an almost unbelievable event of which I was a fortunate participant. There were about twenty-five of us who went, in the company of three teachers. The long journey by train, ferry, and more train took us to this wonderland of green fields bordered by high white mountains. For ten days, we delighted in long walks to spectacular waterfalls, railway rides up mountainsides to snow-clad peaks, exploring nearby towns or small villages, and sampling delicious creamy chocolate cakes such as we had never seen in England. We all got on well, had some marvellous pillow fights in our bedroom, which left feathers everywhere, made eyes at the pretty Swiss maids, and ate like horses everything that we could. I took lots of photos with the camera I had borrowed from Mum and bought some souvenir biscuits to take back to her and a ten-cent cigar from a slot machine on Basel Station for my dad.

Oh, the unkindness of youth; how cruelly I repaid my parents for such a magnificent holiday. Perhaps I made up for it in some other way, like being cheerful and loving (I don't remember), but twelve months later, I was able to twist my father's finger enough to let me go again – this time to St Anton in Austria. The pattern of the holiday was much as before, with a taste of skiing added to it. We did not have ski lifts so had to walk what seemed miles on our unwieldy skis to get to the practice area, where we spent more time horizontal than upright. It was all good clean fun, as were the two maids, Mitzi and Yutsi, who looked after our bedrooms in the hotel. We nicknamed them Misty and Gusty, the local weather forecasters. I found Mitzi to be very attractive, which proves two things. Firstly, I was getting older; secondly, I was obviously quite normal. The occasional kiss behind the wardrobe was soon spotted by my companions, who quickly spread the news. It had probably taken me ten days to pluck up the courage for the first kiss, but two days later, she came to the station to see us all off, where she kissed me goodbye to the roars of approval from the whole school party.

School holidays were generally fun, with never a dull moment that I remember. There was always something to do around the farm, so there were usually friends there to do it with: clearing the manure, playing cricket, camping in the fields, trying out Dad's golf clubs (which he never used himself), shooting targets with my air gun, cleaning Dad's car and driving it around the farm with all the cleaners on board, milking the cows, helping ourselves to some of the rich creamy cold milk straight from the churns in the dairy, even riding Margaret's horse. Yes, young sister Margaret had managed to cajole my father into buying her a pony. All girls seem to go through the horsy stage, and she wasn't going to be left out. It was lovely for her to have a beast which she could feed, show off, talk about, and very occasionally ride. But horses need regular exercise, regular riding, or they become frisky. Hers did! She came off a couple of times, after which I was the one expected to do both my excessive homework and take out the horse. It was a battle to get the horse halfway around the two-mile circuit; the second half flashed past as it realised it was again heading for home. I came off a couple of times in a hayfield, fortunately, where in spite of being dragged a few yards with a foot caught in a stirrup, no harm was done. It wasn't long before we said goodbye to the horse and, regrettably, to the farm as well.

It came as no surprise, as Dad and Jim were not agreeing on how the farm was being run. Dad seemed to be supplying all the money for Jim to spend as he wished. At the same time, three of us were now going to school in Watford, while Joan was a weekly boarder at Mill Hill. Dad was travelling daily to his office, and Mum went to town once a week for the usual shopping, which again she had to lug along the mile-long drive home from the bus stop.

We moved into Watford to a house only one hundred yards from my school. I now found that if I was even slightly late leaving home, it was impossible to get to school on time.

I was sad to leave Aldenham, where we had many happy times but before long had put it behind me, as I was fully immersed in study for the final big exam. What I was going to do when it was over, I did not know; something would turn up. Apart from homework, I made various aero-models, cycled off with friends to their houses, joined in life-saving instruction to gain my award of merit and experienced some blissful hours walking through Cassiobury Park with my latest girlfriend.

The results came and went, being no cause for great celebration, although I met a former classmate from Berkhamsted School, who was surprised that I had passed, where he and others in the same class had failed. Dad decided I should stay on at school for another two years to gain, if possible, my higher school certificate. I was doubtful about that, yet with no alternative in mind, carried on the normal routine. One Easter holiday, I cycled with Johnny Fowler, a good school friend, from Watford to the Isle of Wight, where we spent three days seeing the island and sleeping at various youth hostels. We called on Rose, who was then married and lived at Cowes in a little cottage, similar to the one in Brendon but with an inside flush toilet. That summer, I set off on my bike once more to the Isle of Anglesey, to join up with the Crusaders, the summer camp of our local bible class. I had a very ordinary bike, which I had equipped via birthday and Christmas presents with a dynamo light set and a speedometer. School cadets had taught me how to read a map, which the youth hostel association had provided. What was not provided for was a guarantee of getting into the youth hostel on arrival. The first day, I found I had travelled 110 miles before I could get into the third hostel that I tried. Next day was easier, but on the third day, in North Wales, I failed again, ending up eventually at my Aunt Emmie's house at about 9 p.m., totally unexpected.

She was a brick! Gave me a warm welcome and put the frying pan on to cook me a big supper, while her husband Jim was arranging a bed for me to sleep in that night.

I did not know Emmie and Jim very well. They had spent a lot of time in India, where Jim was in the Indian Army. They had two sons (my cousins), who were both now adult and away from home, one of them also in the army. It was fortunate that Mum had given me their address before leaving home – just in case – as otherwise, I do not know where I would have spent that night. I was reluctant to leave next day, having been made so welcome, hence it was afternoon before I set off again on the last short leg, to find a field of tents on Anglesey. The camp was nicely situated, overlooking a sandy bay. There must have been thirty or forty tents, with four of us allocated to each one. In the centre was a large marquee, which was our main dining room and games room (if it was wet), and also used for films or lectures. One of these was on the subject of sex, a subject which surprised us all and embarrassed many, it being an almost taboo topic in that day and age. But from what I remember, it was well put over and accompanied by stern warnings of not to do it.

Another subject of interest was a talk on careers, with a little advice on where to go for more information. The rest of the time we played games, went for walks, and ate good hearty meals, which very occasionally we cooked ourselves over small camp fires. Before bed, we had a short prayer meeting and then slept the sleep of the just.

Time sped by very rapidly, until the day came to set off on my bicycle once more for home, this time by a different route so that I could see some more of the country. The weather turned wet, making the trip much less enjoyable than when outward bound. I don't recollect any weather forecasts in those days, however right or wrong they may have been, but churning away in my mind as I pedalled away was firstly all I had learnt about sex and secondly that perhaps the Navy would be a good career to follow.

Back at home, my parents were no help at all about joining the Navy. I think Dad would have liked me to help him in his office, which was steadily expanding. My view was that I did not wish to be stuck in an office from dawn to dusk, as he was. I wanted open spaces, room to move, to travel, adventure, and excitement.

I found an advertisement in the Sunday paper: "Join the Navy and See the World as a Seaman Boy." Two shillings and sixpence a day! I was sorely tempted and spoke about it to Cecil Payne, a neighbour of ours when on the farm in Aldenham. He happened to be a county education officer, full of good sense, and a friend with whom I used to hit golf balls in a field and watch television in his house. He scoffed at my idea. "Rubbish," he said. "If you want to join the Navy, you must go to Dartmouth College." Three days later, he provided me with details and an application form for Dartmouth.

To get anywhere near the Royal Naval College at Dartmouth, you first have to pass what I considered to be a stiff exam. I know because I attempted it some weeks later, sitting in County Hall London with maybe a hundred and fifty other applicants from southern England. I had time off from school for the four days of exams, but when the results came out, I was not amongst those accepted to progress.

I was disappointed but not surprised, as exams had never been my forte. I was more surprised by my dad, who found for me a tutor who got hold of the exam syllabus and then gave me tutorials and homework for the next three months, until knowledge was coming out of my ears. All that on top of my schoolwork meant that all I had learnt about sex was well and truly forgotten. Suffice to say that when I sat the exams again, I made a much better showing but my name was three below the line of those accepted. I had failed again.

But the gods must have been looking down on my efforts, as with the results of the Dartmouth examinations came an information sheet from their Lordships of the Admiralty, with details of an eight-year short service commission with the Royal Naval Air Service, the old Fleet Air Arm. Subject to medical fitness and aptitude tests (no more examinations), I could spend eight years in the Royal Navy as a pilot or observer flying naval aircraft from the decks of aircraft carriers. If I was interested, I should complete the enclosed application form.

Was I interested? It seemed too good to be true. I had not realised that the Fleet Air Arm or its successor was still in existence after the war. To be able to fly aeroplanes and travel the world in ships was more than I had ever dreamed of. There was no need for discussion with the family or anyone else except to make sure the application form was correctly completed prior to its urgent despatch back to their Lordships. At last I knew exactly what I wanted to do, if only for eight years. The only thing left was to pass the tests when called to take them.

Chapter 2

The Royal Navy

I was summoned to attend interviews and selection tests at the RAF Station at Hornchurch during the last week of November; I was to bring spare clothing for a possible three-night stay. I travelled there on a cold, miserable day, hoping for the best but with no idea of what would be required of me.

On arrival, it transpired that there were well over one hundred of us to be "processed," starting with medical examinations. These were very thorough, reducing considerably the number who remained for the second day's aptitude tests of putting round pegs into round holes and square pegs into square ones. Along with that, there were exercises in the gymnasium, testing individual leadership qualities, when as class leader, in turn we had to lead our team over imaginary chasms and minefields using the bare essentials of ropes, mats, and benches. These exercises I found to be stimulating and enjoyable, as I had always been keen on gymnastics, so it was not surprising that I was still there next day.

More co-ordination tests followed: keeping a wandering spot of light within a small square on a radar screen by the use of a control stick, while lights which went on to one side or the other had to be switched off by switches on the opposite sides. Together with such practical exercises were more written intelligence tests, all of which had to be completed within a set time.

The last afternoon was spent on individual selection in front of a panel of six men, who desired to know my motives for wanting to join the Royal Navy as a pilot. They queried my background, my schooling, my hobbies, my hopes, and my fears, delving into me to see if I was of the material required to make a naval pilot.

Finally, after two minutes' preparation and thought, I had to give a three-minute talk on one of four chosen subjects. That was, to me, the most difficult, as I had never been a great talker – quite the reverse. What I had to say took less than the three minutes, but at least I spoke up and said what I had to say with conviction.

When we departed from Hornchurch, having been measured for uniforms by Messrs Gieves (Gentlemen's Outfitters), there were only about forty of us left, feeling somewhat the worse for wear. I had spent my eighteenth birthday being tested.

Christmas came without any news of whether I had succeeded. I was very miserable. Then just before the New Year, the magic letter arrived: I had made it and was to join HMS *Indefatigable* at Portland Harbour on 28 January.

Our New Year celebrations more than made up for our unhappy Christmas, as once again I went around with a big smile on my face, no longer the dampening influence on those around me. I still did not know very much about the future, except that I was to spend eight years in the navy with a commission and would be trained to fly aeroplanes from aircraft carriers. It was to start with six months' basic seamanship training.

So three days after joining the Navy, together with the forty other successful aviation cadets, several hundred trainee seamen, and the ship's company, we sailed from Portland Harbour in the training carrier HMS *Indefatigable,* bound for Gibraltar, where we arrived a week later. Getting there had been quite a trial, as in typical naval fashion, on joining the ship, we had been given injections and vaccinations against every likely disease under the sun. Then we had to find our way around this enormous ship, where one deck looked much like the next; all had heavy bulkhead doors, all were connected by ladders which disappeared up or down through small holes, and frequently there were hard protuberances which dug into your body should you perhaps stagger during the unaccustomed pitching or rolling of the ship. Petty officers were forever chasing us around to do various jobs: sweeping, polishing the decks, cleaning the heads, tidying and stowing our hammocks, and then falling in on parade.

I well remember: As we sailed through rough seas in the Bay of Biscay, I felt very seasick. Two POs were teaching us the rudiments of drill in the lower aircraft hangar. As the ship rolled from side to side, so our squad would stagger together with the roll of the ship: first to one side and then back again, commands of "Stand still!" being of no avail. The instructors would try to smarten our stances and come up behind us and pull our bruised and punctured arms down to the side, saying, "Keep your arms straight!" Periodically, one of us had to make a smart right turn and dash off to the heads, if we could find them, or vomit over the side of the ship. But it was all worthwhile when, a few days later, we sailed in the sunshine along the coast of Portugal. Next morning, we lined the flight deck in our best uniforms as, with the band playing, we steamed slowly into Gibraltar Harbour. That was the life!

As I had previously visited Switzerland and Austria on school journeys, I found Gibraltar to be very different. Its narrow streets were filled with many brightly coloured drapes, as the goods from the small shops spilled out of the doorways to attract buyers. Bright silken dressing gowns with gold embroidered dragons, intricately woven mats, sheepskin rugs, and postcards of the Rock and its Barbary apes were all surmounted by the warm sun from a clear blue sky.

But our seamanship training only allowed us a minimum amount of time for exploring. Mostly, we were busily studying, with hours of lectures on ring mains, steam boilers, gyro control mechanisms for torpedoes, tying Turks head knots, and learning the functions of different parts of the ship. Drill continued but on a more stable platform. Cleaning continued with as much vigour as ever, as did our eating and sleeping. We soon realised it did not matter much whether we were at Gibraltar, Portland, or anywhere else: Our routine progressed in much the same way.

After about six months, we had a general idea of how the navy worked, as well as how to find our way around the ship. Our final exams were written and passed, and we celebrated with a Cadet's Ball in our Gunroom on board, at which our girlfriends were naturally guests of honour. Then at last, two weeks' leave at home with families as midshipmen of the Royal Navy.

I made the most of those two weeks, capitalising on my vastly improved knowledge of the world and the Senior Service, of which I was a representative. I proudly donned my uniform one Saturday morning and walked over to my old school to watch the cadets exercising, as I had done only a few months before.

My mother was pleased to have me home, serving me up lots of my favourite dishes, which tasted better than ever when contrasted with our food on board. My father for his part was easily persuaded to help out with a personal taxi service on numerous evenings, as I found suddenly that I had a number of girlfriends who had been neither interested in me nor so interesting to me during my schooldays. Naturally, I made the most of it until my leave ran out, and I found myself entrained for Donibristle on the Firth of Forth, where I was to spend the next three months doing preflight training.

We were now getting to the various aspects of how and why an aeroplane flies, with explanations of lift, drag, thrust, and weight. Instruction was given on meteorology, with its effect on flying, as well as air traffic control signals from ground to aircraft and vice versa. Navigation and map reading were hammered into us so that we could find our way around. We also had a flight in a de Havilland Dominie to give us some air experience. I don't think the twenty-minute flight made any of us sick – just queasy – but it did make some wonder whether we had chosen the right way of life and whether we should continue. Fortunately, I continued.

Flying training

Flying training started at RAF Syerston, near Nottingham, in a light aircraft with turned-up wing tips: the Percival Prentice. It looked a bit small and flimsy, even though it was all metal. When I got into the cockpit, with my instructor alongside me, encumbered by parachute, helmet, mask, and goggles, there was no room to spare. At the same time, we were enveloped in the unmistakable aeroplane smell: a mixture of high-octane fuel, electric wiring, and painted metal. It was almost overpowering at first, but as the weeks and months went past, it became almost addictive (like glue sniffing today).

In front of me were numerous dials, knobs, and levers, which my instructor carefully explained as he manipulated them and switched on, bringing the engine to life. Almost too soon, it seemed, we were moving, with my feet and hands following my instructor's movements on the dual controls. Suddenly, effortlessly, we were in the air, with only my hands on the control column, following directions from the voice of experience alongside me. My very enjoyable flying training had begun, and I started learning to manoeuvre an aircraft around the sky by smoothly and progressively manipulating the control column.

"Keep a good lookout," my instructor insisted, even when he was explaining something about the instrument panel. This paid dividends almost straight away, as with my instructor's attention directed at the artificial horizon, I spotted a Mosquito plane heading directly for us. Not having the time to say anything, I simply grabbed the controls, much to the surprise of my instructor, and put the aircraft into a steep turn out of the path of the other plane.

After six hours and twenty minutes of training, I made my first solo flight when, unexpectedly, my instructor climbed out of the plane at the start of the runway and said, "Go and make one circuit and land by yourself." As any pilot will know, one's first solo flight is never to be forgotten. Being up in the air all alone for the first time is a tremendous thrill, with almost the only thought being, *How do I now get this thing down again?* I made it, even if I did do a bit of a ground loop after landing (which I don't think my instructor saw).

After three months on the Prentice, I progressed to a Harvard, a more advanced trainer with a bigger, noisier engine; the instructor sat behind me in the rear cockpit. It seemed as though we were progressing too quickly, with everything happening so much faster than in the slower Prentice. But the excellent RAF training instructors ensured our safety, provided we stuck carefully to practising the exercises we were briefed to practice during our solo flights. Flying was dangerous and could be a killer, as one of our course found out when "beating up" the house of his girlfriend. The effect was sobering on all of us, as we progressed to cross-country navigation exercises (both daytime and later at night). These exercises took us on triangular routes over the lovely Nottinghamshire and Lincolnshire countryside, with large, easily recognisable landmarks at each turning point. On night flights, I sometimes battled to keep awake and would slide open the canopy to allow some cold, crisp air into the cockpit to freshen me up. It did so quite successfully, but I would then spend the next ten minutes trying to keep the plane flying where it was supposed to go whilst retrieving my pencils, maps, and flight log from the corners of the cockpit whence they had been blown. It was always a triumph to get back to base after an hour and a half away over strange land.

Our course was now reduced to twenty-six enthusiastic nineteen- to twenty-one-year-old budding aviators, as several had dropped out in the early stages of the flying training. We had a room each in the accommodation block adjoining the airfield, where surrounded by our personal items, we could relax or study as we thought fit. At weekends, we were free to travel by bus to Newark or Nottingham, meeting up in the evening at pubs like Ye Trip to Jerusalem (reputedly the oldest pub in England) for a general chat and discussion on our progress over a glass of beer (or, in my case, cider).

Once a month, we had long weekends, in which we stopped work at lunch time on Friday, giving us time to get home for most of Saturday and Sunday. My savings had grown sufficiently to enable me to purchase my own transport, in the form of a BSA 250cc motorbike, which an old schoolfriend had sold me. This gave me freedom of movement around the countryside as well as easy travel to and from Watford. For the rest of the time, we worked hard, with lectures for half of every day and flying during the other half. Tests were frequent, and the competition amongst us was fierce, as we knew that if we did not come up to the high standard set, our services would no longer be required. This was perhaps where I first learned how much one can apply oneself if one really wants to succeed.

Final examinations were written and passed prior to our flying off to Arbroath in Scotland for two weeks, during which we had our final flying handling tests. I managed to do everything right on my test, even doing a three-point glide landing right on the touchdown point. Before sending me on my way, rejoicing, my instructor asked me if there was any other manoeuvre that I would like to try in the aircraft. As we had heard and learnt a lot about spins, I asked him if we could do one which would get well wound up. He took us in a climb much higher than usual, before doing the usual pre-spin checks. We then went into a spin, which did get very wound up, such that we were both rocking the control column back and forward together, as well as applying power at selected times to get the plane out of its flat spin. I remember the rough sea spinning steadily up to meet us and wondering if I had asked too much of my mentor. Suddenly, the spin changed and we came rapidly out of it, with about a thousand feet to spare, my confidence in flying instructors undiminished (however shaken we both may have been).

So after an enjoyable two weeks, we went back to Syerston for our graduation day and the presentation to us of our wings. It was a proud day for all the twenty-six of us who had successfully qualified, as watched by parents and friends we saluted and shook hands with the Third Sea Lord, Admiral Sir Michael Denny K.C.B., C.B.E., D.S.O., who then pinned our wings on to our left sleeves. Mum and Dad were there to view my great moment and enjoyed looking around the aeroplanes in the hangar as well as the classrooms, where so much hard work had taken place. A celebration lunch was laid on for us all in the Officer's Mess, after which we were free to collect our bags and make off home for two weeks of well-earned leave.

The next move was back to Scotland, to Lossiemouth, for operational flying training on Fireflies and Seafires.

The Firefly was again a tandem two-seater with at least twice the power of the Harvard. It was altogether bigger, heavier, and faster and used as a stepping-stone to the single-seater naval version of the Spitfire: the Seafire. It was exactly the same as the Spitfire, with its wonderful, roaring Merlin engine, but had the addition of a retractable hook under the tail to engage the arrester wires when landing aboard aircraft carriers. We had to be extremely careful during take-off in the Seafire, as the torque from the powerful engine could easily pull you off the straight line of the runway.

After the training hacks, some of us had graduated to the thoroughbreds. I say some of us, as our course was now split into two groups: those selected to fly fighter aircraft and those who would continue on anti-submarine aircraft such as the Firefly. After three months, we were split again, as four of us were selected to continue our training on jets. We were sent to Culdrose in Cornwall near Helston, the home of the Morris dancers. There we met the sleek twin-engine Meteor trainer, which flew so swiftly and smoothly through the air, with barely a sound or vibration in the cockpit but a much louder noise, very audible to those outside. We now had the jet engines driving us forward, with the RPM gauges measured in thousands instead of hundreds, the temperature gauges in hundreds rather than tens.

Four other qualified pilots had joined up with our course of four; the most senior got too slow on the downwind leg whilst practising some circuits and landings. Regrettably, he did not survive the crash after the plane stalled, falling out of the sky like a stone. A second one was more fortunate: After landing too fast, he crashed through two Cornish stone walls after running off the end of the runway. He climbed out of the plane uninjured but with such a twitch that he left the navy shortly after. Such were the hazards of learning to fly.

We were not deterred, just more careful and determined to be successful as we continued on the single-seater Attacker. This was the latest jet in operational service with the Royal Navy, capable of firing its four wing cannons, dropping bombs from under-wing racks, or firing off rockets. Unusual for jets, it had a tail wheel instead of a nose wheel, which had to be locked straight before takeoff, otherwise it was extremely difficult to maintain direction down the runway, as I found out one day to my chagrin. We had progressed to formation flying, which included taking off in formation. I was to take off a short distance behind three others, when, caught in the turbulence of their jet stream, I found that my tail wheel had not locked. I found myself careering from side to side of the runway as I struggled to keep the plane straight. The tail wheel locked as I sped off the straight and narrow over the wet grassy airfield. I immediately closed the throttle and shut off the fuel to the engine, allowing the soft, muddy ground to bring me to a rapid standstill and tilting the plane slowly onto its nose before settling back gently on to its recalcitrant tail wheel. Apart from feeling a bit shook up, no damage was done, and the emergency services crew enjoyed the exercise.

In my spare time in Cornwall, I enjoyed exploring the villages and landmarks on my motorcycle, buying small mementoes as souvenirs of my visits. Daphne du Maurier was my favourite author at this time, with her vivid tales, *Jamaica Inn* and *Rebecca*. I had to go and search out exciting places, imagining myself to be back in the days of the smugglers and ship-wreckers of the Cornish coast.

First deck landings

The three months at Culdrose came to an end, completing our training, which had taken just over two years. The six of us were now designated to join two front-line squadrons based at Ford in Sussex: 800 and (for me) 803 Squadron. Our flying became more war-minded as we exercised in battle formations, fired guns at towed banners or ground targets, and more excitingly fired rockets at the wreck of a ship on the coast. In preparation for flying aboard HMS *Eagle*, a large aircraft carrier, we practised numerous airfield dummy deck landings (ADDLs) under the guidance and supervision of an experienced deck landing guidance officer, or batsman, whose signals with a couple of fluorescent bats helped us fly the plane into a position from which, after we closed the throttle, we could expect the hook to catch the arresting wire on the deck. On the airfield, we naturally did not use the hook, as we had no wires, but all the other actions, including our low-level circuits of the airfield, were the same.

The ADDLs were fun, even though we were preparing for landing fast aeroplanes on a very small area of a ship's deck, which in turn was moving up and down on its fluid medium. When the big day arrived, we had our final briefing before flying off in sections of four to put our practise into effect. We each made one dummy run at the carrier, discovering just how small it was. It appeared much higher out of the water, too, with a lot of churning water behind the ship and some blue smoke from the funnel drifting in its wake. These things I noticed before dropping into the previously practised pattern with the utmost care. I saw the batsman give me the "cut" signal, whereupon I immediately closed the throttle, and the hook engaged the arrestor wire. With a bump followed by a rapid deceleration, which caught me by surprise at the suddenness of it, I came to a stop to see various deck-handlers giving me signals to apply my brakes, raise my hook, fold my wings, and taxi forward. My commanding officer gave me a big smile and thumbs-up signal. I had arrived.

The rest of that day, after the remaining aircraft had all arrived safely, was spent settling into our small cabins before trying to find our way around the ship. Getting accustomed to the unusual motion of the ship was also necessary, but by the evening, we were at home enough to celebrate our arrival with a couple of drinks in the wardroom. There was a great sense of achievement amongst us, as well as a certain amount of relief. Tomorrow, we would have the chance of doing it again, four times for each of us.

We were briefed about catapult take-offs from the bows of the carrier and rehearsed the signals and actions we were to take. What had not got home to me clearly was the rapid acceleration effect of increasing speed from nothing to about one hundred and fifty miles an hour in less than one hundred and fifty feet. Yes, I had my head back against the headrest; yes, I had my arms straight and locked against the fully open throttle; and yes, my other arm held the control stick central and immovable. When the acceleration came, it felt as though a giant had his foot in my back, booting me off the bow of the ship while at the same time trying to pull the sides of my mouth and my head back through the headrest. Fortunately, it didn't last long, as within a few seconds, I was safely airborne, away from that vicious instrument of torture, which took a lot of getting used to.

We got accustomed to our shipboard routine as the *Eagle* steamed gently towards the sunny climes of the Mediterranean, where we could expect to exercise without the limitations of rough seas. Once again, we had the sun shining down on us from clear blue skies as we sailed into Gibraltar Harbour to show off the Royal Navy's largest and most modern fleet carrier. There were runs ashore to such exotic places as La Linea and Malaga, across the border in Spain, the red light districts being well known by Jolly Jack, as were numerous waterside bars. For officers such as us, who naturally would not be seen in such places, there was tennis at the Officers Club and numerous cocktail parties. We could all let our hair down in our own way.

Over the next few months, we called in at Toulon, Naples, Oran, and Valetta, before the two jet squadrons disembarked to Halfar in Malta, as *Eagle* was due for some maintenance back in England. A few weeks prior to disembarking, in December 1953, I celebrated my twenty-first birthday on board. The C.O. had arranged a cake for me, and the squadron pilots made the most of the occasion. With the Navy, then as now, any excuse was a good enough reason for a party. We had one. Being at sea, our celebratory activities were somewhat limited to eating, drinking, and singing raucous songs, with a few wardroom games thrown in for good measure. High Cockolorum, a dangerous game of trying to bring down a line of joined bending figures by leap-frogging onto their backs, was always good for a laugh and some painful bruises, whilst balancing on two beer bottles and trying to place one of them as far away as possible was much more a game of skill. Certainly parties on board were entirely different from those of my youth, which my thoughts turned to later that evening.

Once the drab few months of winter had passed, we started into summer routine, in our white short-sleeved shirts with epaulettes and white shorts, long stockings, and white shoes. I used to wake up just before six o'clock as the re-diffusion service of Radio Malta started each day with the wonderful recording of Gounod's version of "*Ave Maria.*" It was a lovely way to start a new day.

By seven o'clock, we were all assembled in our squadron crew rooms for meteorological briefing and details of the morning's flying programme. By twelve thirty, we were finished and back to the wardroom for lunch.

Many afternoons were spent on the beach not far away, sun bathing asleep on the rocks before cooling off in the crystal-clear waters. Snorkelling with flippers around the many little inlets was fascinating, as was water-skiing behind the captain's motor boat. After tea back at the wardroom, we would have time for an hour of tennis in the cool of the evening before showering and getting ready for the evening meal.

The relaxed way of life in the sunny climate certainly appealed to me, and I made the most of it very happily.

At the end of 1954, our squadron was re-equipped with a brand new aeroplane, the Sea Hawk, which was a delightful plane to fly; it looked right, and it flew right. It looked right with its sleek fuselage and air intakes set in the roots of its slender straight wings, while the jet exhausts were moulded into the trailing edges of the wings and fuselage, which in turn tapered to a rounded fin with the hook underneath, completing the streamline effect. The aircraft sat on a balanced tricycle undercarriage, while the pilot was positioned well towards the nose in his spacious bubble-hooded cockpit. It flew right with its quiet, smooth-running jet engine and, equally important, its power-assisted controls, which made fingertip control of the plane an absolute joy. It was not a fast jet, being perhaps slightly underpowered, but it was very docile and forgiving and a vast improvement on the Attacker, which had been a bit of a pig to fly.

We flew by commercial airliner from Malta to England in order to take delivery and familiarise ourselves in the new plane. Naturally we had the weekend off on our arrival to see families and girlfriends, impressing them with our suntans and knowledge of distant lands. We considered ourselves to be the elite of the flying world having a number of deck landings to our credit, a new plane to fly plus a reasonable few pounds accumulating in our bank accounts.

Two weeks later, we flew back to Halfar, landing at Istres in southern France en route to refuel. Back at base, we quickly became accustomed to our new machine, which was just as well, since three months later, we were to fly back on board a smaller aircraft carrier, which had an angled deck and a mirror deck to help in landing instead of a batsman.

This was the HMS *Albion*, a very happy ship with some familiar faces on board. The angled deck had only five wires stretched across it to arrest the landing aircraft, instead of about fifteen on board the HMS *Eagle*. If the aircraft were to miss all five, it would continue on its way over the side of the ship, and since it still had flying speed and power on, it could have another go. Without the angled deck, a crash barrier was necessary to prevent collisions with aircraft parked in the area on the forward part of the ship. The mirror landing aid gave the pilot a steady descent angle to the touchdown point, as the gyro-stabilised mirror reflected a beam of light at just the right angle for a stable descent, whatever movement the ship might make. The pilot could adjust his flight path by keeping the reflected beam of light level with a datum line of lights on either side. We were most impressed by the advancements made in this deck-landing technology, which made our job of landing on the small moving decks so much easier. In fact, when we changed ships to the HMS *Centaur* a few months later, we were so used to our steady descent path system that we landed on the *Centaur* without either mirror or batsman. We were not blasé about deck landings, as they could kill if you made a serious mistake, but we took these things in our stride, as one does in one's youth, in spite of the hazards involved.

When I left the squadron in Malta in May 1955, I drove back to England with a friend in a 1923 Lagonda. We had the hood down all the way through Italy, Switzerland, and France, only meeting rain after we had crossed the Channel back into England. The tourist boom had not really got into full swing in 1955 so the roads, the bed-and-breakfast pensions, and the restaurants were not crowded. Viewing the sights such as Lake Maggiore was easy, as we could park the car wherever there was a picturesque spot for our cameras and take our time. There would not be queues of cars waiting impatiently for us to move on when we returned. Even in the middle of Paris, where we went to the Moulin Rouge, we were able to park the car nearby without fear of its not being there on our return. In fact, the only problem I encountered was that of being able to double-clutch, as the car did not have a syncromesh gearbox. We were back in England before I learnt the secret, by which time my compatriot was tearing his hair out. A strange coincidence was that after the many miles that we drove together, we discovered that we lived within five miles of each other.

After two weeks leave, my next posting was to the RAF Central Flying School at South Cerney and Little Rissington, in the delightful Gloucestershire Cotswolds. While I may have thought I knew how to fly before going there, the CFS literally took the mechanics of flying completely to pieces, both theoretically and practically, in teaching me to become a qualified flying instructor. It was an intensive course, calling on us to learn a great amount of knowledge about how and why an aeroplane flies but also to be able to demonstrate exactly any manoeuvre that the plane was capable of performing while explaining in clear patter just what was happening. Similarly, in the classroom, we were expected to give well-constructed lessons on any subject pertaining to flying training and to be able to answer awkward questions.

After three months' practise on piston-engined Provost aeroplanes and three months on jet Vampires, I qualified with the knowledge that I had completed the finest training course that any pilot could experience. Little did I realise how much use I would make of that training in the next forty or so years.

With the course behind me, the navy immediately put me to work, back at Lossiemouth in Scotland, where I had done some of my training. I spent the next two years converting pilots who had received their basic training in America, to Vampire and Sea Hawk aeroplanes and teaching them how to fly a plane on instruments. In Pensacola, Florida, the skies were always blue, with never a cloud in them. The reverse was the case in the UK, so that the ability to pilot an aircraft solely by reference to its instruments was paramount. As a result, it was quite normal to take off and spend an hour or more in solid cloud, practising instrument flying with radio- and radar-controlled approaches guiding us back to the airfield, where we would see the ground again a few seconds before landing.

Scotland was a lovely place to live in the summer, with its very long, light evenings. I played golf on several of the courses around Lossiemouth, including Nairn, which had one of the deepest sand bunkers I've ever had the misfortune to meet. It was also a place where you could play golf at midnight on the longest day of the year, when it never really got dark.

It was in Scotland I met up with the girl who was to become my wife. Sally Cullen, born in southern Ireland of English parents, had joined the W.R.N.S. on the secretarial side several years before. I met her in the wardroom at Lossiemouth, where she was a third officer and the captain's assistant secretary. I suppose I was attracted by her pretty face, curly hair, and lovely figure: a combination of factors to which I have always reacted. She was vivacious, dynamic, and cheerful, and it wasn't long before we were playing tennis together, going on long walks along the beaches, or having tea on weekend afternoons in various tea-rooms in Elgin. Sally, I know, had been attracted to me for my gleaming old Alvis Speed 20 sports car. She knew that to get her hands on that, she had to accept me as well. Our romance flourished, and some six months later, we were engaged – just before I left Lossiemouth to go to the Royal Naval Air Station at Ford, in southern England, to join 700X Flight. This was formed to evaluate the performance of the latest jet aircraft, which was planned to enter service with the navy. It was called the Scimitar and built by Supermarine. Powered by two enormous Rolls Royce Avon engines and with only one person in the aircraft, it was a fast, powerful monster. Ours was the elite flight of the navy at that time; we were watched with envy by the rest of the naval pilots.

Gradually, as the planes were produced and delivered to us, we set off on our trial flights, accompanied by stopwatches and clipboards to perform evaluation exercises. The commanding officer arranged a seven o'clock take-off flight for the duty pilot each morning, and I remember on one occasion, I arranged my tasks so that I ended up over the Naval Air Station at Culdrose. There I flew low over the airfield and the naval quarters at high speed, just to let them see and hear the latest naval aircraft. It was a noisy beast, the Scimitar, and flying low overhead at nearly 500 miles an hour was unforgettable. The plane would rocket past and then the noise caught up and hit you like an explosion. Fortunately, that sort of thing has been banned these days, but it was exciting in 1957 for all concerned, particularly the pilot.

Wedding

A few months later, Sally and I were married. We spent Christmas together with Sally's parents in Cork, Eire, where she had been born in December 1933. Both her parents ran a hair salon and lived in a comfortable house in Ballinlough Road, just outside the town. Sally's strict rules meant that her parents did not know that we were engaged. I was to get her father's permission first. In preparation for this and perhaps for her own insurance, Sally took me to Blarney Castle to kiss the horrible-looking, lipstick-covered Blarney stone which was reputed to give one the gift of the gab. Next lunch time, being Sunday, Sally engineered it so that I was in the lounge with her father while she and her mother were preparing lunch. Permission was sought and obtained. The diamond and sapphire engagement ring was produced and slipped on the appropriate finger (once again), and stiff drinks were served all round to mark the occasion. Sally's father promised to make the wedding cake for the big day, which we were planning for the end of March, just before the end of the tax year, so that we could get a tax rebate as a married couple.

Organising the wedding at Watford Parish Church from Ford in Sussex, with Sally still in Scotland and her parents in Ireland, was in itself no mean feat. My parents were in South Africa for three months prior to the wedding, so frequent weekends in Watford and daily letters to and from Sally were essential. My younger sister Margaret was to be chief bridesmaid, accompanied by my cousin Carol and Sally's cousin Andrea. My other sisters were both overseas: Audrey in South Africa, where she had gone nursing several years before and had married there, and Joan in Singapore with her husband, who was a squadron leader in the Royal Air Force. Invitations were despatched to relatives, friends, wardrooms, and squadrons. Dresses were made, banns read, flowers booked, and caterers, music, service sheets, ushers, best man and even honeymoon organised.

When the day came, all went as planned, even though Sally's dad got lost wandering around Watford but was fortunately spotted just in time to get his daughter to the church on time. We both said, "I will," at the appropriate place, before passing through the naval guard of honour with its raised swords, relieved and happy smiles on our faces. The rest of the day was to be spent relaxing at the reception in the Oakley Studios, amongst our many happy friends and family. A surprise treat was the singing of three beautiful songs, "This Is My Lovely Day," "*Ave Maria*," and "Oh My Beloved," by my Aunt Maisie Fleming, who had a superb sweet voice which, with the emotion of the day, brought the glistening of tears to many an eye that afternoon.

The three-tiered cake, surmounted by a model of a Sea Hawk aircraft, was cut with a Damascan scimitar which had been purchased in an antique shop some months before and re-chromed especially for the event.

Too quickly, the time came for us to depart, as we were driving to Lydd for our first night prior to flying with the Alvis to Le Touquet. From there, we went on to Lucerne in Switzerland, picnicking en route with bottles of champagne to celebrate our honeymoon. We had fun in Lucerne, seeing the sights, driving up the Brunig Pass, throwing snow balls, doing childish things, and thoroughly enjoying ourselves. We had a race up to our room on the third floor of the hotel, where Sally, just in the lead, rushed in and jumped on the bed, which promptly collapsed under her! A long discussion then took place about how to tell the management, who knew we were on our honeymoon. Suffice to say, a new bed was quickly found to replace the broken one, which was removed by a couple of men, broad smiles on their faces.

It was indeed a happy honeymoon, during which the Alvis served us proudly, so much so that on our return to Ford, where I had rented a small bungalow, I wrote to the Alvis motor company, praising the quality of their vehicles – expecting with this unsolicited reference to at least get a new set of tyres. I got a letter back a week later, saying, "We are very pleased to hear how well your Alvis Speed 20 performed during your honeymoon trip to Switzerland. We do hope it continues to do so throughout your married life!"

Sally and I settled into our new way of life, which was so strange to both of us after many years of living in wardroom messes. I would go off to work each morning, leaving Sally who had retired from the W.R.N.S., as was the custom of the day, to tidy the small bungalow while thinking up some exotic meal for later in the day, when I would be home again. Our abode was at Wick on the outskirts of Littlehampton, so I did not have far to travel each day. Initially, after sorting out our many useful wedding presents, Sally was able to make a list of other essentials, for which we searched Littlehampton and Arundel on Saturday mornings. We entertained Mum and Dad when we thought we could manage, with our brand-new wedding gift crockery, cutlery, and glassware very much in evidence, while pre-lunch sherry was offered on our silver salver, a present from the officers of 700X Flight. On some evenings, we joined other married couples from Ford, having a sociable drink at one of the many country pubs in the area, or having supper at the very popular Stetson Club in Littlehampton.

As soon as my duties with X flight were finished, I was moved on to 700 Squadron, which was a small squadron with a large variety of aircraft used for a range of exercises and trials, from aerial photography in Gannets to deck trails with Scimitars. I soon found myself being converted to the relatively slow twin-Mamba-engined turbo prop Gannet, with its contra-rotating propellers, the pilot seat high above the ground, and an observer sitting behind, surrounded by electronics and a radar screen. Within ten days, I also had my first familiarisation flight in the de Havilland Venom – a more exciting aircraft, with its twin booms and side-by-side seating for pilot and observer, and pushed along by a powerful Ghost engine. It was a bit like an enlarged Vampire but much more advanced, capable of carrying more weapons for longer distances at much greater speeds.

I returned to three different aircraft carriers during my time with 700 Squadron, once for an interesting trial with the Venom. Several had apparently stalled into the sea after night catapult takeoffs, with both pilots and aircraft lost. Our trial, which we had simulated on the airfield, was to pull the control stick back hard just at the end of the launch, to see whether there was any problem from stalling or anything else. We had additional instruments to make readings of the angles of climb, together with our indicated speeds. Two of us therefore were in the cockpit, doing two launches each.

I'm not sure who scared the other the most, but we were able to state categorically at the end that the cause of the crashes had nothing to do with pulling the stick back too hard after the takeoff. It was a spectacular exercise, as thrilling in the cockpit as it was to the many goofers.

HMS *Victorious* was the navy's newest carrier and was due to be the home of the first Scimitar squadron. Prior to this, some pilots from our squadron flew on board with the Scimitar, initially to do launches and landing, to ensure all was well with aircraft and carrier. We returned there a few weeks later to do more trials, including heavy launches in the Scimitar at 37,500-pounds, launches and landings in the Venom, and simple wire stretching with the Gannet – all carefully planned and executed in naval fashion. Regrettably, when the Scimitar squadron flew aboard a few weeks later and the eyes of the media watching and recording every detail, the commanding officer had the hook pulled out from his aircraft, which then slowly trickled over the side of the ship into the water. He did not escape. Accidents did happen, it was a dangerous life, a fact of which we were well aware. Therefore, we were always as careful as possible.

My last carrier visit was in November 1958 to HMS *Centaur*, which had been my home in the Mediterranean some years before with 803 Squadron. On this occasion, it was fairly simple wire pulling with a Gannet and other trial launches and landings in the Venom. Twenty-two carrier landings in six days was a good way to end up my career with the Royal Navy, which had taught me so much and which I had thoroughly enjoyed. December was to be my last month of flying with the navy; I was due for a month's end-of-service leave after the Christmas break. However, I was made use of right to the last moment, and the beginning of December found me back at Lossiemouth for an ultra high frequency radar trial, in which the trial operator and I flew a Gannet far to the north of Scotland. There we steadily approached a line of very large storms, which were flashing away with their electrical discharges. I was a bit apprehensive, even more so when all of a sudden, the propellers and windscreen of the Gannet also started to join in with a spectacular display. It was my first encounter with St Elmo's fire, caused by a build-up of static electricity. Completely harmless, it was very pretty to watch, with its tree-like patterns on the windscreen and dancing ring of fire from the props. But it certainly scared the pants off me when it first started.

So after nearly eight years in the Royal Navy, my service career was drawing to an end. I had some two thousand hours in my flying log book on twenty different types of aeroplane, and I had completed over two hundred deck landings in five of these craft. More importantly, as I only discovered in later years, I had completed one of the best flying courses in the world of aviation, that of the Central Flying School's instructors' course. I was a qualified flying instructor, with an A2 category. Altogether, I was a well-experienced pilot who should not have any difficulty finding a new job in the aviation world. The question was where.

In our caravan, where we now lived at Yeovilton, I discussed the future with Sally. Others of my ilk had written and passed the commercial pilot's licence test, subsequent to which they quickly signed up with BOAC or BEA, who were expanding UK airlines in 1958. There was glamour attached to the air crew, especially to the stewardesses (who were at that time I think called air hostesses). Being newly married, the idea of a week away on flights followed by four days at home sounded like a recipe for marital disaster, as it had proved to be for a number of pilots. We therefore agreed that I should search around for some other job, either in aviation or perhaps to do with farming – a secondary interest of mine as a result of living on or around farms. I was as vague about what I would do as I was at the end of my school days. As a result of naval training, I had plenty of confidence in myself, genuinely believing that anyone could do anything. I was an optimist, positive that something would turn up. The first step was to keep some money coming in so that I would not have to touch the fifteen hundred pounds bonus I was to receive from their Lordships at the end of my eight years. I therefore applied to the chief pilot of airwork at Hurn Airport, where they operated naval aircraft in a similar way to 700 Squadron. The result was negative, as they had sufficient pilots for the present.

I was not deterred but discussed the future with all around me. One morning shortly afterwards, Tim Dooley, who was an air traffic controller living with his family in a caravan nearby, brought over a copy of an Admiralty Fleet Order.

"This is what you want," he said. It said: "A retired officer's scheme for starting up a farm in Rhodesia."

He gave me the AFO to study the details: £3,000 to £5,000 cash needed, fit, interview and selection board to pass, two years learning to grow tobacco, then on to a piece of virgin land to start up a farm. The government would assist with a long-term loan, equivalent to that invested by the successful applicants, and pay them £20 per month during the two years of training. Those with £3,000 would go to a scheme in northern Rhodesia, those with £5,000 would go to a more developed area in southern Rhodesia. Interested persons were to write with full details to the chairman of the Rhodesian Immigrants Selection Board in London.

The word "Rhodesia" took my mind back a few years to Watford and my Uncle Fred, a very likeable rogue, husband to Aunt Maisie, who had sung so beautifully at our wedding. He had a wonderful zest for life, and as a bomb disposal expert during the war, he had to be sharp witted. He was. Numerous lifts in RAF flights to the Continent after the war enabled him to operate a nice little business trading in nylons, watches, cigarettes, liqueurs, and other commodities for ready takers in a deprived war-weary world. Although petrol was scarce and carefully rationed, Uncle Fred never went short. He would don his old flight lieutenant's uniform and drive to the nearby RAF station and fill up his car once a week. Not that we knew very much about it, as he did not brag about his exploits; he just found the way around any obstacle that got in his path, as any good cockney would. He and my father were the best of friends and had been for many years – thus he was an "uncle" to my three sisters and me. My father and mother were great ones for giving parties, especially at Christmas time, and Uncle Fred would always be there with his family to entertain us with some of his more amusing episodes since the last meeting. He had a wonderful way of storytelling, so that his tales came alive and you would be with him when he used just a little too much explosive to demolish some tree stumps in a farmer's field, so the blast blew out the farmhouse windows. You would also be in his overloaded, rickety old truck as it dumped the remainder of the stumps in another farmer's field some miles away. Of course, it would be Uncle Fred who was the last to leave our parties, and it would be his car that we would have to push in order to get it started in the early hours of the morning. He would be the one to waken the neighbours with the revving up and the backfiring as he disappeared down the road, leaving us gasping in a cloud of smoke.

It was Uncle Fred who first painted us a picture of Rhodesia, having spent a few weeks there with his daughter Margaret. His description was vivid about the clear blue skies, wide open landscapes, dusty roads, new towns and buildings going up, the wonderful opportunities, and the marvellous way of life for all its inhabitants. The superlatives would not stop, and he left his listeners enthralled by a land of milk and honey, where the sun shone down continuously. It sounded particularly good on a cold wet evening in Watford. The impressions were just filed away in my memory. Rhodesia, after all, was several thousand miles away, and you could not just move there without a job to go to.

Now some years later, it looked as though there was a chance of going to this far-off land, where we could sample its bountiful milk and honey.

Sally, Tim Dooley, his wife Elaine, and I discussed the subject very fully that evening over a few drinks. The more we talked about it, the rosier the picture became, until it was obvious that we were all going to go there and make our fortune. Our application forms were completed and sent in. Tim's was accepted, but mine wasn't.

"No chance," *said the board.* "This scheme is designed for prematurely retired [axed] offices of mature age and experience."

Once again, I had been slapped down. It was another cold, wet, miserable Christmas.

Two days after Christmas came a phone call from Airwork, offering me a temporary job on a monthly basis, and they wanted me to start next day! I accepted the job but refused to start until the first Monday in January, so that we could complete our festivities and find somewhere to live near Hurn Airport.

Perhaps this offer revitalised me, as at this time, I wrote another letter to the Rhodesian Selection Board, listing all the good points about Richard Jenkins: physically fit, in the prime of life, with a background of farming experience, dynamic, cash available, able to spend more years at the job than doddery axed officers, mentally alert and therefore quick to learn, with a very capable wife who had secretarial qualifications, which would be most useful on a farm. It was probably the one and only time in my life that I made the most of blowing my own trumpet in an endeavour to persuade the selectors that they could not afford to miss such a bargain as us.

Before long, at the end of January, a letter came back from them:

"As you obviously will not take 'no' for an answer you had better come for an interview."

We did, three weeks later. Armed with carefully typed sheets of how we would manage to support ourselves financially during the two years of training and anything else that we thought would strengthen our case, we arrived for our interviews as Tim and his wife, Elaine, departed from theirs.

We spent an hour before the board members and some of their wives – initially, I was with the men while Sally was with the women, then all of us together. They were trying to make sure that our characters were such that we could put up with the privations of life in the outback or bush of a new country, with rough roads, few stores, little in the way of entertainment, and a very different race of people. They gave us a lot of information about the country, having spent many years there themselves. It certainly sounded as though there would be hardships before our fortune was made.

While waiting for the result of the board's deliberations, I had an interview with Peter Twiss, of air-speed record fame. Fairey Aviation, with whom he was associated and who produced the Gannet aircraft offered me a job effectively starting up an Indonesian Air Force, equipped with Gannets. They had learnt that I was a QF1 with plenty of experience on Gannets and was now finished with the navy. If I was interested, they would pay me £4,000 a year with another £4,000 for expenses if I would accompany the aircraft in their crates to Indonesia, see them assembled there, and test-fly them prior to training local pilots to operate them.

The money made it a very tempting offer, but at that time, a lot of rival parties were using Tommy guns to settle their political differences in Indonesia. I felt that perhaps I would become a target for more than one group; in any case, I was already after a job at £20 a month! I therefore declined their offer. Just before I went for the interview with Fairey Aviation, who had contacted Airwork's chief pilot, as a matter of courtesy, Airwork also offered me a permanent job with them, one that I similarly declined, pinning my hopes now on a successful outcome for Rhodesia.

Fortunately, it came after a generous guarantee from my father that he could assist us financially if all else failed. We were to spend our two years of training in southern Rhodesia at the British South Africa Company's estate in Umtali, under the sponsorship of Lord Robins, the chairman of the selection board, who had taken an interest in us. So the decision was made – Rhodesia it would be, goodbye to flying, hello to a farming life.

Little did we really know of Rhodesia or of what our future held in store in that new country. We felt we were going there not just as settlers but as adventurers, pioneers. We were fully prepared to accept whatever came to us and to make the most of it. We were confident it would be good.

Chapter 3
Farming in Africa

Getting There

It is amazing how quickly you collect things around you and do not realise it until the time comes to pack them all up for a move. So it was with us; we took several weeks packing away into crates the numerous things we were to take with us and tried to find homes for the many items we were leaving behind.

My Alvis Speed 20 was up for sale, but very few people were interested in purchasing it, even at the most reasonable price of £150. None of the family were in need of a reliable old sports car, as they were more concerned with comfort than style.

In amongst all this came the vaccinations and inoculations again, to ensure that we would not be prone to the strange diseases of far-off countries. Passports were checked and tickets obtained for the Union Castle Motor Vessel *Athlone Castle,* leaving from Southampton for Cape Town. Several crates of our personal effects were sent off by rail to the ship, with the hope that we would see them again at the other end of our journey.

Then there were the farewells to our many friends and relations, with parties given to explain why we were leaving and what our hopes were for the future.

We spent a few days in Ireland, bidding goodbye to Sally's parents. There we told Mrs Vickery, a neighbour, where we were going.

"Rhodesia?" *she said*. "That's very nice – where's Rhodesia?"

"In Africa," Sally replied, smiling.

"Oh, Africa," *she said, nodding her head sagely.* "That's very nice – where's that?"

Strange to say, it was during the few days in Cork that we first came across the saying "the Black North." We had gone to tea with another family friend – by appointment. The bone china was out and the silver tea service had been brought into commission. Cucumber sandwiches were also in evidence. The daughter-in-law had recently returned from Rhodesia, where her husband was doing very nicely in business. We had an ideal opportunity to discuss the country, its climate, and people with her and to tell her of our plans. It was when we said that we would be going to northern Rhodesia after our two years of training that she drew back, aghast.

"Rhodesia is an idyllic place" she said, "but I would advise you to never go to the Black North." We left with the impression that northern Rhodesia was full of hostile natives who were all troublemakers and that, as a result, there were hardly any white people there.

To say that we were alarmed by this first-hand news would be understating the situation. We had no desire to uproot ourselves, travel some five thousand miles, and put our lives in jeopardy. But we decided that things could not be as bad as had been depicted, and since we were now committed to going, we would continue and assess the situation when we arrived in Rhodesia.

The final day arrived, with plenty of last-minute packing followed by emotional goodbyes, and then we were off by train to the ship at Southampton. Although we had sent our heavy crates of luggage in advance, we still somehow ended up with fifteen pieces of luggage, which included an ironing board. They all arrived on board the ship and were mostly stowed away in the hold, with only two suitcases with our en-route requirements being taken to our small cabin.

We busily settled ourselves in and then rushed off to explore the ship. People were still arriving, so there was a general hubbub of action everywhere: porters carrying three or four suitcases at a time along narrow passageways, uniformed officers hurrying up or down the gangways with sheaves of papers, while passengers called to friends and relatives on the quay side from the haven of the ship. All this came to a climax as the mooring ropes were singled up and cast loose, the streamers between those departing and those left on shore gently broke. Tears involuntarily came to the eyes and blurred the last images.

With a deep resounding farewell trumpet of sound from the ship's siren, we set off for new lands.

The *Athlone Castle* was a nice-looking ship, with cabins which seemed luxurious after the sparseness of those on board aircraft carriers. It was quite full of people who, like us, soon became accustomed to a shipboard routine, which was to last for just two weeks. The seas were calm, and the weather became warmer and sunnier by the day. On the fourth day out from England, we spent a few hours in Las Palmas, where a taxi driver showed us some of his favourite souvenir shops and a few sites of the island. By this time, we had made friends with many of our fellow travellers, with whom we enjoyed our meals or the various deck games designed to keep us occupied during the days of leisure.

I had a big book on practical building, which I half-heartedly tried to study whilst sitting in my deck-chair in the sunshine each morning. I knew that I should know about such things but must admit that I did not get very far in my search for knowledge. I was also growing a beard as part of my new image and had bought a briar pipe to complete the picture. The beard growing gave me no difficulty, as I had previously had to shave twice a day to keep down the bristles. It even came in handy for our fancy dress ball, when Sally and I went as Dr Jekyll and Mr Hyde.

But the pipe was a bit of a problem. I had never been a cigarette smoker, having experimented with it unsuccessfully at the age of seven in some backwoods of Devonshire. I was accompanied then by two girlfriends of similar age, and we had one cigarette and a box of matches between us. In those days, it was not the done thing to put to your lips anything which had touched those of another person, so this one cigarette was broken into three pieces – I got the little piece in the middle. Apart from singeing my nose as I tried to light it, I had nasty little bits of tobacco straying around my mouth, and just enough smoke to set me coughing. A couple of attempts a few years later, when clearing out my rabbit house, in an attempt to overpower with smoke its attendant acrid stench, was the sum total of my smoking experience. So it was not surprising that I could not keep my pipe going – and I did not like the taste when I did. By the time we reached Cape Town, my beard was fine, the pipe almost a thing of the past.

We lazed away most of the days in the sunshine by the pool, talking to the variety of people on board, many of whom had been to England on long leave and were going back to Rhodesia or South Africa. They included school teachers, nurses, mechanics, farmers, and their wives; all were cheerful and sociable, participating in all the events laid on for our entertainment. A Bulawayo farmer had started up his farm in the way prescribed for me, so naturally I found him to be a source of valuable information and one of the most interesting people I could hope to meet at that time. I spent a lot of time with him, trying to understand the many aspects of farming in a new land.

The end of the voyage came, as we arrived at Cape Town on a cold morning with low clouds and rain pouring down. It was unbelievable. We had left England to get away from that sort of weather, and our first steps on the African continent were across a wet and windswept wharf.

Inside the customs shed, we soon forgot about that as, surrounded by our numerous cases and boxes (plus ironing board), we dealt with customs and immigration officials. It did not take long, and we arranged for everything to be sent on to Johannesburg, where we were spending a few days with my elder sister Audrey and her family. As we had a few hours to spare before catching the train, we were able to have a look around at some of the landmarks, the parks with lovely flowers, the wide streets, and the modern shops. Fortunately, the sun soon broke through the clouds, the tablecloth was lifted from Table Mountain, and we were able to enjoy the sight, of which Cape Town is justly proud.

Darkness had fallen as we settled ourselves into our coupe on the train, where our two beds were already prepared for the night. This was our home for the next two nights and a day, as we rolled our way steadily along the rails to the north. We missed the scenery of the Cape Province, and by daylight next morning, which was again wet and miserable, the view was flat, dull, and uninteresting. We passed the time playing cards and draughts or just reading our books. Our day was enlivened by the calls for our meals, which were conveyed to us by a smiling ebony-faced native wearing a spotlessly white starched uniform.

This was our first contact with the black Africans, who were to play such an important part in our lives for the next thirty years. He was very concerned that we were comfortable and had all that we required, talking politely in his best broken English with ever varying facial expressions and hand gestures. He was completely uninhibited and at home with his job. We, on the other hand, were at a bit of a loss, faced with unknown foreigners, so to start with, we showed the true British reserve. Our friends on the ship had warned us that we would have to learn how to handle the natives correctly and not be too friendly with them. But by 5.30 the next morning, when the same cheerful face brought us our early tea prior to our arrival in Johannesburg, we could not help ourselves from responding to him with smiles to match his.

Big sister Audrey became a state registered nurse in Watford, and soon after receiving her silver buckle, she and another nurse friend decided to try their hands in foreign countries. South Africa was crying out for qualified nurses, and they were gladly accepted. They quickly found the country and the people to their liking; the way of life was much more free and sociable than it had been in the UK, so it was not many years before they had settled themselves in with husbands, homes, and children, with the intention of staying forever in the country they had grown to love.

Audrey had married Bill Collins, who had been born in the country of Scottish parents. He was a very successful irrigation engineer and an astute businessman. At home, he was not the handiest of men inside the house; his speciality was outdoors. There, cooking on the *braaivlais* (or barbecue), with a tankard of beer in his hand, he reigned supreme.

They were both at the station to meet us as we arrived, and after introductions and greetings, we piled into their car and were whisked away to their home for breakfast. Home was a delightful thatched house with two large circular rooms, or *rondavels,* at the front linked by conventional rectangular rooms behind. It had a large garden in which several trees were shedding their autumn leaves by the barrow load, and where one little boy was busily occupied with his toys. He in turn was watched over by two enormous great Danes that looked more like lion cubs than dogs. The house was in a little developed suburb, with the rolling countryside and a small river easily in view.

In our few days there, strengthening the family bonds with those who were to be our nearest living relatives, we were shown around the city of Johannesburg. We were impressed by the tall modern buildings and the elegant stores with their beautifully arranged window displays. More surprising were the very wide roads taking several lanes of traffic in each direction and crossing other roads at right angles at the "robots" or stop streets. The stream of cars and lorries was never ending, as in any large town, but here it seemed to go faster and included a great many sleek Mercedes and other such expensive limousines.

We had a panoramic view of the area from the top of the eight-hundred-foot Strijdom Tower. We could see some of the gold-tinted mine dumps along the reef, where numerous gold mines were situated, the source of the town's riches. Like the mine dumps of any city, these mounds were an eyesore, and we were quite happy to leave the concrete jungle and head back to the calm of its suburbs.

Hospitality plays a major role in the African way of life, and we were introduced to it on Sunday morning. A few friends had been invited around to meet us and to have a lunch time drink. They started arriving before noon and chatted happily and continuously to all and sundry on all topics under the sun, meanwhile keeping their vocal chords well-oiled with the free drinks! It was a very successful gathering we decided, as the last of the thirty-odd guests departed some three hours later.

Next morning, after fond farewells and promises to keep in touch, we were back on the train for another two days on the final stage of our journey to Umtali.

The miles did not speed past, as the rail system was not exactly express. At times, we stopped at a remote outpost, and while the engine was topped up with water, we the passengers had tea provided on the platform (or rather where you would expect the platform to be). At other times, we waited endlessly until a slow goods train had passed along the line going in the other direction. We watched the changing scenery, noting the drying maize crops and waterless river beds. We searched unsuccessfully for wild animals in the many miles of wide-open landscape, completely undeveloped, with only scrubby, stunted-looking trees dotted around on the flat Karoo Plain.

As we approached Salisbury, capital of Rhodesia, there was some evidence of development, with scattered farms and occasional small villages. We bid goodbye to two friends who had been with us from Johannesburg, as we changed trains there for the last leg to Umtali.

Gradually, as we neared our journey's end, the scenery become more varied, with large rock outcrops and big balancing boulders and occasional ranges of hills in the distance. There were many more trees, including large eucalyptus or gum trees, with their straight silver trunks holding their branches high in the air.

We were not sorry as, with darkness falling once again at what seemed an unusually early hour, we rolled slowly into Umtali Station. In all our planning, I do not think that we had given a single thought on what would happen on our arrival at the end of the journey. I suppose we had subconsciously reckoned that if we could get that far, we would easily manage the last few miles. Fortunately, the estate manager, Bob Perrett, was there to meet us and welcome us to Umtali. He quickly organised our fifteen pieces of luggage and ourselves and gently drove us through the town, up over the Christmas Pass to the hotel of that name, where we were to stay until we got our house furnished.

So our journey had ended, and another exciting new phase was about to begin. Early next morning, as we threw open the glass doors on the balcony outside our bedroom, we were stunned by the beautiful panorama which stretched before us.

Our balcony overlooked the hotel garden, full of exotic, brightly coloured flowers and shrubs. Across the road stretched open land with clumps of tall eucalyptus trees and a plantation of orange trees leading up to the foothills of some bare rocky hills. In the distance were higher hills, almost purple in colour they were so far away. But above all was the clear deep blue sky, around us fresh crisp air with an indescribably delicious smell to it.

We had arrived.

Premier Estate Umtali

I have always found that travelling to different places in the world is a fascinating experience. To arrive at an entirely new scene, hundreds or thousands of miles from what you know of as home, is exciting and stimulating, and you take in the difference through all your senses. In this case, having travelled so far to a place which was to be our new home for years to come, our faculties were sharpened to the utmost.

Mr Perrett, the estate manager, called for us at the hotel after we had breakfasted on the veranda on fresh orange juice, bacon and eggs, toast, and coffee, whilst revelling in the warmth of the morning sunshine. In his comfortable company car, he took us back over the Christmas Pass, the road over the hills to the west of Umtali (named after the early white pioneers who camped there on Christmas Day in 1890), and down the other side into the town. Umtali, third largest town in Rhodesia, was surrounded by hills and situated right on the border with Portuguese East Africa, or Mozambique.

Once again, we were struck by the wide streets, this time lined with trees which had bright orange-red blossoms. The modern buildings were set well back from the roads, with plenty of space between them; the general orderliness and relaxed atmosphere was apparent, as people appeared to have time to stop and have a chat. Certainly there was no sign of a rat race, just men and women getting on with their business, quite happily. There was a settled, stable feeling about Umtali, as though the established way of life was the best and only way and would never change. The gardens were well kept by the native gardeners, whilst the cars in the driveways shone with their regular morning polishing. The shops appeared to have a plentiful supply of goods of every description and because of the spaciousness, the displays seemed more attractive.

Over everything was the clear blue sky, adding to the picture of this clean and pleasant place; who could not but feel happy to have arrived at such a spot? After a general look at Umtali, we were driven back over the Christmas Pass to the estate, where we expected to stay for two years of training in tobacco growing and general farm management.

We had our first experience of dirt roads as we turned off the main tarmac road and headed towards the hills. The dust we had been warned about by Uncle Fred, but the corrugations which came with well-used, fast unsurfaced roads were something else. Even in the well-sprung estate car, we felt the roughness whilst the whole car rattled and shook, and the accumulated dust from the roof linings, floor mats, and all the nooks and crannies of the vehicle formed a general haze around us. Opening the windows let in more dust from the cars passing in the opposite direction, so we were relieved to turn off onto the farm road, where the surface, although holed, was much smoother.

We wound through some tall eucalyptus trees past a lush garden of vegetables, which was being irrigated from a cement-lined furrow of water, and arrived at the heart of the sixteen-thousand-acre estate.

The office was fronted by two beautifully thatched rondavels which had whitewashed walls and a red-tiled covered pathway between them, which led to the more conventional building at the rear. This was to become the future centre of much of Sally's working hours, but this morning, we just passed by to a large house nearby: the manager's residence. We walked up the stone pathway through a delightful garden, in which stood several native gardeners watching our arrival, and were greeted warmly by Mrs Perrett. A smallish woman, with a bubbling personality and very Rhodesian accent, she quickly made us feel welcome as she served the tea and biscuits which had been brought out by a white-uniformed, barefooted servant.

From the veranda or *stoep,* where we sat in cushioned easy chairs with flat wooden arms, we looked down over a wide valley towards some steeply rising hills. In between was a vast dark green grove of orange trees, with the fruit standing out clearly for all to see. To one side of this was a pasture land, with the grass yellowing through lack of rain, and on the other side a maize field, where workers could be seen cutting the stalks of the plants and building giant stooks, in which the cobs would steadily dry off. Near the office in the foreground was what was obviously a workshop, surrounded by tractors and pieces of agricultural machinery and the usual assortment of old iron, tyres, and drums which seem to go with such a place. On a level with the manager's house were four others, well set out so that each had plenty of space and privacy. Ours was to be the one next door, and we all walked over there to view our new home.

A single-storey building would in England have been called a bungalow, but that name did not seem to apply to the normal type of town or country house in Rhodesia. As space was plentiful, there was no need to build upwards, when it was easier to build outwards. Our new abode was no exception, and we explored the vast building with great interest. The design was simple, with a large living room in the centre, from which led doors to two bedrooms on each of two sides, a bathroom and a kitchen at the rear, and a large roof extending to cover it. A veranda circled three sides of the house, with a framework of mosquito netting to keep out unwanted visitors. Whilst the floors of the main rooms were wooden, those of the verandas were of cement, tinted with red ochre and polished with red polish. The corrugated iron roof was painted a similar colour, contrasting with the green of the doors and netting, while the washable interior walls were a standard cream.

Whilst we eagerly explored each room and our footsteps echoed noisily around us, a certain unease came into my mind. Apart from an electric cooker in the kitchen, the whole house was empty. Our twenty-three pieces of luggage, trunks, and suitcases – plus ironing board – which were on the way would most likely lose themselves in this new habitat.

In England, when carefully planning our expenses, we had budgeted for coal for winter fires, but we had not considered furnishing a house, buying a refrigerator, or even purchasing a car. With rent-free accommodation provided for two years, we had visualised all the comforts of home life, with a bus service or bicycle to get us around. But buoyed up with the fascinating glimpses of our future, we were not going to let minor things upset us, and we were taken back to our hotel to think and plan our next step.

We had in fact allowed a small financial reserve for unforeseen contingencies, and it was obvious that the first of these had already arrived. So next morning, we were taken back to Umtali to a reputable second-hand car dealer, where we purchased a comfortable black Ford Zephyr on hire purchase. At the end of the day, with a few technicalities such as insurance and driving licence complied with, we drove back to our hotel, very pleased with our new acquisition and our first day's work in Rhodesia.

Next morning, we woke early, with the sun rising over the distant Vumba Mountains into another cloudless blue sky. The fresh air on the balcony was invigorating and as intoxicating as champagne. It seemed that everyone started work with the dawn. The natives in the hotel gardens were calling and chatting to each other, quite oblivious of the residents who might still be hoping for a jot more sleep. The birds too were wide awake, and it was probably their dawn chorus, contributed to by a multitude of different varieties, that had roused us from our slumbers. It was Saturday, and again we enjoyed the luxury of breakfast in the open air before leisurely cruising off to see more of the estate.

The office this time was a hub of gentle activity as, with the imminent closure for the weekend, the week's work was being tidied up and reported upon, duties arranged to cover emergencies, loans given against pay earned, leave allowed to see sick relatives, and cars driven off to be supplied with petrol. People were coming and going in a steady stream, whilst others sat in the shade of the trees, awaiting their turn or for a decision to be made. Amidst this, Sally and I were introduced to numerous of the senior staff members, who found time to greet us and offer us cups of tea and words of advice and help. One offered us lunch at his nearby house, whilst the manager promised to take us to the tobacco section later that afternoon.

Everyone was very friendly and cheerful, whether they had white faces or black. We heard a lot of the native language being spoken and doubted whether we would ever get to understand the strange sounds, which were unlike any that we had heard before.

Leaving them to get on with their work, we walked up the track to have another look at our house. The garden was rather parched and` dusty, as we investigated the surrounds of the building. A large cylindrical tank stood close to the back door, with a pipe leading to it from the roof gutter. This, we learned later, was our drinking water supply, whilst the normal tap water came from the irrigation furrow we had seen the day before.

Up on a slight rise was a strange-looking contraption consisting of two forty-five-gallon fuel drums bricked into a position over what was obviously an open fireplace. Yes, this turned out to be our hot water supply from our "Rhodesian boiler." Cheap to build and surprisingly efficient, we came to know these contrivances intimately and to recognise them as part of the normal scene in central Africa.

Behind the boiler was a large stack of firewood and then open ground, rising steadily to a hill several miles long. Small trees and scrub grew among the rocks and tall dry grasses covering the hill, while occasional small brown pinnacles of earth, which we later learned to be anthills, stood out against the yellowing grass. This we were to learn was the African bush, where lived wild animals and snakes and other frightening creatures. "Darkest Africa" started at our back door, and we looked at it with trepidation.

Clive, the estate accountant, found us listing our requirements for the interior of the house and walked us over to his residence nearby for lunch. Bespectacled, as are so many who deal with numbers, he wore a loose-fitting safari suit over his sparse frame.

His wife, Fira, more than made up for his leanness, as not only was she small and round, but this was emphasised by her being seven months pregnant. She had a jolly personality with a most noticeable South African accent, and we soon felt at home, as Clive served up cold Castle beers. We discussed all the impressions we had gained so far, whilst our empty house soon became a major topic. We were given advice on where to go in Umtali to find household items at reasonable prices and directions to an auction market, where second-hand furnishings were generally available. News of the estate lorry's visit to town was also useful, as it could collect any large purchases for us and deliver them to our door.

Our talk went on steadily whilst we lunched, and we gleaned information about the other five white families who lived on the estate. We in turn gave some of our history and discussed our hopes for the future. To people who had lived in the country for many years, we probably seemed naive, as we only had the skeleton knowledge of the basic plan we were to follow. With their cognition of what it took to start up a farm miles from anywhere in the raw African bush, whilst looking at two English rookies, they could not hide the occasional surreptitious smile at each other. We realised that we had a tremendous amount to learn but were undeterred. It was obvious from the friendliness of all the people we had met so far that we would get all the help we would need. Rhodesia and the white Rhodesians were only too happy to have more white settlers in the country, and we were being made most welcome.

That afternoon, the Perretts took us for a tour of the estate in the company car. The girls sat in the back, enabling them to discuss domestic matters; Bobsey, as his wife called him, and I sat in the front to consider the more serious aspects of farm life. We passed by the now quiet workshop and a large-roofed building, which was used for washing and grading the citrus crop. Oranges, lemons, and grapefruit were grown on the estate from several hundred acres of trees. Sale of the fruit was the major source of income and gave employment to about one hundred and fifty native labourers, whose compound of houses we saw from the road as we passed by. Apart from three or four brick houses for the "boss boys" or supervisors, they were all made of poles, plastered with mud, and roofed with a rough grass thatch in various states of disrepair. Smoke rose through the roofs of many of the houses, natives wandered around, and children chased about, scattering chickens into patches of maize stalks which were interspersed with the huts and disturbing the scruffy-looking dogs. Bicycles were much in evidence, and two dilapidated cars indicated visitors to the weekly beer party.

The dirt road wound gently through a gap in the hills, which were steep-sided, rocky, and covered in scrub and *msasa* trees. On the other side of the hills, the panorama opened up again, and we could see for miles the gently undulating, grass-covered land with rocky outcrops and always the hills in the distance. We passed more orange trees at an earlier stage of growth, with a network of black plastic pipes leading water to the base of each tree. On our other side was another plantation, this time heavy with fruit.

Then came some cattle paddocks, with shiny brown and black Afrikaner cattle desultorily chewing at the dried grasses. Beside the paddock was a dip, which was unfamiliar to us. It was to be used once a week to immerse the animals in a soluble insecticide and give them protection against ticks: inhabitants of the bush which fed on the blood of passing creatures.

We parked the car after half an hour beneath some giant eucalyptus trees, their shiny silvery trunks soaring upwards, each as straight as a die, into the sparse covering of long narrow leaves. Nearby, rising not quite so high, were the tobacco barns in a continuous line – eight of them. The purpose of these buildings would be revealed to me in the course of my training; for the present, we just looked and wondered.

Close at hand was another large, low building, for which we were heading. Unlocking the padlock and flooding the interior with light from the fluorescent bulbs overhead, we stepped into the sight and smell of Virginia tobacco for the first time. Our noses worked overtime, trying to sift and analyse the intriguing aroma, unlike anything we had smelt before. It was slightly musky, sharp enough to catch at the back of your nostrils, but overlaid with a sweet smell like honey that made you breathe it in deeply and enjoyably. It certainly did not resemble that acrid harshness I associated with cigarettes.

Various-sized heaps of cured leaves were stacked on one side of the shed, with packed bales ready for the auction floors arranged along another wall. Tables were neatly aligned on the opposite side of the shed, and it was there that the graders would stand to sort out the different grades (or qualities) of the leaves. These varied from pure unspotted golden yellow to fragmenting brown, depending upon the ripeness of the leaves when picked in the fields. In three rooms leading from the main one were large stacks or bulks of tobacco leaves, about fifteen feet square and eight feet high. These were all awaiting their turn to be sorted, and as this stage of tobacco growing was currently in progress, it would be the first with which I would be initiated. Again, it looked a daunting task, as a quick calculation showed that we had been viewing about eight million leaves, which all had to be hand sorted.

Back in the car, with Bobsey answering our questions as far as possible and telling us of future plans for expansion, we drove to another section of the estate, which was the nursery for the fruit trees. Here we had a quick view of hundreds of small seedling lemon trees, which would later be budded or grafted with the variety of orange tree required. They stood in small black plastic pots under slatted wooden sun shelters, while larger, ready-to-plant saplings with white name tags were arranged along the side. Elsewhere were other varieties of fruit trees in different stages of growth. Some were being used for experimentation by the nurseryman; others, with names new to us like the lychee, were grown for their delectable fruit. One renowned product of this nursery had been a delicious, sweet seedless grapefruit, which sold well in the local market.

Our tour ended as we continued past various lands which held either drying maize plants or the bare stalks of the previous season's tobacco plants. The latter had been pulled out of the ground and put into heaps for drying prior to their being burned, so that any pests or beetles could be destroyed before the next season started. The ground between had been lightly cultivated before the hot sun dried it rocklike, so everywhere looked very tidy and ship-shape.

Sally and I were pleased to get back to our hotel late that afternoon, where we could continue talking over the many things we had seen and heard that day. The sun went down behind the hills as we arrived, and within thirty minutes, the landscape was plunged into pitch darkness.

Getting Started

It did not take us long to get ourselves organised with a few basic necessities for our house. The auction rooms had a good supply of furnishing at very reasonable prices, and we had soon selected a double bed and mattress, two old oak chests of drawers, a table and four chairs, an electric refrigerator, and a kitchen dresser. The fridge we looked on as an absolute bargain, as it was almost new. The previous owner had suddenly been transferred to an outlying district with no electricity supply and had exchanged it for a paraffin-operated model. These purchases were delivered to our front door by the farm lorry next afternoon and off-loaded by some of the labourers, all giving loud and diverse instructions to each other.

As these major items of furniture were swallowed up into positions of importance in our mansion, we learned that our trunks and packing cases had arrived at the railway station and would be collected next morning.

By the end of the week, we had unpacked everything and scattered our small hoard of valued belongings around the appropriate rooms. These still looked bare, but the essentials were there, to which we could add as the months went past. So, with just the addition of a variety of foodstuffs, we left the comfort of the hotel and moved in.

Our first job then was to choose our house-staff – this being the normal and expected thing to do. We were not sure what jobs he would perform, as we had been used to doing everything for ourselves, but as several cheerful and willing bodies were queuing up at the kitchen door, we decided to take on one, Sebastian, who had been highly recommended by his previous employer. For thirty shillings a month, Sebastian took over the running of our residence. At dawn, he would arrive and get the fire of our Rhodesian boiler going with a blaze. Then we would hear our electric kettle whistling as he made our early morning tea. This would arrive on a tray beside our bed a few minutes later. He did not cook but would prepare the table for our meals, peel the potatoes, wash up the dirty dishes, clean and polish the house, and do any other jobs as required. He could wash and iron clothes as well as any laundry.

Sebastian could speak enough English to be readily understood, so he became a useful interpreter when other natives came to the door – generally again looking for work. He carried a *situpa,* or identification book, well worn from being carried in his trousers pocket for some years. This held a few details of where and when he was born, a photograph of his smiling face, plus details of his employer and monthly pay. In this book, he also kept sundry pieces of note paper on which were references from previous employers. It was obvious from these that jobs lasted for periods of one to four years and that the monthly pay remained very much the same. He was married and lived in a thatched house at a nearby mission station. He walked to and from work each day.

One evening, he came back to our house to tell me in his broken English that his wife was suffering from a very bad stomach pain; could I help? My medical knowledge was at this time very limited, and our resources in the house even more so. I gave him two aspirin, suggested he take his wife to the mission hospital for a check, bade him goodnight, and went off to bed. Next morning, as he brought the tea, Sally asked him how his wife was faring.

"She much better," he replied, smiling broadly. "She have lovely baby girl!" Aspirin, it seemed, worked wonders!

Home now being established, we were able to set off for work on the following Monday. Sally had been accepted for a secretarial job in the estate office a short walk from our front door, so she was able to more than double our monthly income. She quickly settled into the routine, which was a bit tedious, with some systems somewhat antiquated when compared with those of Royal Naval offices in which she had been schooled.

I set forth in the Zephyr at dawn to arrive at the tobacco section for 6 a.m., at which time the labourers would be gathering around a small brushwood fire for roll-call. I had previously met David Scott, the manager of this section. In his mid-thirties, he came to typify the average white Rhodesian male. Short and solid in build with a strong, squat neck surmounted by a square head with closely cropped hair, David had been a sergeant in the Rhodesian

Army until a year before. Rugby football was his favourite pastime, although drinking cool Castles, a product of the local brewery, appeared, by his paunch, to be usurping this. With a lopsided grin below his short, bristly moustache, his attitude was that of a tough world-beater. Nobody could get the better of him and get away with it. He was his own master, and Rhodesia belonged to him. He was not too keen on having a Pommy around him, but he had no choice in the matter. He would therefore teach me, not by instruction and explanation, but by example that I could copy as I pleased.

So, dressed to kill in what I thought would be a good rig-of-the-day, ex-naval tropical shirt and knee-length shorts dyed khaki, long socks encased in tall brown leather boots, all-purpose sheath-knife on a wide brown belt, plus a wide-brimmed hat on my head, I arrived for my first day at work, ready for anything.

That day, like many subsequent days, was spent in the grading shed. The crop, having been reaped from the lands, cured in the barns, and then stored in the enormous bulks, was now being sorted for market on the auction floors in Salisbury. Pipes led steam from a boiler outside to condition, or give suppleness to, the piles of compressed leaves being taken from the bulk and weighed out into even heaps by the scales. These heaps would be taken one at a time by the graders, whose job it was to bring order out of the mixed variety of leaves. The colours varied from a clear lemon gold, with perhaps a tinge of green, through to heavily spotted reddish brown, and the object was to get leaves of the same likeness together. As no two leaves were really alike, this was more easily said than done, but the graders did their best to differentiate into about sixteen to twenty grades. Leaves reaped from the bottom of the plant also differed in quality from those taken from the middle or the top, and the tobacco plants varied with the different lands on which they were grown. So care was necessary when storing the leaves to ensure a gradual transition from the first to the last reapings, whilst the crops from differing lands were kept apart. In this way, the grades from one harvesting would hopefully blend in with those of the next from the same land.

I spent many hours standing behind the tables with the natives, watching them sort from their piles of leaves. Some were easy to identify, as they stood out in their golden perfection. Others at the other end of the spread were also easy, but those in between had me bewildered, and I found myself mesmerised by the task of identifying which leaf went onto which pile.

Checkers would come round each table and take the individual heaps to ensure the grader had done his job correctly. Then those leaves would be placed before a "tier," who was often an *mfazi* or *piccanin* (a woman labourer or child). Their job was to collect up a small handful of leaves with their butts all carefully levelled together and bind them at the stub end with a similar rolled leaf. These were called "hands" of tobacco and were stooked in heaps until there was enough of that variety to make a bale of tobacco, weighing over two hundred pounds. In one corner was the baling box and press. Into the box in a precise pattern would be loaded the hands of leaves, being compacted several times to get more and more into what was becoming a solid bale. When it was all loaded and compressed, the sides of the box were unlocked, clamps were positioned at either end of the bale to hold the wooden top and bottom in situ, the press was slackened off, and the solid block lifted out and placed to one side. Next day, it would maintain its shape without the need for clamps and would be neatly wrapped in waterproof paper and stitched up into hessian before labelling, ready for sale.

All these activities were taking place at one time, so tobacco leaves were literally everywhere, and part of the job of supervising was to make sure that none got walked on and thus broken. Tobacco wasted was money thrown away. The whole shed was kept fairly humid by the steam and other conditioners, so that the leaves remained pliable. Dry leaves fractured easily and formed a lot of scrap or waste. Conversely, anything which got damp or wet could easily and quickly become mouldy. This could spread through a bale or bulk, with a resultant loss through its being unsaleable.

The shed was like a factory, with artificial lighting overhead to give an even light throughout, while below this, the forty-odd workers shuffled the piles of leaves from place to place. Provided there was some organisation behind the apparent chaos, the end result was an ever increasing line of neatly stacked bales of tobacco ready for the lorry to take to Salisbury to the auction. This happened every two weeks when there would be about eighty of them waiting, and only then did there appear to be any real progress.

We had a two-hour break at midday so that, whilst sustaining ourselves for a further three hours of work in the afternoon, we could get our eyeballs back to normal and breathe some fresh air. It was a welcome interlude, and I used it to drive home to lunch with Sally and discuss the events of the morning. We soon found the idea of a *siesta* for a short while after our light lunch was very nice and certainly rejuvenated me, so that I no longer felt myself dozing off back at work.

The afternoon work followed a similar pattern to that of the morning, but as the graders completed their allotted number of scales, they would sort out saleable tobacco scrap from the rubbish accumulated from the day's work and then leave for their nearby homes. Gradually, the tables cleared and the tying heaps decreased until only the sweepers were left, ensuring an orderly start next day.

Opposite the nearby line of tobacco barns, work was in progress building another eight similar barns and another storage shed. As I had no previous building experience, it was of great value to study their progress. Tobacco curing barns for the Virginia flue-cured variety that we were growing stood about sixteen feet square and thirty feet high. Inside were eight tiers of strong poles, stretching from side to side of the barn, about four feet apart and three feet between each level. On these racks would be placed the tobacco sticks to which had been tied newly reaped green leaves. So the object of each barn was to support about six hundred and fifty sticks full of leaves, and to allow hot drying air from the furnace and flue pipe heating system on the floor to rise though them and exit via a ventilator in the roof, taking the moisture from the leaves with it.

The new barns were only at the foundation stage; over the next few weeks, I was able to watch them grow. Metal door frames were placed in position, concrete lintels built over the furnace positions, and lower ventilation windows incorporated at ground level. Then came the scaffolding. This did not compare with what I had previously understood to be scaffolding: those perpendicular pipes with others at right angles, all rigidly braced and looking as strong and steady as the building under construction – not here!

Small holes were dug into the ground at intervals, into which were stuck young thirty-foot trees cut from the bush. These had been trimmed of their branches but had only a rough resemblance to being straight. Much of the bark had been stripped from these uprights, and after soaking in a drum of water for a day, it was used to bind similar thinner saplings as the horizontals. Sometimes a few spare planks might be used to give a really good working surface, but the whole resembled a contraption designed by Ronald Searle! Amazingly enough, I never heard of an accident from such scaffolding, which supported numerous builders, piles of bricks, and heaps of mud. The mud was used to bind the bricks together, instead of cement, and was just as effective. When baked in the heat of the sun, it dried out almost as hard. But as it could easily be eroded by the torrential tropical rains, the finished buildings were often protected with a cement plaster.

So observing the building construction and grading of the tobacco were my chief interests, which continued over the next two months, as the weather cooled off and the nights called for blazing wood fires to give us warmth. Occasionally, there was some light drizzle from the overcast sky, just enough to make the dirt roads slippery and a nice mess of the car. We got into the routine of going to town once a week for groceries and would combine that with a film show. This normally happened on a Thursday afternoon, which we had off, so armed with a few pounds and a long list, we accomplished as much as we could. Dinner before the bioscope consisted of take-away fish cakes, which we ate in the car with a cool drink to wash them down.

We welcomed the weekly break and would get one more item for our house each time. In the evening, having turned one veranda into a workshop, I did some woodwork. First I constructed a workbench, and then I later made a kitchen table and a mahogany bookcase. In a joint production, we made a padded easy chair and renovated the chests of drawers, which Sally painted. So a new tool for my collection was my aim each week. I looked on them as investments for the future. Sally bought a kit for making a rug and spent many hours in the evenings with a crochet hook, plodding away until at last we had a rug in front of the fireplace. For pictures on the walls, we bought some glass and with passe-partout around the sides, we framed some of Constable's prints, such as *The Old Mill* and *The Haywain*. These had been given as part of a special offer at a new supermarket in Umtali and looked very nice on our bare walls. We also had a couple of my old Scimitar aeroplane photographs framed in the same way, to remind me of another way of life. Over the fireplace hung a bow and some arrows made by Sebastian. I felt it would add character to our sitting room to have some local hunting weapons around us, so these were the first of the collection, happily exchanged with Sebastian for a pair of my old socks. Sally was mortified, but both Sebastian and I were quite happy with our deal.

We had fresh milk delivered every day from the dairy, and once a week, we were treated to several pints of thick cream. This went well with the luscious fruit, which was always in abundant supply, but we found that we churned most of the cream into butter. Also supplied regularly were bags of oranges, grapefruit, and, if required, lemons. Many of these were squeezed for the fresh juice and kept readily available in the refrigerator. Neither of us was interested in alcoholic drinks at that time and could hardly have afforded them anyway, so the nutritious juice was always in demand. Finally, from the estate gardens came quantities of vegetables of all kinds. We never ran short and always had a selection on hand. These perks from the farm were much appreciated and helped to stretch out our meagre monthly pay cheques.

Back at the tobacco section, once a week we supplied rations to the labourers, as was the practice on each farm. These consisted of a large tinful of maize meal or "mealy meal," either some dried fish or fresh meat, fruit and vegetables, and some salt. Most of these commodities would be divided equally into the requisite number of piles for the number of labourers, and when their name was called out, a labourer or his wife would come forward and collect the weekly ration. The maize meal would go into their four-gallon tin or maybe an old maize bag, whilst the rest would go into their baskets. The fifty or sixty of them would gather outside the ration shed, talking noisily until all was ready and their name called. There never appeared to be any hurry, each one content to wait his or her turn. As town shops were some twelve miles away and village stores few and far between, this method did ensure that everyone had a basic supply of foodstuffs each week. The better the farmer, or the more considerate he was, the better and greater variety the food, indirectly giving him a more stable labour force, as he became known in the district as a good boss. There was, however, much left to be desired in the way of hygiene, as butchering an animal and cutting up its carcass with an axe on the floor of a shed, in a temperature sometimes around one hundred degrees Fahrenheit, brought a great hoard of bluebottles only too keen to join in the feast. These things made an impression on me, as I always associated meat with spotlessly clean butchers' shops, free of both flies and smell. But when I started to consider ways of improving the system, I found that without having a similar setup as a butcher's shop, with a cool room and air conditioning and maybe a band-saw, there was little that could be done except to try to keep the ration area well and truly clean. But I never liked ration days and was glad in later years when the system changed – but that was a long way off.

Spring

The tobacco grading and the building progressed steadily into July, while the weather continued cool during the day and distinctly cold at night. Dave and I took time off each day to check on other activities that were going on in our domain. One gang of labourers, or span, had been employed to stump out a new land. This meant that they had to dig down around the base of the many trees and chop off the stem some twelve inches below ground level. With just the primitive hoes and axes, it was not an easy task. Inevitably, the tree would continue to be held upright by its numerous roots, which had to be excavated in turn. But it was important that the job was done well, lest the plough at a later stage was damaged by hitting a solid stump hidden just below ground. Each labourer would be given a task each day to uproot some of these twenty-foot indigenous trees, the number depending on the size of the trunks. A boss boy would stand and supervise the span, having allotted the task (*ngwaza*) to each. Others in their tatty shorts and bare chests were busy chopping up the branches into lengths of about three feet and assembling them into regular-sized cords or stacks of wood, eight feet long by five feet high. One such cord was their assignment each day, and they could disappear home after the boss boy had checked it. Dave pointed out to me how the sizes of these stacks easily shrunk by the way they might incorporate a mound of earth or a tree stump at the base, visually helping to fill the pile for the axe man but of no use later when the wood was required for the furnaces. The various ruses were shown to me in front of the worker, and the explanations and protestations from him were laughable. We would laugh at his excuse while he would laugh back, aware that he had been caught out on this one occasion, but knowing too that he had got away with it several times before. Similarly, a reprimand would not stop him from trying the same trick again. Elsewhere, we had three labourers busy fencing a new paddock for the cattle. These three, led by Sixpence, a wiry little man who boasted an old bowler hat on his hairless head, walked several miles each day to get to the area where they were to continue fencing. Our job was simply to mark out the baseline for each week's work and ensure they had the necessary supplies of fence posts and barbed wire. At the same time, we checked on the straightness and tension of the completed section. It was a tough job, hammering in steel posts at regular intervals, and the barbs of the wire would often catch you unawares and dig deeply into your soft flesh.

It was on these excursions that I saw the occasional inhabitants of the bush. Often a small family of baboons crossed our path, with the babies sitting on their mothers' backs. On the Koppies or rock outcrops lived families of rock-rabbits, or hyraxes, who watched our progress with interest but disappeared quickly if we showed our own curiosity in them. Occasionally, a small buck started up at our approach. If we had any natives with us, they immediately set off in hot pursuit and often ran a mile or more in the hope of a tasty feast. Their chase was usually accompanied by shouts and directions, which alerted others ahead. These would also down tools and join in. The job at hand could be completed later.

Plans were made for the next season's crop, and it was determined that we were to grow eighty-five acres of tobacco on our section. The appropriate lands were decided upon, including the new virgin lands, where stumping was still in progress and which could be expected to grow some of the best disease-free leaf.

Then a site for the seedbeds was chosen, close to a reservoir for a reliable water supply. This was given a sound mechanical cultivation before *Sixpence* was brought in to fence the area and seal it off from both man and beast. It became very much a protected area in which any form of tobacco from previous years was taboo, as disease could be transmitted from old leaf to the new seedlings. After the perimeter was fenced with grass six feet high, one hundred seed beds were carefully laid out and meticulously prepared. A pipeline was laid from the reservoir to supply open drums at strategic points, from which water for the seedlings would be taken. A thatched hut was built in one corner to hold all the paraphernalia employed in the production of healthy plants: hoes, watering cans, fertiliser, insecticides, seed, and fumigants, plus a log book giving a record of the sowings. As the beds were progressively prepared, they were covered with a plastic sheet held off the ground on wire hoops. The sides and ends of the sheets were buried in the soil and sealed with several cans of water. Three tins of methyl bromide were then released under the tents to fumigate the soil, killing off nematodes and weeds. The process took forty-eight hours to complete, whereupon the sheets would be moved on to the next beds. It was a time-consuming business, and as the grading drew to a close, I found myself spending more time supervising the seedbeds than in the grading shed.

The weather was also changing, with a strange sense of awakening in the air, a smell of spring. The birds, of which there were infinite multicoloured varieties, like hoopoes, lilac breasted rollers, waxbills, red breasted cardinals, turtle doves, and weavers, were much more active. It was not so cool during the day, and woollen jerseys were left in the car. The trees started to blossom forth with new growth, whilst at the same time, they shed their old leaves of red and gold. Vivid blue jacaranda trees stood out in all their glory, without a trace of green to be seen. Small flowers started to blossom in the bush; life was starting again. So in the seedbeds, it was time to sow the next crop. Tobacco seed is extremely fine. To achieve our target of evenly spaced seedlings, with enough in one bed to plant out one acre of land, we needed only two level teaspoons of seed. One spoonful was added to a can of water and carefully watered one side of the bed through the rose whilst stirring the water with a stick at the same time to keep the seed distributed. The operation was repeated on the other side of the bed, making sure that the water pattern met in the centre. It was, of course, essential that this was done in calm conditions, which was a good reason for getting up at 4.30 in the morning and sowing at first light.

And that was perhaps the easy part. The newly sown bed was evenly and lightly covered with previously prepared chopped grass, to stop the sun from drying out the soil and to give some protection to the sensitive seedlings when they emerged six days later. Then the watering span was set to sprinkling cans of water evenly on each bed. My working day thus became fully engaged in organising the small span of selected labourers making up new beds, fertilising, fumigating, sowing, and continually watering the new growth.

As a reward for my efforts and for my further education, Bobsey proposed that Sally and I should go with Dave to the next tobacco sale, which was being held in Salisbury the following week. We had just over one hundred bales on the auction floor due for auctioning at 9.15 on the Tuesday morning. This again meant an early start to drive the hundred and fifty miles there, but by now, dawn awakenings and long distances were becoming quite acceptable.

Tuesday morning came and, armed with a flask of coffee and some fried egg sandwiches, we set off at speed in Dave's powerful old jalopy and reached Salisbury just three hours later.

We approached this vibrant young city from the southeast, with our eyes open wide to absorb all the wonders of a new discovery. The broad, straight streets allowed us good views of the tall buildings of offices and stores on either side. Robots stood at the main road crossings, which all went at right angles to the road on which we were travelling. The cleanliness of streets and pathways was very apparent, and we were impressed by the smart appearance of all the people we saw. Many men wore comfortable safari suits whilst others were clothed in open-necked shirts and neatly pressed shorts. Ladies bedecked themselves in brightly coloured dresses, which added a certain gaiety to the scene. Not to be outdone, nature embellished the picture with its blue jacaranda trees, which lined several avenues, carpeting the road with fallen blossoms. Lush green hedges fenced many residential houses, with brilliant red hibiscus flowers trumpeting into prominence like a scarlet fever. Well-laid-out and carefully tended parks, with beds full of exotic tropical flowers which contrasted with the green of the lawns, allowed tranquil sites in the midst of the bustle of the city. It was in just such a park that we relaxed for a few minutes with our coffee and sandwiches before driving on to the industrial area, where were situated the three tobacco auction floors. Tobacco in the Federation of Rhodesia and Nyasaland was big business and a major source of revenue for the young developing country.

Rhodesians themselves were quite heavy smokers, and the tobacco for the local cigarette factories was bought at these auctions. But the type of tobacco grown, and the going rate for it, brought it into favour with the buyers from the European and Japanese markets. The price paid at the auctions varied not only with the quality or grade of leaf being offered, but also with the competition between the buyers, who took into consideration such factors as the cost of transport and the size of the previous crop in the United States. All the tobacco grown in the federation was channelled to these three auction floors for sale, so there was great competition between them to provide an efficient service to both grower and buyer in an optimum environment.

The "floors" were basically enormous warehouses where row upon row of tobacco bales were paraded, awaiting the attention of the auctioneer and his followers. There was room for them to pass down the sides of each line of bales or even to squeeze through into the next line without going to the end of the row. A grid system of letters and numbers overhead helped to identify where our tobacco was placed, and the scheduled time for the auctioneer to pass our bales was promulgated on the day's sales board.

Overhead, the natural light of day flooded the area with the best lighting possible through large, evenly spaced windows and roof lights. The intriguing smell of the tobacco mixed with that of hessian pervaded the atmosphere, whilst the sound of voices of the many people talking was absorbed by the vastness of the building.

We located our bales, which had been correctly arranged in numerical order and filled two and a half rows. Our best bales were offered at the start, with the inferior grades and scrap coming at the end. Native workers were opening the bales along the top side and pulling out a few hands of leaf, ready for inspection by the buyers. We had time to make our own check on how the grades looked and the condition they had maintained since being pressed some weeks before. We saw and heard the auctioneer walking steadily along the previous rows towards our first bale, singing out the price and watching the line of up to twelve buyers for their signals of bids, increasing the offer until the final price was fixed. All that took about four or five seconds before he would move on to the next bale. The buyers who had inspected the tobacco briefly beforehand would, if interested in it, scramble to catch the eye of the auctioneer, so that facing him across the open bale of tobacco, they were often squeezed together like the bale itself.

The melodious incantations and shouts were incomprehensible to growers like us, but fortunately, behind them came a translator who was engaged in snatching up the sales ticket, quickly scribbling the price of the sale with the buyer's name, and finally throwing it back to the appropriate bale. Just as in the grading shed, we had seen order emerge from apparent chaos, so here order re-emerged once the chant faded into the next line.

We were now able to inspect each bale and consider whether the price paid for each pound of tobacco was good, bad, or indifferent. We still had the chance of cancelling the sale if we felt the price was not as good as it should be.

As we left the scene for a further cup of coffee at the restaurant overlooking the floor, native workers were busy stitching up the open bales and wheeling them away on their two-wheeled trolleys to the waiting lorries outside. They all worked with a will and speedily, often scooting back precariously on their unladen trolley. Others would be bringing in fresh loads, ready for the next day's sales, while sweepers continually went the rounds, keeping everywhere spick and span.

The sales sheet arrived after another half an hour, listing the prices received for each lot. It did not mean much to me at that stage, but Dave seemed quite happy with the final result, so, the business of the day being finished, we were able to go and have a look at the shops before setting off back to Umtali.

The days grew steadily hotter and hotter, and the seedlings got bigger and thirstier. The lands were being ploughed, harrowed, and ridged into lines a set distance apart. In the midst of the heat, the natives were called on to mark the planting spots with pre-cut straws and then inject each place with a fumigating gun. This was to kill the nematodes in the soil, which could stunt the growth of the tobacco plant. It was a hot, dry, and dusty job and sapped the energy of the best workers. By midday, we would call a halt until the next morning. Bush fires became a threat to the dry maize lands where the harvesting was not complete. Sometimes caused by combustion as a result of the concentration of the sun's rays through glass bottles, or by discarded cigarette ends, these fires rapidly spread though the tinder dry bush. As they increased in size, they also generated their own wind, which fanned the blaze into a travelling disaster. When smoke was seen near our boundaries, the alarm would be given, summoning all workers to board the tractor and trailer and rush off to the source. There, armed with branches of leaves or hastily pulled shrubs, they would attempt to beat out the flames. With major outbreaks they would burn back towards the fire from a roadway or previously constructed fire break, as directed by the manager in charge. Everyone available joined in the fight, which could last for several hours. Hopefully, we would end up near the farmhouse of somebody we knew, and there, whilst the natives quenched their thirst from the nearest garden hose pipe, the bosses would down an ice--cold beer. We might spend twenty minutes there discussing the fire, tobacco sales, and the latest political matters before setting off for home and a good cleanup.

Walking through the bush a few days after a big fire was a new experience. For once, with all the grass and shrubs gone, it was possible to see for considerable distances. Small rock outcrops appeared where it had seemed none previously existed. Skeletons of bush animals were discovered, some with snares attached to nearby trees; anthills became clear, standing many feet high like enormous stalagmites, with their colonies of termites safely working away below ground. The smell of the bush also changed from that of burnt wood to a delicate sweet smell as a carpet of small pink and white flowers blossomed forth, only days after the inferno.

It was after one of these bush fires had blackened the hills behind our house that Tim Dooley and Elaine arrived from England on their way to Karoi. They had sailed to Beira with their Morris shooting brake car, which was well laden with many of their prized possessions, themselves, and their three young children. We knew approximately when they were coming and so had plenty of food in the house to give them a welcome break on their journey. But we had little to offer them in the way of beds. However, that did not worry them. They were prepared to camp out along the side of the road on the way to Salisbury until we advised them against it, what with lions and other wild animals about. After a good meal and lots of discussion about Rhodesia and how we were liking it, and of course our hopes for the future, they all dossed down on rugs on the floor, or in our not-too-comfortable deck chairs.

They departed in the early hours of the next morning, determined to get to their new home at Karoi in good time to unpack and get started in their new life. It was lovely to see them again, even though it was only a brief visit. It was a source of great comfort to us to know that there was now somebody else from our previous way of life living in the same country, just up the road, just two hundred and fifty miles away.

Summer

October was known as "suicide month," as the heat often drove people beyond the limit of their endurance. Air-conditioned offices and shops were still things of the future – gently revolving fans stirring the hot air was the reality of the time. Out in the tobacco seedbeds, the heat and the continual watering encouraged vigorous and rapid growth of the young plants, and it was now time to toughen up the first sowing, ready for their transplanting into the lands.

This hardening-up process started with a clipping of the leaves with garden shears, taking care not to cut across the heart of the plant. Then we stopped watering them completely for up to two weeks. From the lush, rich green, sturdy upright plants standing six inches or so high, they steadily changed until they looked rather sad and limp, with singed brown outer leaves. I thought the system was rather drastic, but each morning after the cool night, the plants would be standing up again and ready for another hot day.

The preparation of the last lands was almost complete, and trailers with water tanks and hose pipes were being readied for the next operation: planting out nearly seven thousand plants on each acre. Each day, we would watch the sky for any sign of rain. Small cumulus clouds would appear at midmorning, grow steadily, and then disappear by midafternoon. The rain was fairly predictable each year, however, and we were told to expect it in our area about 10 November. So about two weeks before that, the appointed day arrived for starting the planting operation. The first four seedbeds were soaked with water overnight and again in the early morning, to loosen the soil around the roots of the seedlings. Then at the crack of dawn, all the available labourers assembled on the site and religiously washed their hands as directed, before starting to pull out the plants from the beds. An hour and a half later, the beds looked decimated, whilst the seedlings had been carefully stacked on a trailer and covered with wet sacking. We moved off to the first land, where buckets and tins were available to take water from the hoses to the planting holes. There the many labourers, who again included the mfazis and piccanins, were organised. One filled the holes with water, another dropped a plant close by the hole, a third planted the plant with a trowel, whilst others kept supplies of water and plants coming from the tractors and trailers. As one tank was emptied, the operation came to a halt, and everyone took a well-earned rest. The next tank was brought into position on the nearby roadway, and the first was driven off several miles to the main water supply to be refilled.

It was a "Heath Robinson" affair: very inefficient and labour intensive, but as dusk approached, we had about three acres planted out and would expect to do about the same each day until the job was finished. If rain came, we would manage without the water from the tankers, but the prospects at that time did not look good. Each day seemed to get hotter as we worked from dawn until 11 a.m. and resumed about 2.30 p.m. until dusk about four hours later. There was no shade about in the lands, and tempers at times flared when something went wrong: punctures in the trailer wheel, taps left on (wasting valuable water), seedlings left uncovered with their roots drying out, labourers disappearing in the distance to relieve themselves and returning, unhurriedly, twenty minutes later.

At the end of each day, we could just see the new plants looking a bit lost in the open spaces. Those of the previous days were hardly visible, as they had shrivelled up considerably. But again, they came back to life in the cool of the night and were sustained by the water with which they had been planted. So first thing in the morning, as we arrived in the lands, the previous planting stood gamely a few inches above the surrounding soil. After two weeks with still no rain, we went back over the first day's work, and where a plant had obviously died, another was put in. By doing this, we hoped not to have many gaps when they started to grow.

Farmers around us were similarly occupied with their various systems: some better, others worse than ours. Several felt it better to await the first steady rain and just plant with that, so doing away with water tanks. Such matters were the subjects of discussion at Field Days, held each month on different farms under the auspices of the local tobacco conservation and extension officer. He was able to co-ordinate local farmers and discuss the pros and cons of different methods of each stage of tobacco growing, backed up by reports from tobacco research stations. We had been to a Field Day the previous month in which the main topic had been seedbeds and had offered to have the next gathering on Premier Estate, where we could discuss planting and show off the new tobacco barns.

So, with a week to go and only occasional showers around on distant farms, our tobacco was not looking too good for visitors. The new barns, on the other hand, were just about finished. Dave and the builders had spent many days struggling to erect the new tier poles in each of the barns and also to install air blowers to force-circulate the hot air throughout the drying leaves (a new idea). Now, with the roofs on and top vents in place, the carpenter was putting on the double doors while the builder completed the furnaces.

One old man – a *mandala* – with a wheel barrow of about the same age had the job of tidying up around the new buildings, clearing the old broken bricks, pieces of wood from the now dismantled scaffolding, and the oddments of rubbish which new buildings seem to attract. Many useful items had already disappeared, having found ready use in the nearby compounds. Why, for instance, leave scaffolding lying around when it can be used for firewood? Similarly, the wire holding it together had a multitude of uses, from fixing bicycles to making snares. So the mandala was not overworked, and on the Field Day morning, all was looking ship-shape. Work was to continue as usual in the afternoon, and the boss boys were briefed accordingly and warned that visiting "*bwanas*" would be coming to see them in action – action being what we hoped to see, as each farmer was convinced that his labourers worked better than those of the neighbouring farmer.

The morning had been hot, as usual, and very sultry, more clouds than normal building up over the lunch time break. At half past two, as some twenty farmers arrived for our meeting, so did the rain – a steady downpour for the next two hours. Naturally, we were considered to be most fortunate, and everyone speculated on how widespread the rain might be. Had it reached their particular farm twenty miles away? Most were optimistic, and the sudden cooling of the temperature and freshening of the air, with that unbelievable smell of sweet fragrant earth that comes with the first rains, put new life and cheerfulness into the gathering.

The discussions ranged from buildings, such as the new barns, to the new machines being tried out for tying the tobacco leaves onto the tobacco sticks. Many questions were asked, many methods discussed, and much advice given. It was obvious to me, as a newcomer, that there were a lot of ways of growing and handling the crop. I would have to investigate each one and decide which I considered to be the most practical for my circumstances.

Because of the rain, we did not move the conclave to the scene of the planting, staying instead in the shelter of the building until nearly five o'clock. As the visitors dispersed, so the rain also stopped, and Dave and I rushed off quickly to see how well the water had soaked into the soil. We found that the labourers were plodding on, albeit a bit bedraggled and muddy. Most had on their new bright yellow rain capes with hoods, which had been issued to them a week before, so that they all looked very much alike.

The number one boss boy was identifiable by his umbrella, the status symbol from under which he was quietly supervising the situation. Water was still being tipped into the planting holes, as the soil was still dry two inches below the surface. The rain, which had seemed a lot, was still insufficient to enable us to discard the water tanks. We would just have to hope for more. Meanwhile, it would certainly bring new life to the first acres.

It was about this time that we received a telegram from my younger sister, Margaret, in Bombay. She would be arriving in Beira a week later and asked us to meet her off the ship, the *Karanji*. Margaret had been Daddy's favourite daughter, probably as a result of her being at a more amenable age when our father returned from Burma after the war. She had progressed through her adolescence to become a resourceful individualist with a flair for mathematics, which had been passed on to all four children from our father. With this talent, Margaret had worked for several years in my father's office before eventually deciding to see some other parts of the world, going on an overland trip to India. We had received several postcards from her along the way and had now received confirmation of the date of her arrival at Beira. She would then spend two weeks with us before continuing to Johannesburg to stay with Audrey.

Beira, in those days, was a favourite weekend watering place for many Rhodesian families. It was the nearest seaside resort, with a good road from Umtali. The town itself boasted some good hotels and a great variety of restaurants which specialised in prawns *piri-piri* and Portuguese wines such as Lagosta. It was a Portuguese settlement, as opposed to British, and had a very different atmosphere from Rhodesia – more exotic, more exciting. In the middle of the afternoon, we collected Margaret, and another girl she had befriended en route, from the small steamer in which they had travelled third class, with numerous Asian families. We then spent a while wandering around Beira and seeing the sights before sampling their delicious prawns and driving home.

It had been hot as usual and very humid by the sea. As we started on our way, the skies opened and the rain teemed down. By itself, it was not a problem, as the windscreen wipers were able to cope, but combined with the rain came clouds of vapour from the hot tarmac road. Away from the town, there was no definition to the edges of the road, there being just grass and undergrowth and trees. So the next hour's drive until the steam disappeared was very difficult and not eased by the excited chatter of the passengers. As we got farther inland, the steam and the rain disappeared, and the stars came out into a clear night sky. After a few difficulties, we found the residence to drop off Margaret's friend, taking them by surprise to say the least, before continuing to our home.

It was fun hearing all the news of what had been home from Margaret, in her animated, squeaky voice. In return, we showed her all around our new locality, emphasising the many excellent features of our new life, quite convinced that our move had been the right thing to do and that we would be in Africa forever. We had a small party in her honour, serving a quite lethal car smash cocktail, which had even Bobsey letting down his hair. As the guests had only to drive home along quiet farm roads, there were no misfortunes reported next morning.

After a flying visit to see the Victoria Falls, Margaret continued her journey to Johannesburg, where she stayed for several weeks, working to gain some funds for her return to England. Then back to us for a final week before boarding another bus in Salisbury on the next stage of her interesting journey. This bus was driven by Cyril, the same driver as on the trip to India; surprisingly, they married several months later! Together, they made one more overland trip to Northern India, with Cyril as driver and Margaret as hostess, after which they packed their bags and emigrated to Adelaide, Australia. They still live near there now.

Back at the lands, the plants continued to struggle with the lack of steady rains. Since our Field Day five weeks before, we had felt only a few drops. The first lands had managed to get away and were standing nearly two feet high, with their leaves drooping during the day. The later plantings were stationary, to such an extent that we had suspended the planting out of the last thirty acres until steady rain arrived. Meanwhile, the labourers were kept busy hoeing and cultivating the first lands, where the weeds were quite happy to grow. Others were engaged in carting in the cords of firewood for the furnaces, stacking it carefully at the back of the new barns. New tobacco sticks were being cut from the bush, each labourer being given the task of finding fifty straight saplings about six feet long, trimming them, stripping off the bark, and carrying them to the nearest road for the tractor and trailer to collect.

At our house, we had progressed to building a chicken house, with a lot of assistance from Sebastian, and obtaining ten "point-of-lay" chickens to provide us with eggs. It seemed a great scheme and had full support from Sebastian, who obviously realised that he too would be on to a good thing. But before the first hen reached the production stage, a snake took a fancy to it, and we ended up with one dead hen. Sebastian had heard the commotion and retaliated by killing the snake, which he proudly kept to show us, along with the chicken. Both disappeared thereafter – the snake into the fire of the boiler, the chicken, I fancy, into the cooking pot at Sebastian's house.

Snakes were plentiful around Umtali; I had already met several types in the bush and the lands. I had a certain amount of fear of them, having heard numerous exaggerated stories of their power and speed. But, as I had to live with snakes around me, I decided I had better find out all that I could about them, and the best way to do that was to catch some. I enlisted Dave's assistance, and whenever one was seen, we would do our best to capture it. Sometimes, we had an old sack or box in the back of the car and we would carefully manoeuvre the serpent into it with the assistance of a stick. On one occasion, with nothing else to hand, I took off one of my Wellington boots and carried home a puff adder in the foot of it. We were careful in what we did, not risking any bites from the sharp end. We kept the current snake in the tobacco bailing box, whose sides were too high for most snakes to escape. There, we could study them, and with the help of a field guide to snakes we identified them and found out whether they were poisonous. On our next visit to town, one of us would take them to the local snake park. We were not looked on too favourably by the natives, who instinctively killed all snakes and often brought enormous dead ones for us to see. These included a fifteen-foot python, which had apparently attacked a small child. The python was declared a protected species in the federation, but it also had a superstition about it – if you killed one, the rains would not come. This certainly seemed to be the case this year, as it had been brought in to us at the beginning of September and now, in mid-December, we were still desperate for some good rain.

As we progressed in our knowledge of snakes, we handled more and would pick them up by their tails. An eighteen-inch night adder I found had a large frog in its mouth, not having had a chance to swallow it. The head and half the body of the frog were not visible, but all four legs were doing their best to stop further progress. I thought the snake would be quite safe to lift by its tail, but fortunately, I had a small stick with me. As I placed the stick across the neck of the adder, it ejected the frog from its mouth instantly and was ready to do battle. I was amazed at its quick reaction and was also surprised to see the frog making a rapid retreat, hopping smartly down the row, none the worse for its experience.

Three days before Christmas, the rains set in, and we were able to complete the operation we had started eight weeks before. The ground was now soaked, the soil sticky, puddles on the slippery dirt roads, and everywhere beginning to show green. This allowed us to celebrate the festive season without the threat of a continuing drought.

On Christmas Eve, we distributed extra rations to all the workers, with both meat and fish plus lots of vegetables, salt, and the usual large tin of maize meal. For the wives and piccanins, there were special additions of sugar, biscuits, and sweets, and everyone was given a bonus of spending money to make the holiday a success. We would all have two days off. Permits to brew beer had been given to various employees the previous week, enabling them to brew a forty-five-gallon drum each of rich, potent beer from fermented sorghums. They would do well over the holiday, selling their product at sixpence a cup and really adding to the party spirit.

On Christmas Day, Sally and I exchanged our presents which, due to financial constrictions, were to be practical ones – mine, a vise for my workbench, Sally's a pressure cooker for the kitchen. After dismissing Sebastian for the day, with a new shirt for him and appropriate presents for wife and daughter, we called on our neighbours to exchange greetings before driving up to the Vumba Mountains for a planned Christmas lunch. Imagine our chagrin to find that there was no turkey and ham on the menu, nor Christmas pud with holly on the top. Instead, we had curry. Our disappointment was not complete, as we were unable to get the Queen's speech on our radio. We sat in the car, fiddling for a good reception, with the rain pouring down outside. I think at that time, we were just a bit homesick. So feeling low, we went back to some friends in Umtali, who had invited us to a party that evening. There, we did have the traditional spread in a homely atmosphere with Christmas decorations around us, so that life did not seem that bad after all (although I had my doubts later, when the Scottish dancing on top of my turkey had a distinctly detrimental effect).

We met with new faces of residents who had settled in Rhodesia a number of years before and who were now running businesses of their own or in managerial positions with local companies. They were interested to learn of our plans to start up a farm in Northern Rhodesia after my two years' experience. As usual we heard the advice of "Don't go to the Black North!" which seemed to be the standard remark. On investigation, we never met up with anyone who had actually been to the Black North; they had only heard or known of a third person who had experienced the country and had dreadful tales to tell. These were mainly about the arrogance of the natives who were of very different tribes from those in Southern Rhodesia. As there were far fewer white people in the north, the country was less developed with inferior roads and facilities. In fact, at the later breakup of the federation, it became obvious that much of the development of Southern Rhodesia had been funded from the copper mines of the Black North, to the detriment of that country. Undoubtedly, the white people kept together and will continue to do so as the different cultures in Africa, or anywhere else in the world, do not easily mix. They can generally get along and work together, each hopefully benefiting from the other.

So, in Southern Rhodesia, a country with a small population of white settlers, I think it was a propaganda move to try and persuade any newcomer to stay and swell the ranks. It became apparent that politics was a subject in the forefront of everyone's thoughts, and the latest happenings were chewed over even at Christmas parties. The 1959 elections in the UK had taken place two months before, with the Conservatives winning. The consensus was that this would be good for the federation, whilst many said they would have left if the Labour party had come to power. I was surprised to hear this mentioned, as I could not see how English election results could affect us. Only a few years later did it become clear, but now with a glass of beer in my hand, I listened to the discussions and news of quelled disturbances in which the ringleaders had been jailed, and quietly planned to at least go and have a look at the Black North before making my decision to continue there or to stay in the South.

The first three months of the year were very busy on the tobacco scene, as the next activities commenced. The plants grew rapidly and, when about four feet high, pushed out a flower which had to be topped or broken off. This would then force "the weed," which tobacco was, to put more growth into the leaves whilst trying to produce another flower and so reproduce itself. These attempts, in the form of suckers, growing from the junction of the leaves with the stem, also had to be picked off before they grew too big. This was a job for the piccanins at tuppence an hour, whereas the *mfazis* would be paid a bit more. It was a laborious and never-ending job, but the group who performed it regularly each day seemed quite content, going at it unhurriedly without a care in the world, except having food ready for their husbands on their return from the reaping.

The main labour force was concentrated on reaping the crop. This started before the middle of January when the bottom two leaves were plucked from each stem, carried to waiting wire baskets which, when full, were transported to the tying area near the barns. This might take about four hours each morning, covering each section of the lands in turn and starting over again with the next two leaves when all the lands had been covered. With about sixteen leaves on each stalk, it meant we went around the lands once a week for two months as the leaves ripened from a dark green to a lighter yellowed green. When the set area had been reaped, we moved back to the barns, where some freshly cooked *porter-hye* was available to all. This was a baked mixture of maize meal with sugar liberally applied; it looked like a thick biscuit. It was very popular and sustained the vigour for the next few hours of tying the tobacco leaves on to the sticks for the barns. In this operation, the cabbage-like leaves were strung three at a time on to either side of the *matepe,* until it was full of about a hundred leaves. The string was secured and the full stick carried into the barn, where it was borne aloft by other strong hands and suspended across the topmost empty rack. This work continued for several hours until all the crates had been collected from the land and had been tied and stacked in the now-full barn. It was a relief to see the last few leaves disappear, while the tying area was swept of broken pieces of leaves and the empty crates stacked on the trailer ready for the next day. The natives were weary and so was I, although my job was only supervising and trying to ensure a steady, smooth flowing operation without hold-ups.

Curing the tobacco started immediately after the loading of the barn was complete. Fallen leaves were tied and racked, the barn floor swept, and wet sacks placed on the flue pipes through which warm air started to circulate from the freshly lighted fire. The temperature was kept at about 90 degrees Fahrenheit for the first two days, as the humid air caused the green leaves to change colour to a yellow or orange. As the colour approached that, the wet sacks were dispensed with, the ventilators opened progressively, and the temperature increased by stages up to 160 degrees, which it reached three days later. This meant that the moisture in the leaves was driven out from the web of the leaf into the midribs and then that in turn was dried out at the high temperature. The yellow gold colour would be fixed and the leaves would shrivel up in the heat. It took approximately a week to cure each barn, with a steady roaring wood fire in the furnace, day and night. In the latter stages, fans were used to ensure an even heat, right into the corners of the barn.

Wet midribs in the storing bulks would cause mould and mean lost tobacco.

At the end of the week (as shown from the record on the barn door), if the midribs were found to be dry, the fire would be allowed to die out and the doors opened. If we did this at lunch time, the cool, moist night air would normally be sufficient to condition the cured tobacco and enable it to be taken out next morning. The leaves were now rather like chamois leather, as they had picked up moisture from the air and become pliable. In that condition, they could be handled without getting broken. As they picked up this condition, they also gave off a rich aroma, like sweet honey – a pleasant smell which I had missed, since grading had finished four months earlier.

Keeping the barn temperatures correct was the job of those looking after the fires – normally, one mandala and his younger assistant. It was not an easy job, controlling the heat simply by the size and number of the logs put into the furnace, but somehow they managed. If the temperature went up too soon, the leaf would dry out with a green tinge, whilst a drop in temperature could cause the colour to become a muddy brown, like a sponge.

As part of my training and to save the manager from getting up in the middle of the night, when the barn-boys also liked to relax, I was given the task of sleeping by the barns so that I could check the gauges every three hours. So my routine changed; I left for home in the early afternoon, whilst tying was in full swing, and returned at nine o'clock in the evening, armed with a naval-type hammock, flask of coffee, and alarm clock. Having checked that all was well on arrival, with no fallen leaves or matepes on the flue pipes, which could set the barn afire, I would set my alarm for the next random check, sling my hammock on the verandah where the tying took place, and settle down for a few hours' sleep. This procedure naturally had the barn-boys splitting their sides with mirth, as they had never seen anyone sleep in a string bed before. I would awaken with the bell ringing persistently in my ears, get up, and check the nearest barns. With luck, the gauges were near enough correct, and I could do spot-checks on the rest before having a word with the firemen. When the temperatures were well down, it meant they were asleep on the job and needed to be jolted into action. This could be done with a loud noise in their ears once they were found or perhaps by a can of water up their trouser legs. Both worked effectively, and for the next few nights, the fires were well attended. Weekends were the worst, especially if someone had brewed a few gallons of their favourite drink; then I might find myself doing as much stoking as they did. Natives are not keen on the dark, when their ancestral spirits roam about, and it was easy for them to be frightened. So the changeover at midnight was accompanied by paraffin lights, torches, and much noise to scare off any evil spirits. By five o'clock, dawn had arrived, and the routine of the new day got under way. When Dave came along at six o'clock, fully rested and showered after his night's uninterrupted sleep, all the gauges would be correct.

This routine continued until the end of March, through all sorts of weather and many heavy thunderstorms. Additional labourers were taken on to untie the tobacco from the strings after the curing was complete and then to carefully stack it in the different bulks, awaiting the grading. There was not much time off, and when there was, I used to catch up on missing hours of sleep. Often our reaping had to continue on Sundays, as the ripening leaves were not respecters of the days of the week.

But in spite of that, our idea of a trip to Mkushi in Northern Rhodesia, the fearsome Black North, turned into a planned holiday for three weeks in April, when the curing would be almost at an end. Letters were sent off to the powers-that-be responsible for the settlement scheme, advising them of our intentions and also to the Dooleys in Karoi, who were going to join us on our excursion. Maps were found, distances measured, questions asked. The car was given a de-coke; new bushes put into the steering rods; spare petrol cans loaded into the boot; and hammock, rugs, water bottles, and emergency rations prepared for loading. Soon the day came, and we set off, eager to get away for a well-earned break but with some apprehension about what we would find.

Chapter 4
The Black north

First Look at Mkushi

First port of call was Salisbury, where we went to the tobacco auction floors to see the start of the sales for that season. Knowing just a little bit more than on my last visit, I thought the price was good for the inferior primings and sandlugs, or lower leaves, which were on offer. The sellers were quite content.

After a breakfast in the canteen, we made calls on the B.S.A. Company, seeking an increase in my £20 per month salary for the next year, also on the Home Affairs Department, who were responsible for the land settlement schemes. There we were given names of contacts in Lusaka who would, in turn, update us on progress in the Mkushi Block and give us all the assistance we might require. This sounded reassuring so, armed with that information, we continued our journey for another hundred and fifty miles to the farm at Karoi, where Tim and Elaine were living. It was wonderful to see them, and we greeted each other more like family than friends. Their house was much smaller than ours, being that provided for a farm assistant who was expected to manage without too many modern conveniences. Lighting, for instance, came from pressure lamps or ordinary paraffin lanterns. Similarly, the fridge was run on paraffin. The hot water system we recognised as a Rhodesian boiler similar to ours, giving off lots of very hot water into the second-hand bath in the small bathroom. We were fortunate that two of their children, Marilyn and John, were away at boarding school in Salisbury, and we were thus accommodated in their room for the two nights of our stay.

Elaine was a good cook and quite happy to potter away at the stove, preparing all sorts of homely food in her easygoing disarray. Both she and Tim came from the West Country, where they had been childhood sweethearts. They had placid natures, which helped them to sail unruffled through all sorts of difficulties, which was fortunate, as organisation was not their strong point.

Tim showed me over the farm next day, as we discussed the various aspects of farming with which we now felt familiar. He had had quite a lot to do with cattle on the farm, and he thought cattle might be a better investment in Mkushi than growing tobacco. Both of us had seen some of the maize growing but were unsure how well it would grow five hundred miles farther north. I told him that if Sally and I liked what we saw in Mkushi, we might try to find a farmer to teach me there for my second year of training. In that way, I could learn the problems of the area before actually starting on my own. Tim thought that would be a good idea but with three young children, two at boarding school, he was not prepared to change his situation until he had completed his training at Karoi. However, he was ready for the visit to Northern Rhodesia, his Land Rover laden down with all the likely necessities for the next week. Next morning, this time in convoy with the Dooleys, we set off on the road again.

The countryside became more and more hilly as the narrow road wound its way up to the Zambezi escarpment, from the top of which we were able to look down and across the plain to the mighty Zambezi River some miles away. We zigzagged carefully down to the level ground and kept our eyes open for the elephants which frequented the area, as was evidenced by the enormous visiting cards they left behind them. Across the Beit suspension bridge, we passed, looking down at the turgid river below, then on into more hills, passing small native villages with their usual scattering of chickens and waving piccanins until we came to cross the Kafue

River, on a bridge which had once spanned the Thames in London. A few miles farther on, we drove into Lusaka, the capital city of Northern Rhodesia. Named after the native chief who once ruled over the surrounding area, it was not an impressive town. There was a cement factory some miles south and a stone-crushing plant closer to town, both of which contributed to the dusty look of this windy city. It was set on a flat plain almost devoid of hills or trees. Although the road through the city was wide, there was little else to compare the town with its counterpart in the south. There were no tall buildings with elegant shops and tree-lined pavements. It was a developing rural farming town with various manufacturing companies spread around and a rail head supplying the necessities of life from the outside world.

We found our government contact without any difficulty and had a long discussion with him. He was again most helpful and very enthusiastic about the progress of the Mkushi Block. Some thirty families had settled in the area so far, and more were coming each year. Those already there had been farmers or farm managers in Rhodesia or South Africa and felt that the offer of about two thousand acres of land, of which one-third was guaranteed to be arable, plus a long-term loan, was too good to miss. The area stretched for nearly fifty miles along the road leading from Northern Rhodesia to Tanganyika, spreading twenty miles in depth on the southern side of this road. Nothing had previously existed in the area, just tall indigenous trees and wide grassy drainage areas called *vleis.* A survey had been made by the ministry of lands, which then planned an initial development of one hundred farming units, linked by a network of dirt roads. Each farm was to have an access road bulldozed into it, forty acres of trees would be stumped by bulldozers, and a bore hole would be drilled so that a source of water was available. As two rivers, the Lunsemfwa and the Munshiwemba, ran through the area, some farms would also have a river frontage and could draw their water requirement from there. The costs of these developments would be recovered over thirty years, together with the long-term loan of forty-five hundred pounds.

The good points about Mkushi were naturally explained fully and enthusiastically in the same way that an estate agent will describe the fine features of a house. Other factors – such as the distance of fifty miles to the railhead; town and hospital one hundred miles; deliveries from town once a week; party-line telephones being installed in the distant future – were mentioned in passing. Feeling full of confidence, we parted from him to continue on our way towards Chisamba, where we were to spend the night with another ex-naval officer, Basil Williams, and his wife, Alma. They were just completing the second year of training and were in the process of moving onto their farm. We were warmly welcomed like long-lost friends and feasted on barbecued chops and sausages in the cool evening air. First-hand information was now available on the country; it did not appear to be alarming after all. Basil was full of enthusiasm and well equipped with maps, figures, and drawings and plans of all that he was about to do. We were most impressed. I think we even felt that we were missing out by being a year behind him.

So next morning, sustained once again by a full breakfast, encouraged by all that we had learned, we finally approached Mkushi. The slightly undulating land had become steadily more wooded, with trees now reaching up to about forty feet. Views from the strip road, which had two narrow tracks of tarmac rather like a railway, were limited by these trees, and the scenery only changed as we crossed the infrequent rivers or streams. Amongst the woods, we could see many of the enormous anthills about which we had been told. These often stood half as high as the trees themselves, in their uneven conical shapes, their termite colonies either extinct or working away well below the ground.

Mkushi was first shown on the signpost when we were a few miles past the rail head of Kapiri Mposhi, which boasted both a café and a petrol pump. We followed the sign onto a wide dirt road, which eventually led us to the Mkushi Boma. This was the seat of the area administrator the district commissioner, and his building was clearly recognised by the Union flag fluttering outside. An orderly array of offices was surrounded by a polished red veranda floor and a disciplined garden, which was being continually watered by the expected garden boy with his hose pipe. Government messengers, in short khaki uniform, puttees, shiny black boots, and a red fez atop their curly black hair, sat outside one office, ready to take messages to far-flung villages or to announce (with foot stamping and smart salute) visitors such as ourselves.

We were warmly welcomed by the D.C. and introduced to various other officials including the land settlement officer, Sir Richard Codrington, who would show us over some farms next day. We discussed labour problems, crime, future development, and the many other things which had come into our thoughts and on which we were seeking reassurance. We were persuaded that everything would be done to make the scheme a success, thus opening up good farming land, increasing the agricultural output of the country, and diversifying the economy away from its reliance on copper mining. There were problems with labour, caused partly by the shortage of natives in the area and their general lack of knowledge of tobacco growing, as they had previously been employees of the copper mines. As far as crime was concerned, there was none to worry about, as most were inter-tribal quarrels which would not affect us. Politics, the D.C. admitted, were an unknown factor. Although the federation was expected to continue, there were no guarantees, nor could anyone predict the future.

We spent that night at the Mkushi River Hotel – a very small establishment which justified its title by being the only hostelry within a hundred miles. It was scenically situated amongst some tall trees beside the River Mkushi, which babbled its way noisily southwards towards the Luangwa River. It was quiet and peaceful, with the smell of wood smoke in the air from the usual Rhodesian boilers. Later, the throb of the generator could be heard until lights-out at 11 p.m., when silence again reigned supreme. We tossed and turned for a bit, with our minds full of all we had seen and heard. We were looking forward to seeing some farms and farmers next day, as that would be the ultimate factor in our assessment of the Black North.

We had not met with many of the natives. All that we had met were in the positions of servants or assistants. They were clean, well dressed, cheerful, respectful people. The only others that we had seen from the road were often decked out in clothes that had seen better days many years before. Only the occasional person wore shoes while the piccanins wore nothing at all. None of them appeared at all threatening to us – quite the reverse we could not help smiling at them in the same way that they beamed at us, waving as we drove past them.

We made the rendezvous with the land settlement officer, who showed us on the map of the area where we would tour that day. Then followed him on to the minor roads of the block to finally disappear down a rough track, which turned out to be a farm road. We stopped where there was a large square clearing in which the bulldozed trees had been pushed into lines stretching across the cleared land. There we solemnly studied the ground, the grasses, and the size of the wind-rowed trees before us. We were told of the acreage of the farm, learned the expected output of the bore hole in gallons per hour, and saw the general layout of the farm on the map. All these facts, of course, went into our heads, where no doubt they milled around before largely disappearing. How does one determine what would make a good farm from a piece of wooded Africa miles from anywhere? What, for that matter, were either Tim or I looking for? What should we look for? Our knowledge was limited in the extreme, but buoyed up by youthful aspirations, we inspected, listened, and asked questions.

We called on a farm nearby where the farmer and his wife, Miles and Pamela Cornhill, had been settled for nearly two years. Miles was happy to show us his progress whilst giving his viewpoints on the area and preening himself on the results he had obtained from his first two crops. Tobacco, it seemed, ripened more rapidly in Mkushi than in Southern Rhodesia, where he had previously farmed. But it was top-quality leaf, which fetched good prices on the auction floors. He showed us a few acres of maize which he was growing. Now drying out, the plants stood much higher than those we were used to, the cobs also being much bigger. He led us on to the adjacent farm, which had not been allocated to a new settler. We again wandered through the trees, looking at the vigorous growth of everything.

On our way back to the farmhouse, where the girls were learning the good and bad points of keeping house in a new farming area, we stumbled across some enormous white bones and the skull of a large animal. It could have been a small elephant; we were not sure. It was enough to start us talking on the animals he knew to exist in the area: sable, roan and eland antelopes, smaller duikers and bush buck, occasional lions and leopards, plus the usual baboons and monkeys. Some of these were potential hazards to crops and livestock, others were sought by Afrikaner farmers, who were keen on shooting them for the cooking pot.

Back at the simple farmhouse, a cold lunch had been prepared for us all, quite unexpectedly. We were surprised at the hospitality shown to four complete strangers such as ourselves but came to realise that it was the normal happening, as restaurants or similar facilities did not exist. Also meeting people and exchanging news was a highlight of life in the bush, as the few people around were spread over a wide area, and visitors were few and far between. In return for their friendliness, we happily chatted away on our experiences and views, becoming convinced by now that we would be coming back to Mkushi to join with them in the pioneering adventure they had undertaken.

Our exploration of the area continued during the next two days, using the map to find our way around. Everywhere, we met up with the same warm welcome and were offered refreshments, beds for the night, or just directions to get us back to our country hostelry. Tim and I had finally found the piece of land which we decided would be the best. Its boundaries had not yet been decided, so we hoped it could be split in two, with Tim having the western half, me the eastern half. It fronted the Munshiwemba River, before which Tim was planning to have his house, with rolling green lawns. My plans did not extend quite that far, but we contentedly advised Sir Richard of our chosen areas before bidding farewell to Tim and Elaine, who left on their return to Karoi.

Sally and I remained to see if I could find someone to train me for my second year. That afternoon, we had been told of a get-together of many farmers at a rugby football match on Van Tonder's farm. We went along to watch this spirited entertainment, the main object of which appeared to be to raise a thirst for the cold beers which followed. We were invited to join in the happy throng and partake of the braaivlais held as night quickly fell. Most people were about our age, had just enough money to qualify for the scheme, and had been farm assistants or managers before starting out on their own. They were all convinced that in spite of the enormous amount of work involved, they would be successful and make their fortunes. Van Tonder was a bit older and more astute. He was aware of the potential of the area, especially where maize was concerned. He was already in the process of buying a mill in a township fifty miles away and was planning to grow a large acreage of maize, which he would process through the mill and sell at a much higher price. He not only provided us with beds for the night but offered me a job for my second year. I could grow his tobacco crop for him. He would not pay me but was prepared to house us, so payment would come from experience.

Next day, I was offered another job. This was on the farm of David and Valerie Kaminer, which was situated almost at the start of the block, where the distance to the railhead was only forty miles. David was a small, very wiry man with thick rimmed glasses. He was much the same age as myself, well experienced in farming, with advanced ideas on producing good results. He would not hesitate to invest hard-earned money if he felt it would improve the crop next season. His lay-out of barns and handling sheds was of a standard pattern, with the addition of a well-equipped workshop with oxy-acetylene welding gear. To keep his wife happy, he had built a delightful, large house with a magnificent thatched roof. As a result, it was cool in the hot weather and warm in the winter cold. We lunched with them, during which David said that his farm assistant would shortly be leaving to return to South Africa. He asked if I would be interested in taking his place for a year, during which time he could continue to train me and supplement my income with another sixteen pounds each month – almost doubling my present income. For housing I would take over the building adjoining the tobacco sheds and would be free to alter and improve it as I wished, at his expense. An inspection of it showed that a lot of work was required to make it habitable to our standards, but the offer was too good to miss. Our own hoped-for farm would be only ten miles away, which we could visit and even plan on starting some work ahead of time.

Subject to approval from the powers that be, we accepted the offer and planned for an arrival date four weeks later. This suited them, as they were to holiday in South Africa for four weeks immediately after our arrival, leaving us their house to live in, our abode to renovate, and the farm to run during their absence.

We left Mkushi next morning, called at the Ministry of Lands in Lusaka, on the Dooleys at Karoi, and at the B.S.A. Company in Salisbury on our way back to Umtali.

Our plans were approved, so we started our last few weeks work on Premier Estate, interspersed with farewell parties and packing. About this time, Sally determined that she was pregnant, and naturally, this became a major topic of conversation. Many of our friends said that the future baby would be a girl, as the citrus fruits, which we so enjoyed on the estate, seemed to be responsible for more female babies conceived there than males.

Four weeks later, accompanied by Tom-Tom, our cat, and a car packed with our precious goods, we arrived back in Mkushi on the next stage of our farming life.

Wendy Ann Arrives

Our goods and chattels, which we had locked away in a railway truck in Umtali, arrived at Kapiri Mposhi three days after our arrival in Mkushi. A message passed on from the only farmer nearby with a phone had a tractor and trailer together with four handlers despatched to the station next morning to collect our worldly possessions. On arrival back at the farm, these were stowed away in a barn whilst we were being accommodated by David and Valerie. The first week passed rapidly, as I was shown the organisation of the farm and met the boss boy, the tractor drivers, and the labourers while being briefed on the jobs in hand. My first impression was of a happy farm with a contented labour force. The contrast with a big estate having several different sections to it made it feel more friendly, or homely, as well as more manageable. So when the owners left for their holiday with strict instructions not to call them, I had no qualms; after all, my philosophy remained "Anyone can do anything."

Many of the labourers were occupied shelling maize cobs on a simple tractor-driven machine. The dried leaves of the cobs had first to be removed by hand, thus slowing the progress. The second tractor was busy towing trees off the newly stumped lands into the standing trees around the sides. There, other labourers were busy chopping their cords of wood. Apart from periodic checks, I was able to concentrate with the builder on making a home out of the shed we were taking over. Built against a large tobacco handling shed and designed for similar use in years to come, it had three rough brick partition walls forming a bedroom, living room, kitchen, and bathroom. The water system was very rudimentary, as was the drainage. The previous occupant had chiselled a furrow in the cement floor, through the wall to the outside garden to let the water out! Most of the floors had big cracks in them, so starting with the bathroom, each floor was taken up and new ones laid. The plumbing was sorted out before replacing a newer bath and wash basin, while outside, a new soak-away was dug to accept the waste water. Our toilet was a long drop, about fifty yards away, where you took two steps up and sat on a well-constructed wooden throne.

As soon as the new floors had hardened, the walls were plastered using clay from the small ant heaps, which were produced in profusion in the grassy vleis. These were crushed by being smashed with sticks and mixed with some sand and water to form a plaster, which when dry was almost as strong as cement, at a fraction of the cost. During a trip to Broken Hill for our monthly supplies, we collected some wall paints in delicate pastel colours, ordered a new front door, and bought some curtain material for the windows we had installed. The final move was to tidy up, form a garden in front of our new home, and put a layer of long dried grass on the corrugated iron roof, to reduce the scorching effect of the hot sun. By the time the owners returned, we had finished our new dwelling place and taken up residence. They were somewhat amazed at the transformation of what had been a hovel and must have immediately realised that we were newcomers with high standards. From that moment on, we were the best of friends, working and playing together without fear of upsetting the employer-employee relationship. We felt quite at home in our abode, ready to welcome and entertain the neighbours and visitors who dropped in to see how we were progressing.

Over the weekends following pay day, we listened to the drums of the natives throbbing away in the dark of the night as they celebrated their time off in their traditional way. It was fascinating to hear these drums beating almost monotonously into the early hours of the morning. At times, they caused a certain amount of unease, especially when news of troubles in the nearby Belgian Congo was filtering through to us. The southern boundary of the Congo, Pedicle, was only about twenty miles away, although there were no roads or towns for about one hundred miles. Rumours of native uprisings with slaughtering of missionaries passed along the grapevine and was later substantiated by the BBC World Service, to which we listened for news each day. We heard that the Rhodesian Army was "exercising" along the border areas, ready to pounce on any marauding bands of warriors who might wish to spread the trouble.

Instead of native raiders came a steady stream of white refugees who had literally upped and off at the first sign of trouble, leaving everything behind – even wives and daughters. Being some fifty miles off their route from the Copperbelt to the south, we were unable to offer any assistance but heard from others in Broken Hill and Lusaka of steps taken to assist those frightened people. Unkindly, we criticised the Belgians for fleeing in the way they did, blindly believing that we in Mkushi, being made of sterner stuff, would not have done the same. Surely, we felt, this episode on our borders must strengthen the need for the continuance of the federation.

The hot weather progressed, and our seedbeds grew once again. We were able to cool off each lunch-time in the swimming pool alongside David's house. That was bliss, especially for Sally and Valerie, both of whom were pregnant and expecting in the early months of the next year. We took a much-needed siesta after lunch each day, lying almost naked on our bed, waiting for the heat of the day to pass before starting work again.

It was during one such rest that a rat invaded our privacy from the shed next door and fell off the rafter onto Sally's bare tum. Consternation ruled supreme for the next ten minutes as, accompanied by screams from Sally (now standing on the bed), I chased the rat around the room in my birthday suit until it eventually escaped through the open front door, from whence it had probably come. Ideas of going home to Mum and to a civilised country were eventually met with a compromise of making sure there were no more rats on the farm, and life gradually returned to normal.

I continued to catch the occasional snake and was very fortunate one morning to find a large puff adder in the garden, just before we set off to town. I took it in a sack to the pet shop, where the sale price was sufficient to buy us breakfast. The pet shop was interesting, as it had two large gaboon vipers in a glass box: two of the most deadly snakes to be found in Africa, with their magnificent diamond-shaped patterns giving an amazing camouflage against dry leaves. I don't know where the snakes went to from there and, eating my hearty breakfast, was not really worried.

Much spare time was taken up, costing the equipment, the labour, and the various buildings for our farm. The government had written to say that the area we had earmarked had been split into four farms, and I was offered the one on the side requested. After taking David there for confirmation of my views on its suitability, I accepted the offer and got them to permit me to start some work there before my two years of training were completed. This would allow me to get another forty acres of land stumped out during the coming rains and so enable me to grow that acreage of maize as well as the tobacco. Several new farms were being built around us that year, naturally becoming the focus of our attention to see how they managed and what problems they experienced. Good planning was essential, starting from the clearing of the land for both buildings and crops, as well as laying on a reliable water supply from bore-hole or river to a reservoir where, hopefully, the water could then gravitate to the buildings and gardens.

Organising contract brick-gangs to make the requisite number of bricks was a major undertaking, as they required a constant supply of water, sand, grass, and later firewood. As the buildings went up, so door frames, window frames, furnaces, scaffolding, and finally roofing materials had to be available when required, to prevent unnecessary hold-ups.

Elsewhere, the land preparation for the next crop had to be kept going to schedule, in spite of breakages or unforeseen difficulties. Fortunately, in Mkushi, there was always someone to call on for assistance, in the form of nearby farmers. One would help lay out foundations of intended structures, another repair a break on a tractor linkage with his welding gear, yet another would help with the chimney design for a fireplace.

Agricultural companies in Lusaka could also offer technical assistance when it came to what size of water pump and engine was required, what fertiliser should be applied to the lands for maize or tobacco, or what supports should be provided for large roof areas over the tobacco shed. Gradually, after continuous grappling with ideas, costs, and problems, my plans resolved themselves to such an extent that I had a good blueprint worked out in advance of moving onto our piece of bare African bush.

Meanwhile, at David's farm, planting time had arrived again, and with little fuss, we swung into action, with two tractors towing two-wheeled water tankers into the rows at a slow pace, enabling the four natives at the back time to fill each hole with water. The "waiters" with the seedlings followed with the planters, so that the job progressed in a steady, orderly fashion. The rains arrived two weeks later, as we completed the planting of the fifty acres and immediately continued with sowing the same acreage of maize. In this, the workers were well versed, as they grew their own maize each year for their own larders. Two pips dropped together on the top of each ridge, covered with earth by a useful foot, and the process repeated a pace forward. Within a week, that crop was sown, leaving just a trial ten acres of ground nuts to be put in the ground in much the same way.

The rains were favourable from the start, the crops grew steadily, and we had some of the best-looking tobacco in what was obviously a highly competitive area. But there was a long way to go, with all sorts of hazards still to be faced. We were fortunate just before Christmas to escape much damage when our tobacco was hit by a slight hailstorm. Little harm was done, but it became clear how a crop could be wiped out by a heavy storm. Insurance was available, at a price.

Christmas came and went with the usual celebrations, during which the four of us became quite close. We saw each other each day, the girls comparing notes as they grew in size, we men making plans for the day or night when we would have to make a dash for the Broken Hill Hospital ninety miles away along the now-muddy road. Our cars were equipped with a pair of scissors and a shoe lace – just in case we got stuck – and vague instructions obtained on what to do. Sally came back from the long drop one wet morning very proudly stating that she had killed her first snake. She did not share my liking for these creatures; I was surprised that she had not simply made a hasty retreat. She was reticent about describing the snake or the dangers she had faced, so I decided to have a look. After a careful search for an injured monster, all I found was a poor battered earthworm, which might have been three inches long in its prime. To Sally, it was a snake and has remained so to this day.

Farm work continued, with reaping in full swing using tying machines in the lands so that the picked leaves went straight on to the matepes. The system worked well. Golden tobacco came out of the barns each morning, as we made space for that day's reaping. The maize grew vigorously in the hot and wet conditions, never being short of moisture, as had happened in Umtali. I traded in the Zephyr for a Peugeot vanette, which would be the farm workhorse for fetching supplies from town. I also started a crew of natives stumping on my land and another gang under Alfred, a polite, well-spoken builder, to start cutting poles and erecting a pole-and-dagga house for our first couple of years' residence.

Finances being limited, I had decided that we would not invest in a large brick house until we could afford one. Instead, a well-constructed mud-plastered wooden building with a waterproof asbestos roof would be our first homestead.

The political scene was not improving, with outbreaks of trouble on the Copperbelt, causing a lot of headaches. Sir Roy Walensky, the federal prime minister, was forever reassuring us; he had a lot of support from settlers from miles around at a meeting in Broken Hill. He surely would look after our future, he would be listened to – a respected man like him. But a few weeks later, after the London conference about the future of the federation, we were not so sure. The winds of change were blowing over Mkushi and the federation. The tension was amazing and most noticeable even in the farming areas, where politics were not a major topic but where most settlers had staked everything. We were afraid that in their efforts to progress the indigenous natives, the British government would ignore the advice of the white politicians living in the country and give the natives control of the country by votes for everyone, regardless of whether they had any property or education. We were sure that the votes cast by most of the indigenous population would go to those who promised most for least, leading to innumerable problems for everyone.

There were, as yet, very few black people in positions of responsibility; all of the development of the country so far had been planned and managed by the white man, assisted by the black natives in the lesser positions of power. We considered that there were improvements going on in their lifestyle, more and more being employed as business expanded, enabling them to purchase radios, bicycles, and smart new clothes from the spreading number of trading stores. Many of these were owned and run by Asians or local Africans. We felt that there would be a government run by the people of the country eventually, but why rush it? Let it come gradually.

Valerie produced a son and heir, Roy. Three weeks later, Sally brought forth a daughter, Wendy Ann. All thoughts of farming or political troubles were forgotten. The night that the waters broke was a beautiful moonlit evening, the road unusually smooth as the vanettte purred its way to the maternity wing of the hospital. Some hours later, Wendy arrived and was in my arms in a small blanket, still with forceps on her navel cord, just a few minutes later, whilst Mum was attended to. I walked up and down the veranda outside the delivery room with this blue-eyed bundle of joy in my arms. Life was great. There would be no stopping us, no turning back. Come what may, our home was in Mkushi, and we expected to stay there for years to come.

Foundations

After forty-six inches of accumulated rainfall, the wet season came to an end in the middle of March, just four months after it had started. Curing was already finished, as the excessive amount of rain had made the tobacco ripen at a rapid rate and caused some loss in the land through over-ripeness. Preparations were being made to start grading the crop, and I was given reasonable amounts of time off to work on my farm. There, the first job was to repair the road. This had been built across the vlei drainage areas, without any culverts or water channels being installed. As a result, my access road was completely washed away in three places where the water had broken through. Forty-five-gallon oil drums from the oil depot in Lusaka and surplus to requirements now came in useful as culverts. With the ends cut out by hammer and chisel, several lines of them were laid in position, end to end, as a water channel, with vanette loads of soil packed around and on top. Two weeks later, the road was again useable down past the newly stumped lands to the site where our house was being built.

For ease of building and structural strength, I had designed this in three individual sections. The smallest block, in the form of a square, was the kitchen. A few paces away in line with it was the bedroom block, with two rooms and a bathroom. Parallel to these was our main living room, with a dining area opposite the door to the kitchen. The poles for these buildings had been erected with spaces left for doorways and windows. For the latter, we planned on wooden frames with mosquito netting, saving money on window frames and glass. We did not think it got cold enough to worry about insulation or warmth, so no fireplace was even considered. The poles were stuck into the ground alongside each other and held together by horizontal lengths of thin saplings, a few nails, and some strips of bark in strategic places. To ensure a firm, secure roof, a platform of imported timber was nailed to the top of the poles and well-constructed roof trusses set on top. Once I had nailed the asbestos sheets in position, the builders were able to start the next operation of plastering the wooden poles with a nice clay mud. As the first layer dried out, further layers were added, filling the cracks and unevenness until it passed inspection. Doors and windows were put in, ridging capped the roof, and then a cement floor was carefully laid in each room. The kitchen and bathroom, with its flush toilet, were plumbed, ready for the bath and wash basin from David's farm (these now being surplus to his requirements). Then everything was painted: pastel shades on the inside, as we still had some of this paint left, and white wash around the outside. With some red paint applied liberally on the window frames, our new home looked a treat.

On 3 June, as David no longer required my assistance, we were ready to move in. With bath and washbasin disconnected from one house and me busy reconnecting them in our new home, Sally suddenly went very sick: Malaria had struck! She and Wendy had been spending the day on another farm with Norma and Glehn Curtis whilst I got on with the work. She got progressively worse as the day went on, and when Glehn brought her home at the prearranged time, she was welcomed by Adam, our excellent house boy, and then went straight to bed, where she stayed for the next four days. Norma, one of the kindest, most helpful persons you could ever meet, kept Wendy and happily looked after her for those four days. She loved children, having three of her own, and considered one more as no extra effort. Norma was only about four feet nine inches high and very much a gentle lady. She and Glehn enjoyed entertaining with a well-laid table illuminated by candles and supplied with delicious food cooked by Norma over a hot wood-fired range. Cakes were her speciality, and she rarely visited any of her many friends without taking just a small something with her. She smoked continuously, was not a dynamic personality, but certainly was the boss in her own home and a tower of strength to Glehn as he developed his farm. He was a good farmer, always doing things the right way. Very little flustered Glehn, although he could get quite hot under the collar at times. He was always ready to help anyone in any way possible, sparing no expense in doing so. He and Norma were a perfect match and did much to further the spirit of goodwill that prevailed throughout Mkushi. So after four days in very good hands, having been thoroughly spoilt, Wendy came home to roost to a weak but improving mother.

Malaria used to strike at almost any time, the mosquitoes not being selective about where they took their blood. The natives were at risk most, having no protection in their huts from the nocturnal invaders. We, at least, had mosquito netting over our windows and slept under nets. But the effect was the same for those infected: Firstly, a feeling of not being very well, rapidly followed by feeling chill and shivery whilst the skin felt hot and the temperature went up. Nausea, diarrhoea, and a general feeling of not wanting to live would set in. Bed and medication was the only remedy. The worst of the fever was expected to pass in about two days, leaving you feeling as weak as the day you were born. Many of the natives got malaria each year, having their strength sapped out of them in this way. Fortunately, chloroquine worked wonders on them, and a good supply was always kept on hand to treat them when necessary. These were not the only cures kept in stock, as once we took up our residence, we became the general physicians for all the farm labourers and their families.

After roll call each morning, when jobs were allocated to the growing rank of workers, came sick parade for those who were ailing and others who just liked the taste of the cough or stomach *muti*. "*Muti*" was the African word for medicine and must be known by all farmers and others south of the African equator. To start with, I used to give aspirin if the trouble was above the waist and diarrhoea mixture if it was below. Much of the time, I was correct, but as my knowledge advanced and my need of fit labourers also intensified, so my muti chest expanded until I was even giving penicillin injections to those who were badly sick. There was a clinic at the Boma twenty-five miles away along the dirt road, but during busy times, that was a long way. My injections became sought after, even though the needles became blunt. The opinion of the natives being that the more the injection hurt, the better it was.

Brick making was now in full swing by two contract brick spans, each making one hundred thousand bricks with further contracts to those making the best. Not far from the cleared site for the buildings, two large anthills had been selected for use; the undergrowth was cleared and ground levelled nearby ready to lay out the drying bricks, then work started in earnest. Using hoes, the soil at the base of the ant heap was dug up and water liberally applied to it. Other workers, up to their knees in the mixture, tramped it into a well-blended stiff mud. Enough was prepared each afternoon for the following day's task of filling the requisite number of wooden brick moulds, which were then carefully turned out in lines on the cleared area before being lightly covered with grass. There they would slowly dry and harden in the sun while the process was repeated. Upright grass stalks marked each day's task set by the contractor, until there were enough bricks for the first kiln to be made, holding about fifty thousand bricks.

It would take about a week to collect the bricks together into the carefully built kiln, with evenly spaced tunnels through its base for the fires. The whole would be plastered with a good layer of mud to prevent the fire from breaking out and, instead, burn steadily away inside the oven. Finally, the firewood would be piled in and a burning stick from another cooking fire applied. For the next six days, the furnaces would be stoked; steam would rise steadily from the top of the kiln, which gave off not only a tremendous heat but also an unmistakable sulphurous smell, which could be detected half a mile away. When a clump of dry grass thrown onto the top of the kiln burst into flames immediately, the bricks were considered to have burnt sufficiently and the fires allowed to die out. A week later, as the temperature cooled off, the bricks, now a burnt red colour, with a ring to them when tapped, were ready for use.

Glehn came over one afternoon and helped me lay out the foundations for my barns and sheds. I finally decided to have two sections of four barns facing each other, with a wide roofed area between them and another large shed across the ends of the barns. In this way, I was able to employ two building gangs who operated independently, and by using barn walls which were already there, I obtained roofed areas at minimum cost. With sliding doors on each end, the tractors would be able to drive through the complex, with loads of tobacco or whatever was loaded at the time. But initially, after a full afternoon's work, Glehn and I had just a pattern of sticks and strings criss-crossing over the cleared area. Next morning, the digging of the foundations started, trenches appeared between the strings, mounds of soil alongside. Soon the first bricks were laid, with the usual mud or *dagga* mixture between them to bind them together. About three weeks after the first brick was laid, the foundations were completed. We were back to ground level.

At the end of June, our homestead now running smoothly with the assistance of a cook and a house boy, we invited Valerie and David for dinner one evening, with a rubber of bridge to follow. Our cook, Tamara, was a wizened little man who had come from Nyasaland many years before. He was very versatile, cooking us the meals organised by Sally with little fuss and not too much idea of time. But the end result was usually excellent. Assisting him and doing the many other cleaning jobs in the house was Adam, who was with us for just three months. He was visiting an uncle in our area while on leave from Salisbury where, it transpired, he was a table boy at the governor general's residence. This we were unaware of at the time of taking him into our house, but when Sally saw the way the table gleamed with the shining cutlery and our crystal glasses from which peacock shaped napkins emerged, she asked him where he had learned to set a table so splendidly. Thus our evening commenced on a high note, although we were all beginning to feel rather cool. Until now, a woollen jersey each evening had been sufficient to keep us warm. We did not expect it to get any colder, but that evening it did. For a while, our polite guests stayed with us as we played our bridge, wrapped in warm coats with gloves also in evidence. After a while, we gave up, as outside a frost descended. Our first guests departed, and Sally and I headed for the warmth of our bed.

Next morning, window frames with glass were sought, and the builder started to build a fireplace and chimney. We were to find out that June and July each year often brought some very cold nights. Ice on the windscreen of the vanette was not unusual, leaves of trees and shrubs would turn dark brown as though burnt, and plants such as bananas would go black overnight.

By now, many pieces of necessary equipment had arrived on the farm either in the vanette, which brought a tremendous variety of goods from town on each visit, or by delivery lorry. The engine and water pump had been installed above the flood line of the river, lengths of piping joined together to lead to a storage tank mounted atop another anthill near the building site. The new Massey Ferguson tractor, which was to be the major workhorse of the new farm, had arrived and was already busy with chains towing the tree stumps from the new lands. A smaller second-hand tractor had also arrived, with a new four-wheeled trailer, and was engaged in carting wood for the brick kilns. At the end of the main farm road stood two fuel tanks for petrol and diesel, supplied by the oil company which had solicited my business, knowing the amount of fuel required on expanding farms. Stacked in the trees by the building area were metal door frames, window frames, coils of reinforcing wire, pockets of cement, a drum of oil, and other assorted oddments which would be required in due course.

David had given me a two-wheeled trailer which had been made up from an old lorry chassis (and needed more attention before I was able to put it to use), also a framework with discs for making the tobacco ridges and fertilising them at the same time. From another neighbour, who was changing from Ferguson equipment, I was able to buy a plough and harrow. All these pieces of equipment on which the crop would depend were lined up neatly but almost lost in the trees near the building area.

Agronomist salesmen arrived in turn from the three major fertiliser companies to discuss the planned crop, study the vegetation and take soil samples. On these their recommendations would be based as to how much nitrogen, phosphate, and potash should be applied to the soil to get the best results. They returned a few weeks later, after which one was chosen, the order given, and arrangements made for payment from the first sales of the tobacco crop. Delivery would be made onto the farm by the end of September.

The land settlement officer called each month to see how developments were progressing. As permanent improvements were made, such as the completion of building foundations or newly stumped lands cleared, so I was eligible for amounts of the government loan, at the rate of thirty shillings for each twenty that I had spent. His job was to assess the cost and make sure my work came up to standard. There was much competition amongst the four of us who had started that year, and it was my intention to keep ahead of the field. This was possible thanks to my early start on the land as well as to my knowledge of where to go for the farm requirements.

As the weather started to heat up, so did the pace of development. Seedbeds were prepared, lands ploughed, scaffolding erected around the rising barns, tier poles were cut and built into the wall, task work was given for cutting matepes, timber and corrugated iron arrived ready for the roofing. It was continuous hard work, from dawn to dusk. But still somehow, we managed to join in with the occasional social events occurring in the district, as was expected. A piece of ground had been set aside by the Lands Department as a club site, but as yet there were barely enough farmers with sufficient spare money to build a club. Instead, we had farmers' meetings and socials on people's farms, generally in a swept tobacco shed where bags of maize were arranged as seats and a few crates of beer stacked in a corner.

A cricket team had also come into being, led by a couple of keen Rhodesians: Dennis Bourdillon, who was handy with the bat, and Murray Herron, who could frighten many of our opponents with his fast bowling. Anyone who had ever played cricket was expected to turn up for practise on Thursday afternoons at four o'clock. Matches had been arranged every three or four weeks with friendly teams on the Copperbelt, Broken Hill, and Lusaka. There we would meet on a Saturday afternoon to be greeted by the local team, accommodated in their homes, and given a welcome party in the evening. Next morning, often feeling the worse for wear, we donned our white flannels for a serious game of cricket. Our wives and babies, of course, accompanied us on these excursions, which were welcome interludes from the farming scene. Work permitting, we would spend a further night in town to allow shopping next morning, so that we would arrive home fully laden but refreshed and ready to continue the fray.

By the time the midday temperature each day was in the mid-eighties, the seedbeds were sown and looking green, the lands were being marked out and fumigated, and the main building operation was the roofing of the first barns and sheds. Although carpenters could be found at a price, I had planned that I would roof all my buildings using two or three labourers to assist me. So each morning, after starting off the various other jobs, I found myself precariously perched on beams at dizzying heights, armed with a hammer and roofing nails, affixing the never-ending supply of corrugated iron sheets on the barns and sheds. It's not a difficult job, even though the straight edge that you are trying to achieve cannot easily be checked when it hangs over a thirty-foot drop. The main problem was getting the not-too-sharp nail though the surprisingly hard iron in the position required. Holding the nail was naturally done between finger and thumb, whilst attacking blows were made with the heavy hammer. Periodically, one blow (or more) would miss the nail. Regrettably not being equipped with an automatic stop, it would normally make contact with the nearest thumb, flattening it very successfully and forcing an involuntary gasp of agony from deep within its owner. Many were the times that I wrapped my painful bleeding thumb in my handkerchief, only to hit it again with the next blow! In spite of that, the roofing progressed, a new look was given to the buildings, and some cool shade was available below.

The builders were able to fill the gap between the top of the walls and the roofs, spare labourers used to level the floors and lay broken bricks ready for cementing them, and even the walls of the storage shed were treated to some coats of whitewash. We were really getting organised and experienced a satisfactory sense of achievement, but there was no time to sit back, as planting time had arrived.

The final preparations were made in the lands, with roads every thirty yards across the land, at right angles to the ridges, to allow easy access for the tractors during reaping time. Water carts were readied, with short hose pipes at the back. The seedlings had been clipped, sprayed, and hardened, and on the first Monday of November, everyone except the builders and brick-spans, who were firing the last kiln of bricks, swung smoothly into gear planting out our first crop of tobacco.

We worked steadily for two weeks, and with only a few acres left to plant, the skies opened to give us a wonderful soaking rain. We were able to finish that afternoon, exulting in the fantastic start we had received as we drank in the earthy smell of the first rains of the season. It really looked like *Pennies from Heaven*. I was determined to make the most of them.

First Crop

The following week, the maize lands were ridged, fertilised, and sown with the maize pips, whilst other workers checked for missing plants in the tobacco lands, planting new ones where necessary. All of a sudden, the intense pressure of getting everything ready for planting before the rains came, and getting the roofs on the buildings, was lifted. Now we had a breathing space, whilst the crops grew, to do the hundreds of small jobs that had had to wait just such an opportunity. It also gave me chance to relax at home on a Sunday, and well I remember one such day, when with the rain pouring down outside, we had a traditional English lunch of roast beef and Yorkshire pudding with crispy roast potatoes, green beans, and cabbage from the garden to go with it. A good nap on the settee afterwards was enough to convince me that life really was great. With my organisation and planning, Sally's support at home, and the hard work of my native labourers, we now had a farm on which the first crops were growing. Yes, I had a terrific sense of achievement. I was proud of all that I had accomplished but also realised that there was still a very long way to go. But on such a Sunday, with Wendy the centre of attention as she crawled around the floor, we could really relax for a change, write letters home, and think of what came next. We had just had confirmed that Sally was again going to add to the family in May of the next year, so plans were made for the addition of a son and heir, with great thought going into the choosing of his names, an ideal occupation for a wet Sunday afternoon.

The names of our natives often amused us, as they appeared to have been given them for the nice sounds they had, regardless of meaning. "Sixpence" was quite common, "Spider" unusual and somewhat sinister, while "Stamp" was obviously destined to go far. Many had names influenced by the mission schools, where parents had learned the names of the twelve apostles and had selected their favourite name from them.

When a native came onto our farm looking for work, he would generally go to the compound where the huts were gathered, as in a small village. There he would enquire as to whether it was a good place to work, how good the pay and provisions were, and what the boss boy was like. He would also learn what tribes were represented amongst the workers, not being prepared to join the farm if the majority and boss boy were of a different tribe. If all seemed favourable, he would seek out either me or the boss boy, saying he would like to work – this either in English or Fanakalo, which was a common bastard language used initially in the copper mines and common throughout southern Africa. I had to learn this in order to communicate with the natives but found that a large list of nouns connected with a few verbs and plenty of gesticulations went a long way to some frequent misunderstandings. Fortunately, my boss boy had learnt English at a mission school and was able to translate whenever there was something serious to discuss. For the size of crops I was growing, I needed about forty to fifty labourers, so it took a while to build up to that number.

I would take details of the newcomer from his identity card and allow him a week to build himself a hut to live in and get himself organised. The tractor and trailer would assist him after normal work was finished, to collect poles and thatch for his house, whilst I would often assist with the vanette in collecting his belongings or *Gatundu*: wife, children, and chickens from the place of his previous employment. The huts they built for themselves were very basic pole-and-dagga one-room huts, of a size to suit themselves and their families. Their quality varied from very good to very poor, often an indication of how well they could work and how long they were going to stay. The industrious ones quickly put their hoes into operation in the ground around their hut, where they planted the usual maize pips, sweet potatoes, beans, tomatoes, and pumpkins at the appropriate times.

As Christmas and the reaping season approached once again, I was nearing my required size of labour force, but all was not well, as too many were reporting sick each day. It was not a specific sickness which was easily cured with doses of medicine, but one more sinister, as it had its basis in African folklore. Enquiries uncovered the belief that the boss boy was putting evil spells on various labourers while they slept at night, so that in the morning, they had not the strength to go to work. My medicine was not powerful enough to cure these people, who undoubtedly looked pale and listless. It was of no help my scoffing at their beliefs or telling them to shake themselves out of it. They believed the boss boy had put an evil spirit on them, so they could not be cured unless the boss boy was sent away. Like it or not, I got the message. I fought it for as long as possible, not wanting to discharge someone who was doing a good job, but eventually I had to give him a week's notice and find someone to take his place. Even then my problems were not solved, as seven or eight others decided to leave, as the farm was no longer a good one. By now we were reaping the superb-looking crop but also having teething problems with the furnaces and the associated heating systems inside the barns, which were smoking too much, needing longer chimney flues to get a better draught. So losing nearly a quarter of my labourer force at that time was a tremendous blow. There were very few spare labourers around, as every farmer could utilise extra labourers during the peak season of reaping.

Fortunately, a solution was forthcoming, as one of my better workers, Jonas, said he could find employees at his village near Kanona, about one hundred and twenty miles further northeast along the main dirt road to Tanganyika. He was sure he could find some if I would collect them and then return them when the season's work was finished. Jonas was despatched immediately with money for bus fare and orders to rendezvous at the Kanona Inn at midday the following Sunday, when hopefully I would arrive to find some willing helpers. Meanwhile, we struggled on, concentrating on the main job of getting the tobacco into the barns and curing it.

Sunday dawn came late, as the Congo Air Boundary – where the wet northeasterly winds from the Equatorial Congo Basin met up with the southeasterly winds – was centred overhead. From the heavy leaden sky, the rain poured down continuously. I allowed myself four hours to get to Kanona and set off, ready for anything along the slippery, muddy, potholed road, hoping for the best.

I was very surprised as I passed the turnoff to Mkushi Boma to find a bedraggled white hitch-hiker, complete with backpack, sheltering beneath a big tree, with one arm and thumb stuck out in the direction I was travelling. As I was only going about twenty miles an hour, through the mud I easily slid to a stop alongside him. He slung his pack into the back before climbing into the front alongside me. He was an aircraftsman with a Royal Air Force detachment on the Copperbelt, who had decided to spend his three weeks' leave hitchhiking to Kenya and back. He was not too thrilled with the start of his journey but very pleased to be in a dry place once again, if only for a few hours. We chatted away as we slipped and bumped along our way, peering through the misty windscreen and the ever-wiping wipers to the dismal unvarying scene ahead. We collected two more natives who were glad to shelter in the back and get some assistance along their way. Eventually, the signpost said Kanona, where since it was about half the size of Mkushi Boma, the inn was not difficult to find. Jonas was not in evidence, so John, the hitchhiker, and I went in for some refreshment.

The inn was a relic of the good old days of big-game hunters; it served as a lodge to those who went off on hunting safaris for elephants and large antelopes, which were concentrated in the nearby Luangwa Valley. Various stuffed heads adorned the dim and dusty walls, with several heavy elephant guns also on display. The innkeeper, a widower, matched his hostelry, in that he was perhaps living in the past and would not see many more years to come. Trade was not very good, so he spent his time growing apples, peaches, and plums in his garden. But we were given the traditional welcome, served two bottles of beer, and within half an hour dished up with a homely meal, starting with big bowls of hot vegetable soup, which warmed us from the inside. Over the meal, I suggested to John that rather than spend his leave en route to Nairobi, he might like the experience of nearly three weeks on a farm, where he could assist me supervising the labour and checking the barn temperatures at night. Strangely, he did not need much persuasion, so I was assured of one extra hand on my return. But true to form, Jonas showed up before we had finished our repast with news of several boys waiting for collection at three nearby villages.

We set off along the narrow track to the first village, where we found five natives, all ready to depart with small suitcases, bundles of clothes, pots and pans, and a bicycle. After handshakes and farewells around the village, they climbed into the back, and we set off to the next village. There three more were ready, equipped as before, but this time with a few chickens squawking away, heads sticking out of the flimsy basket made from saplings especially for their conveyance. When everything and everybody was again loaded up, the vanette was well laden, but Jonas said that three more were waiting at his father's village, which we had to visit to enable him to bid farewell to his father. So off we went again, along a narrow, winding track through the bush to another collection of thatched huts. There, the last three unskilled farm workers were ready and waiting, with yet another bicycle.

We removed John's large backpack into the front and, with a lot of pushing and squeezing (even letting the air out of the bicycle tyres), got Jonas and the eleven others wedged into the back. With the accustomed shouts of farewell, especially to Jonas' father, and laughter in spite of the rain, we set off on our return trip back to the farm. Somehow, we made it without so much as a puncture, the rain finally easing off as we reached the farm road. Next morning, all the new labourers and my new assistant were set to work, topping the flowers which had appeared on the tobacco. My labour problems had suddenly ended, sickness stopped, and there was a rise in morale, as everyone got into a steady routine, which continued unchanged for the next two months.

John was a great help to me over the next three weeks, supervising much of the reaping of the crop while I concentrated on untying and baling the cured tobacco. It was then stacked away until the time came to grade it all. I had decided that rather than risk large bulks of tobacco, which could go mouldy on the new and still damp floors, I would make bales instead, which could be turned regularly and be easily inspected.

John also was persuaded to alternate with me for checking the barn temperatures in the middle of the night. He got up one night when a thunderstorm was raging overhead. Bravely, he donned his raincoat and went out to the vanette to drive up to the barns, about half a mile away. The next thing he knew, he was waking up, lying on the wet ground, with the rain pouring down on him. A flash of lightning striking nearby had knocked him out for a couple of minutes, fortunately doing no other damage and giving no after-effects, except a healthy respect for tropical thunderstorms. But that was probably the only exciting event in what must have been rather a dull holiday for him, as it was steady work each day, with very little time for entertainment, which barely existed at that time. Sally and Tamara kept us well fed with a good variety of meals, and John read many of our books in the evenings, but farming life was not for him, so he was pleased to be on his way back to the Copperbelt, a few pounds richer at the end of his hard-working leave.

A month or so later, the last leaves were taken from the stalks, allowing me to breathe a sigh of relief. In spite of various problems, we had kept up with the crop, gathering it in steadily as it ripened without losing anything along the way. As the final barns were cured, the fires died out, and Sally and I were able to head for town once again to replenish our supplies. I was also desperate for a haircut, not having been near a barber for nearly ten weeks; with my beard also very bushy, I could have been mistaken for the wild man of Mkushi. Glehn and Norma had the same idea, whereupon it was decided that Glehn and I should take our golf clubs with us and try a game on the Broken Hill golf course. We did. We played "at" the game of golf, losing several balls as we ploughed a very erratic course, but thoroughly enjoyed ourselves for the one afternoon. We treated our wives to an evening dinner at the Elephant's Head Hotel, where with our last few pounds, we celebrated the end of the curing season and the start of a slightly less strenuous period, which should also see money coming back into our exhausted bank accounts.

A week later, while the labourers were given the task of chopping out the tobacco stalks and putting them in piles on the roadways, we left Wendy with Norma while we headed for Lusaka and some maintenance on the vanette. This sturdy vehicle had clocked up just over twenty thousand miles in the twelve months since we had purchased it. Most of those miles had been heavily laden, on rough dirt or muddy roads, so some new tyres, brake linings, and a front spring were all fitted to keep our workhorse up to the reliable standard we demanded of it. Our son and heir was by now very noticeable, and the vanette was our only transport for when the day arrived. We did not hurry the garage in their work but enjoyed two days there, Sally looking at the wonderful displays in the shops, me tagging along behind, trying to show an interest, while the evenings were spent watching a cabaret at the hotel where we were staying.

Undoubtedly, the two days off were very much of benefit to Sally, who had played such a major part in the background of all that had been going on. She was a sounding board for the various ideas that came out of my head and, as such, was able to keep me on the right track, at times with a few terse words of criticism or prodding me to greater efforts when some project did not work first time. It was not easy for her living in the bush, with our nearest neighbour five miles away along our dirt roads, and the nearest shops a hundred miles or more. She had to plan our food requirements for periods of a month, during which such things as meat, fish, butter, and bread would be kept in our paraffin-operated deep freezer. Milk would be made up from tins of powdered milk, whilst eggs could be obtained from our battery of chickens or one of our neighbours. Vegetables naturally came out of our garden, which was supervised by Sally and which produced a good selection, the most prolific being carrots, beans, and tomatoes. So we both enjoyed our break in the big city, with time to discuss the coming few months on a family basis, leaving the farm and farm work in the background. With a son due to arrive on the scene, it was apparent that he would probably not be content to travel in the back of our vanette, so another form of conveyance would have to be purchased after the opening of the tobacco sales, when money would start coming into the coffers. We liked the Peugeot, which had proved so strong on bad roads, so we decided that a good second-hand station wagon would be ideal for our family of four, together with the monthly shopping. With it, we could also go on holiday, driving down to South Africa, where we could spend a few days with my sister Audrey before continuing on to the Rhodesian favourite holiday spot: Durban. It was now three years of exciting but nonstop hard work since we had arrived in Africa, and over our dinner that evening, we agreed we should have our holiday.

Party line telephones were being installed very slowly in Mkushi. Each district road, which serviced maybe ten farms, was having a line put up, linking those farms to the Mkushi exchange and the outside world. Our road was the next to be done; a span of telephone labourers had already been along, chopping down a swathe of trees where the poles and wires were to go. In spite of the barbarous way the route had been cleared, we were looking forward to having communication with our neighbours and firms in town. Normally, our mail was delivered in a post bag to a depot on the main road once each week, where we would collect it together with any other consignment from town. Otherwise, we could collect our post from the post office at Broken Hill, as we did once to find that a telegram had just missed the previous week's delivery and was now waiting for us five days later, saying that Sally's father had died.

That had been most distressing at the time, emphasising how isolated we were. Now we were able to take time to discuss Sally's mother, Rosa, coming to stay with us permanently on the farm. My parents had also indicated a strong desire to come and see our progress later in the year, so more serious discussion was held on that matter. We decided that if our finances could stretch sufficiently, we would build a self-contained cottage in which the sitting room could be a second bedroom if all three parents arrived together, reverting to its proper purpose for mother-in-law when my folks returned to England. We would build using bricks, fit good metal window frames and door frames, roof with asbestos similar to that on our pole-and-dagga house, and also ceilings – a real luxury. By building just across the garden from our home, there would be sufficient privacy for us all, without the feeling of being isolated in the midst of a hostile environment at night.

With our plans resolved for the next six months and the vanette back on the road in tip-top condition, loaded up in its usual way, we set off back to the farm to complete the seasons' crop and prepare for the next.

Ian Richard Arrives

Whilst the tidying up of the farm went on for a couple of weeks, organisation for the next stage swung into operation. Walls were white-washed in the main shed, whilst brick walls were put up to support table tops for grading the tobacco. For these tops, I went off on several trips to Kapiri Mposhi, just fifty miles away, where new power lines had been erected, taking electricity from the Kariba Dam, which was then being constructed, to the power-hungry mines of the Copperbelt. Discarded wooden drums, on which the cables had been rolled, were lying in the bush. When dismantled and sawn in half, these proved to be the ideal size for semi-circular tables on which to sort the three million or so tobacco leaves.

Thanks to continual dampness in the air, we had not needed any steam to condition our tobacco during the curing period. Now with drier weather approaching, a modified Rhodesian boiler was built to provide a steady output of steam with which to keep the tobacco supple and unbroken.

Boilers were reputed to be quite dangerous pieces of equipment, looked on by most with respect, if not trepidation. However, we did not have regulations requiring safety valves or the like. If anyone had such a thing, I'm sure it never got checked. So with an ever-growing community of farmers each having a boiler of sorts, it was not surprising that the time would come for an incident to occur. It happened to accident-prone Dennis, who on checking his barns in the middle of one night found his boiler boy asleep by a well-stoked furnace. The gauge misleadingly indicated just ten pounds/square inch, having already made one circuit of the dial. This was not good enough for Dennis, who roughly awakened his labourer and exhorted him to greater efforts.

Needless to say, Dennis was awakened an hour or so later, as bricks rained down on his tin roof, following an enormous explosion. Fortunately, it had taken place as his stoker had paid a call of nature in the bush nearby, so that no one was hurt. Very little damage had been done, although the boiler ended up in a nearby tree. Dennis had been a manager on a farm in Southern Rhodesia for some years, before coming to Mkushi with his young, intellectual wife, Angela. He was very dynamic, with many advanced ideas on tobacco growing. His buildings were immaculate, and the quality of crops that he grew were always a credit to him. His only possible weakness lay in his enjoyment of social occasions and the beer that went with them. These were so infrequent that Dennis would always make the most of them, inevitably being the last to leave in the early hours of the morning. Angie would understandingly have got a lift home with a sober neighbour some hours before. One night, Dennis did not quite make it home in his old and trusty Mercedes. Taking the last bend on his farm road, he skidded into the ditch, rolled his car over, and knocked himself out in the process. When he came to, upside down, he really thought his final hour had come, as it appeared that thick blood covered his head and was oozing down his face and neck. He eased his way gently out of the wreck, finding himself to be surprisingly sound, apart from his head. He made his way the last few hundred yards to his house and awakened Angie with his call for help. She burst out laughing when she saw him materialise into the light: His head was covered in broken eggs from a trayful she had left for him to bring safely home.

When asked about it later, Angie used to state quite categorically, "I am not responsible for my husband's actions."

In the first couple of years, many of our get-togethers took place on Oom Danie's farm. He was one of those salt-of-the-earth types who were largely responsible for developing many parts of Africa. An Afrikaner of about sixty years, he was fit, strong, and wiry, with a wizened sunburnt brown face and a typical Dutch goatee on his chin. He had seen the potential of opening up a farm in the bush of Northern Rhodesia and decided it would be ideal for his young unmarried son, Shadow. Not afraid of hard work, he and Shadow had driven tractors and trailers, loaded with the bits and pieces of farm equipment which he had collected over years of leasing farms in the Republic of South Africa, the many hundreds of miles to their piece of Africa, in the wilds of Mkushi. They had been one of the first to arrive in the area, so were a step ahead of most of us. They worked from dawn to dusk each day, sustained by the excellent meals provided by Oom Danie's wife, Aunty Gerty. Their homestead consisted of three elongated thatched rondavels, with another similar open-sided one as the central gathering place for during the day. It was there that our first meetings were held and where plans were first made to build a club for future activities. We had a field on which rugby could be played, this being a favourite pastime of many of the younger Afrikaner farmers. We also had a large garden with a cricket net, where we could practise our batting and fielding once a week. This was supported mainly by the Rhodesians and British, the former being extremely keen on the game. Other than that, our nearest entertainment was in Broken Hill, ninety miles away.

During the initial planning of the area, a site had been put aside for a club. It was central for the Mkushi Block when fully occupied, had a river frontage on the Munshiwemba River, and was on the edge of a range of hills and therefore not suitable for growing crops. Oom Danie was able to get the go-ahead from our land settlement officer to start clearing some of this land for a club house and cricket field. A small collection was made and a gang of labourers employed to stump out the trees on a suitable area. As not much of the ground was flat, it was not difficult to decide where it would be. Work commenced, progressing in fits and starts throughout the dry winter season as and when tractors and machinery became available, until just after the start of the next rains. Then on a Saturday morning, with most of the crops in the ground, about twenty farmers, with ten labourers each, tackled the task of planting grass runners every twelve inches or so over this vast field. We were all greatly surprised when it was finished by lunch time, but then all the labourers had worked with a will, not wanting to miss any of their usual Saturday afternoon activity: beer drinking with friends in the farm compounds. We were able to take them back to our farms in our vanettes, knowing that a start had been made on a club where we might be able to play cricket in seven or eight months' time.

But that was all in the future. Our main task now was again grading and baling the tobacco and sending it off in the Central African Road Services (CARS) lorries to the auction floors in Salisbury, five hundred miles away. We had had many visitors calling on the farm to see how the season had treated the new Mkushi farmers. These were generally experts from fertiliser companies, the Tobacco Research Board, conservation and extension services, the auction floors, and even the federal minister of agriculture, Mr John Graylin, with his group of advisers. They all wanted to have a look at the end product and get a preview of what would soon be appearing at the auctions.

Naturally, I was encouraged by their expert opinions of my first crop and was looking forward to my first sale of some fifty bales, scheduled to be auctioned around the middle of May. Whenever possible, farmers would drive down for their sales, or if they were doing particularly well, like David Kaminer and Colin Clark, they could even charter a small plane and do the return trip easily in one day. I planned to drive there, if possible, but a great deal depended on when Sally was going to do her bit and produce our hoped-for son and heir. Like any good farmer's wife, she timed it to perfection. I drove her to the Broken Hill Hospital in the very early hours of the morning on the day of the auction, then continued the further three hundred-odd miles to see what turned out to be an excellent sale and got back to the hospital next morning to find Ian, a superb little son, waiting for me in his mother's arms. I was not surprised that it was a boy, as right from the start Sally and I had decided that having got a lovely little girl, a baby brother would have to follow. Thus we had his name ready for his arrival.

A feeling of euphoria came over me, as I spent the day in town alternating between farm stores and the hospital. The vanette got a quick service, the bank manager was called on to be informed of money en route to the empty coffers, whilst everyone was told of my brand-new son. Late that evening, after a fond farewell to Sally and Ian, I set off on my return to the farm, with the usual load in the back of the truck. Twenty miles out of Broken Hill, I found the engine overheating. I stopped to investigate, striking matches over the engine to give me some light. It did not take long to discover that the radiator cap had come off, allowing much of the water to escape. There were no other vehicles on the road at that time of night and no farms or houses within ten miles. But I knew I had crossed a stream about a mile before I had stopped. I searched the vehicle for an appropriate water container, but the only suitable items turned out to be my Wellington boots – the same ones I used for catching snakes. Armed with these, I walked back to the stream, scrambled down the bank, filled my boots, and carefully carried them all the way back to the car. By this time, the engine was cool, so the water went straight into the radiator. I sealed the top with a piece of sacking before starting the engine. Now I found that the cylinder head gasket had blown, so although I could drive the vehicle, it had very little power. The best I could do under the circumstances was to return to Broken Hill, where it could be fixed next morning.

I got back to town, but my troubles were not quite over, as at the only hotel – the Elephant's Head – no room was available. Eventually, after some discussion, the night duty manager took pity on me and for seven and sixpence allowed me to use the bed in the ladies' powder room, insisting it should be vacated by 7 a.m. It was!

A few days later, we were all back at home, settling into a busier family routine. A wife of one of the labourers was employed as a nanny to help keep an eye on Wendy and to assist with the washing and ironing. Wendy, although only eighteen months old, was already proving how agile she could be, especially at getting into places where she shouldn't. We had not progressed as far as a paddling pool in the garden so were free of that source of worry. Some months before, Norma's two-year-old daughter Vanessa was tragically drowned in just a few inches of water, when only a few minutes out of sight.

The new house went up easily under the auspices of Alfred Chanda, the builder who was still resident on the farm, doing all required construction work or brick making. He was a very clean, polite, well-spoken African whose skill was much better than most. He had been educated and trained at one of the mission schools in Northern Rhodesia, where he had also learned his excellent English. At some time in his career, he had either bought or been given a very nice felt trilby hat – a very unusual one for a farming district. This was a prized possession of Alfred's, as I rarely saw him without it over the next ten years, and it was always in immaculate condition.

Alfred would be engaged on a contract basis, whether it was for making fifty thousand or so bricks or erecting tobacco barns or other buildings. There was always a going rate for the job, at which price we could start negotiating. The layout of building foundations was always my responsibility, as was the positioning of doors and windows. It was my job too to supply the bricks, sand, water, and other necessities to the site, and to provide an agreed amount of dried fish and maize meal at regular intervals for the builders. Alfred would engage his team of workers, which included brick layers down to the humble mud-mixers for cementing the bricks together. There was no doubt that he could get greater results from his unkempt scallywags than I would ever get from a similar span.

Work progressed on all fronts, with most rewarding tobacco sales as a result of our endeavours. We were able to purchase the second-hand Peugeot station wagon, which when loaded up with everything, except the kitchen sink, took us away on our well-earned holiday to Durban. To get there was a good three-day journey, with night stops at Salisbury and Johannesburg. In Salisbury, our stop coincided with one of our sales, whilst in Jo'burg, we were able to spend a few happy days with Audrey, Bill, and family, bringing them up to date with our pioneering adventures. The political situation, of course, was discussed, as South Africans were worried about the shape of things to come. They hoped to get some idea of their possible future from the events in countries to the north, in the meantime putting on a brave face to convince themselves that South Africa would always be different, always be governed by sensible white men. For my part, I was optimistic that our future in Northern Rhodesia would continue to thrive happily, even if the federation was dismantled (as then seemed likely). But as a determined and fit thirty-year-old with a lovely young family, on a developing farm which had already produced one excellent crop, why should I concern myself with politics? We farmers might fear that there would be some changes but we would adapt as necessary; the main job was to produce good crops of tobacco and maize.

One who was able to foresee some future changes was my bank manager; when I went for travellers cheques for our holiday, he recommended that I take out a considerable sum of surplus cash and invest it in a savings account in the republic. He was expecting finance control measures to be brought into effect before long, and funds outside of the country could be most useful. For my part, I did not understand what he was getting at; in any case, I expected to be on a cash basis for my next crop and would need every available penny for that. Eventually, I took out an extra £250; it was some years before I realised the opportunity that I had missed.

The holiday in hot and humid Durban was restful, up to a point. All our time was spent with Wendy and Ian, although nannies were available during the evenings, as we dined on some delicious seafood. Unfortunately, Ian suffered from colic and diarrhoea much of the time, necessitating visits to a nearby doctor. Naturally, Mother was distraught, so we were not sorry to bid farewell to R.S.A. and get ourselves back to the farm and the routine which we now knew so well.

Strike

The year drew to a close with good weather conditions for the start of the new crop, which now included some ground nuts, where maize had been grown previously. Two cows and half a dozen ducks had been added to our thirty chickens for our household requirements of food while my parents and mother-in-law were with us. It was not easy for them to spend some weeks in the bush, in spite of the royal welcome we gave them. All were impressed by our achievements on the farm and, naturally, with their grandchildren. My dad, who had helped us financially, was fascinated and would spend the days with me watching all that was going on. He had arthritis in one hip, which prevented much walking about, but he never complained. We were able to repay half of the money loaned to us during his visit.

My mother was a Londoner who liked the hustle and bustle of towns. One morning, she called to Sally and said, "Listen."

Sally listened hard and said, "I cannot hear anything," to which my mother replied, "Yes, that's just the trouble; it's too quiet!"

Mother-in-law, who stayed on for twelve months, was similarly ill at ease so far from the way of life that she knew. Dirty, muddy, slippery roads; possible snakes in the garden; no one else living within five miles except the natives (of whom she was afraid); and inquisitive cows who were bigger than she was all made for a rather tense, frightened episode in her otherwise tranquil life. But she loved the children, and we managed to get her to collect the eggs from the chickens each day as part of her duty on the farm. Babysitting, if we wanted to go out to dinner in the evening, was definitely not on, as in her mind, anything could happen during our absence.

Admittedly, some things were changing, as the federation had come to an end, with Northern Rhodesia now having an interim government prior to full independence in 1964. Certain labourers were beginning to expect great benefits with the coming of an African government. With this in mind, they would try to get the backing of the labour force to coerce the farmer into higher wages or different food supplies. These people were looked on as troublemakers by the farmers, and the agreed system amongst us was to pay them off and sign their employment record card – or *Situpa* – with our Christian name. This would be a warning to the next employer. In the Mkushi area, these agitators all belonged to the ever growing United Nationalist Independence Party (UNIP), who now had party members touring the farms and telling the people what was going to happen, what they should do, and when the time came who they should vote for.

One Sunday morning, the milk did not arrive. A quick check proved the herdsman to be absent from the farm, leaving the Bwana to do the job himself. Once completed, I let the two cows loose in the paddock for the rest of the day, knowing there was plenty of grass for them to eat. But that night, one broke out to go in search of a mate. After milking the other cow next morning, the now-chastened herdsman set off to find the missing beast and bring her home. At the end of the day, he found her on a farm some seven miles away. Using his head, he asked the farmer to keep her overnight and milk her next morning, by which time he would be back to collect her. This almost worked to plan, but as they set off to return home, the cow again took off at a run in the opposite direction. Fortunately, at the end of the day, they arrived back on home ground after what turned out to be a very satisfactory excursion, as some months later, she produced a lovely bull calf (which we named Ferdinand).

Much of this escapade I only learned after another journey to Kanona. One of my labourers had died suddenly during the night, and rather than being buried on the farm, as was the custom, there was some persuasion put upon me to return him to his home village. We were in the middle of the curing season once again but so far without any undue problems – all had been running smoothly. I decided that I could be spared for the day, organised the work to be done, and then set off with the body and four of his compatriots, back along the muddy Great North Road. In this way, I hoped to keep my labour force happy and show that not all Bwanas were bad guys.

Mission accomplished, I returned home to find the work done but a delegation awaiting me. This was the last of the total labour span of thirty-eight who had materialised in the garden, asking for me and frightening Sally out of her wits. For some reason, they thought I was already back from my journey to Kanona. Sally told them I was not there and that they could wait for me, but away from the house. She then phoned through to the club and raised the alarm, not knowing what to expect. Fortunately, a number of farmers were there. They immediately jumped into their cars with beers in their hands and raced to her assistance. Reaching her, they found the situation well under control, as most of the thirty-eight men had dispersed to their homes. Buoyed up by their rapid response to the alarm call, the farmers made themselves at home for a while, emptying most of my bottles containing anything alcoholic, except one crate of beer, on which someone was sitting. By the time I got back, my small stock of booze was gone, as were all the farmers, except for Glehn, who stayed to make sure all remained calm. I went out to the surly group, where the boss boy explained that the labourers felt they should all be paid more for their efforts and would not do any more work unless I increased their wages. I thus had a strike on my hands. No one else in the area had experienced such a thing (although it had been talked about as a possibility). I considered myself very much a moderate or fair handler of labour with slightly better-than-average wages, better rations, and generally good working conditions. Yet it was on my farm that there was trouble. I was stunned and frightened. This had come out of the blue, after I had done what I considered to be a good deed for my employees by returning their dead compatriot to his village one hundred miles away. I told the foreman we would discuss it next morning. I then went into our home to think.

The family were very worried. Arrangements were quickly made for Mother-in-law to sleep with Sally for the night, whilst

I would bunk down on the sofa. Bottles and strings were set around the outside of the house to give us advance warning of any marauders. The shotgun was brought out of hiding and placed in a readily available position. Phone calls on our party-line informed neighbours of what was happening, in return for which a great deal of advice was forthcoming. They would be ready to help throughout the night if a call was made; meanwhile, I should not give in to the strikers: "Pay them all off!" Sound and good advice? Easy to give if you are not affected, difficult to follow when the farm is at its busiest and no spare labourers around. I could not expect to get others from neighbouring farms, who were just as busy as myself.

Next morning, after an undisturbed night, I started paying off those who did not want to continue in their jobs. I interviewed each one in turn and paid off twelve of the twenty-five who refused to continue. By then I had run out of money. Sally was despatched to a nearby store, which had sufficient money to cash a cheque to pay the remainder. That left me only fourteen workers and no boss boy. Yet another trip to Kanona was called for, and I set off two days later, happy in the knowledge that I had diffused the tense situation.

In the villages around Kanona, fortune smiled on me once again, as I picked up nine willing fit young men who were prepared to have a go on a farm for six months, after which I agreed to return them to their villages. As usual, they were all inexperienced in farm work but they each had two hands and the usual smile on their face. It looked as though I might make out after all. Back on the farm, eight of those previously paid off had had second thoughts and requested to be taken back to work. As they had obviously been led to strike against their own inclination, I quickly gave my assent. I had passed the critical point and was back on the road to recovery, short-handed by only eight labourers. From that moment onwards, everything went very smoothly, and Alfred Chanda stepped in as my boss boy for the rest of the season, until it was time to make more bricks for new barns. Then he brought along his younger brother John, who took over and worked well with me for many years to come.

The club was now in being with an appropriately impressive title: the Mkushi Country Club. With the cricket field getting greener, a simple building had been put up as the centre for our community. Contributions of all kinds had been sought by Oom Danie, in the form of bricks, cement, door frames, window frames, labour, and, of course, cash. The State Lottery and Breweries also donated to our cause, much to our great surprise. Again it fell on Oom Danie to employ and supervise the construction, which consisted of a hall, kitchen, toilets, and very importantly a bar, with a large veranda extending the length of the building on the side of the cricket field. A small generator provided power for lighting and the very useful long fridge, which was given to us by the Copperbelt Brewery. As soon as it was completed, we had a grand opening with a simple fete, braaivleis, and a film show in the evening.

The number of farmers was steadily increasing in Mkushi, and as the nearest alternative entertainment was a minimum of ninety miles away, it was not surprising that families steadily increased in size, and the club became a very popular meeting place. A small committee was formed with Oom Danie the first chairman, assisted by a representative from each of the six telephone lines. This made it easy for one person to contact others on his line or road without going through the telephone exchange.

Over the years, the club expanded, with two tennis courts, badminton in the hall, and all kinds of social events. Two natives were employed as caretakers and generally to assist by cleaning up after the members had gone home. Other work was done voluntarily by the farmers in turn, who would bring the requisite farm implements and labourers to complete the task at hand. Thursdays became the recognised club day, with an ever-growing library which was well supported, and a bank agency would operate there twice a month. Weekends were favoured for sporting activities, after which hot showers, liquid refreshment, darts, and food became available. Whilst the men took it in turn to run the bar, it was up to the wives to supply the food. This ranged from simple bacon and eggs at the start to delectable joints of roast beef, roast potatoes, fresh vegetables, and a sweet as the competition between members of each road developed. The cooking facilities at the club were very basic, so most of the preparation had to be done on the farms beforehand.

There was always this element of competitiveness around as the different sectors took over the running of the club for their four-week period. There were cricket matches against the teams that we had been playing before our own field came into being. Inevitably, a dance would be scheduled for the Saturday evening, with music from records on loan for the occasion. Sometimes there would be a theme to the evening, like a "Hawaiian Dance," "Roman Orgy," or a "Turnabout Dance," where the ladies went as men and had to run the bar and the men went as women with the cooking duties to contend with. On that occasion, I shaved off my beard and dressed in one of Sally's twin sets. We went into the club house separately. Although I was on the committee and acquainted with everyone there, I was not recognised until I made myself known an hour later. My main recollection is of men dressed in female apparel sitting with their knees wide apart, skirts stretched between them, being served beers by their spouses.

New Year's Eve was always a big night and a dress affair, too. Occasionally at some exorbitant cost, we managed to get a live band. The hall would be decorated, an excellent spread of food would be available, tables would have been booked to the appropriate member well in advance, and we would drive through mud and rain to attend, in all our finery, this magical event of the year. Drinking and dancing would go on until all hours, with the children all asleep in the cars. The highlight, naturally, was midnight, when handshakes and kisses were exchanged with everybody. We all knew each other well and liked each other greatly. Very rarely was there an altercation or incident of impropriety. In fact, we maintained a high standard of morals, which was rarely transgressed.

After one social evening, it did appear that a young lady had done so. A seventeen-year-old girl who had recently left school, and was now bored with life on her father's farm in the bush, was out for a good time that evening. Whether she got it or not, I don't think anyone ever found out, but on the following morning, as we turned up for cricket, she came staggering out of the club house in a long, very bedraggled evening dress, asking for one of us to drive her home. She was only eligible for membership some months later when she reached her eighteenth birthday. Believe it or not, she was blackballed in the vote and was unable to join until several years later.

By that time, we had other problems to worry about, as membership in the early years was restricted, by our committee, to farm owners, farm managers, and their families. This meant in effect it was a whites-only club until several years after independence, when all clubs had to be open for anyone to join. Suddenly, the Caledonian Society had an influx of black-faced Scots with kilts – or so the story went at the time.

One of the early African visitors to the club to address a farmers meeting prior to independence was Mr Simon Kapepwe, the minister of agriculture for N. Rhodesia. A leading member of Mr Kenneth Kaunda's UNIP, he came to set our minds at rest about our being wanted in the country once a black majority government was in power. He arrived a little late, with his retinue of minor officials and police attendants in various modes of dress. Kapepwe himself was smartly turned out in a dark safari suit and carried a walking stick with an entwined snake carved around it. All the visitors expected to sit at the top table facing the farmers – even the drivers!

Somehow, we managed to settle everyone and listened with much interest to what Mr Kapapwe had to say. In a letter to my father some days later, I wrote:

"Our impressions are that the leaders of both UNIP and ANC – the African National Congress Party – are all apparently quite logical in their plans and reasonable sensible men in themselves. Perhaps if there were more like them we would have little to fear. Kapepwe certainly gave us reassurances on all major points and in fact told us what we liked to hear. He seemed genuine. But behind the scenes there is a great deal of intimidation of the Africans and this will almost inevitably lead to a one party UNIP government at the next election. However I feel that we may be very fortunate in Northern Rhodesia and may be sitting pretty as there has without doubt been steady progress towards multi-racialism over the past decade. The fact that we have now had a 'Black' government in power for the last nine months without many changes is surely a good omen for the future. Certainly our future lies in expansion and I'm sure Mkushi will do just that."

Wary but optimistic views similar to those of our neighbours. We had started from nothing, progressed to a viable farming business after much hardship and exertion, and would not give up easily. We certainly could not sell our farms at that time, nor were we able to pack up and take them with us. We had no choice but to stay and hope for the best.

What of Southern Rhodesia at this time? My letter gave a clue:

"We had a visitor here the other evening who is farming in Southern Rhodesia. His views being entirely the opposite of ours were most interesting to listen to, and I feel they give an indication of harder times ahead for the White South."

Our connections with the land to the south were still very strong. Many farmers had family relations living there, and the auction floors were centred there, as were the various research stations. It had larger towns with more shops, schools, hospitals, hotels, and better roads than we had in the North. We continued to look on it as civilisation. There was an older generation of white settlers there, living in lovely houses with beautiful, well-kept gardens and the usual highly polished car in the garage. Little old ladies smartly dressed carrying flat handbags could be seen walking into the Birdcage, the tea room of Barbours, a major store in Salisbury, at 11 a.m. each weekday for their regular tea and gossip. Southern Rhodesia was still a land of milk and honey for the white settlers, with its lovely climate and apparent stability. But much of its development had been paid for in federal days by the income from the copper mines in the North, or so said the new politicians who were about to change all that.

Independence day was getting closer when the government of the United Kingdom was going to hand over the country to the mainly black politicians of the country. We waited and watched anxiously.

Chapter 5

Independence

On 24 October 1964, Northern Rhodesia was no more. It had become Zambia, under the government of Kenneth Kaunda and his majority United National Independence Party, with a few seats available for the ANC party and for a few white members of NPP. An Independence Stadium had been built in Lusaka for the happy celebrations, which consisted of speeches, singing and dancing, and a football match. It was absolutely packed out by the natives from all the surrounding areas. A few white faces belonging to new ambassadors to Zambia, UNIP advisors and supporters, and representatives of the United Kingdom, who were symbolically transferring the mantle of power to the new ruler. Promises were made to improve the African's living conditions: his wages, housing, schools, and hospitals. Everything would be better under the new government. No one asked how all this would be paid for, as Zambia had the copper mines and was a rich country.

Back on the farms, the labourers were all given two days' holiday, with extra rations to help them celebrate the occasion. Drums of beer had been brewed in most of the compounds, and some celebrations were planned at the Boma – too far away for most.

The farmers themselves kept a low profile. The club was closed lest it became a source of annoyance to anyone; we spent the day quietly with Glehn and Norma and the family, hoping that it would pass off without any incidents and that we could then get back to normal.

We happily sat in the cool sitting room of our pole-and-dagga house, with the doors wide open and the children running in and out. They had an inflatable pool on the grass outside, in which they had great fun, with Wendy the ringleader in all their games. Beer, coca colas, and good food was in plentiful supply.

Wendy had now recovered from primary tuberculosis, which had been diagnosed following X-rays when she had suffered bronchitis earlier in the year. We had rushed her into the Broken Hill Hospital with an ever worsening chest cold. Three days later, we were told the bad news: primary T.B. But it had been discovered at a very early stage, with treatment available promising 100 per cent cure. Tests of our cows, house staff, and ourselves failed to trace any possible source of the infection, the result of which was that little Wendy, only two years old, had to remain in the children's ward of the hospital for another four weeks. This was heart-breaking, both for her and for us. Sally phoned each morning to check on her progress, and we drove to town to see her every four days, upsetting her and ourselves on every parting. Ian, as a result, was spoilt by the extra care and attention lavished on him. He was now starting to say a few words, going straight to the important ones like "Dad," "tractor," and "ducks."

Eventually, the day came for us to bring Wendy home and continue the treatment with daily injections to be given by an ex-nurse, now a farmer's wife, living a few miles away. On the morning when Sally phoned the doctor to confirm all was well, he laughingly advised her that apart from a few mosquito bites, Wendy was fit for home. At this, Sally let loose a tremendous tirade of which she was most capable. She told the doctor in no uncertain terms just what would happen to him if Wendy got home and then went down with malaria. They turned out not to be mosquito bites but spots from measles, and Wendy had to return to the hospital for another week. Fortunately for the doctor, he lived to tell the tale. The treatment continued for a further five months before the final X-ray showed Wendy's lungs to be quite clear. We were very, very relieved and bought a lovely present for the nurse who had helped us so much with the daily injections.

Moira, with her Welsh accent and slight build, continued her life as a farmer's wife as the archetypal nursing sister. It was easy to imagine a ward full of patients lying to attention as she did her rounds. Many of us had an indubitable fear of her, such that we gave her a wide berth. She had friends in high places, such as the High Commission, whose names she would casually drop into conversation, and while gossip was the accepted way of passing on information in Mkushi, hers often had a slight edge to it. Her husband Harold was kept very well under her thumb in spite of his sturdy build. He was a pleasant-natured ex-army man whose farming methods were advanced and meticulous. He was one of the first to build a nice house on his farm and furnish it with better quality possessions than most farms. Harold was also a golfer who made up the fourth on an occasion of an outing to a golf course in Kitwe, on the Copperbelt – men only! Suffice it to say that after the golf, we stayed on for an evening meal, with a few drinks in a night club. We returned home rather later than expected to find three of the four wives sitting in state in Moira's sitting room, worked up into a state of frenzy over what might have happened to us. The police had been contacted, but their response that we were probably just having "a bit of fun" only added fuel to the fire.

To our great surprise at the time, we were met with torrents of words of censure, delivered with the backing of an icy blast before being taken to our respective homes to be kept "in Coventry" for several days. Ever afterwards, our wives accompanied us to all golf games, but none was as memorable as that one in Kitwe. The fear had been that of an accident on the way home from the Copperbelt. Thoughts perhaps fanned by Moira, with reminiscences of accident wards in English hospitals, had alarmed the others, not without grounds. Although much of the road was tarmac, the last fifty miles was still corrugated dirt. That in itself, whilst hazardous, was not the main danger. That came from vehicles parked without any signs or lights on the shoulders of the road, as their occupants visited native houses nearby. These were as lethal as drunken drivers, but as police patrols were impossible over the hundreds of miles of country roads, the problem only deteriorated as the numbers of worn-out vehicles increased. Two of our golfing four were later to die in road accidents.

But danger was not limited to our roads. As the new crop was being planted into the lands, David Kaminer was killed by a tractor accident on his farm. He had been jacking up a water cart to connect to a tractor. Instead of then getting out of the way, he beckoned the driver to reverse for the connecting hitch. Regrettably, the backing tractor driver miscalculated in such a way that David was crushed beneath a wheel. He died instantly.

The shock reverberated throughout Mkushi, and many of us drove to Broken Hill for his funeral service several days later. We were numbed at how quickly we could lose a friend, a leading farmer, a valued respected member of our small community, one of us. He was buried in the graveyard just outside Broken Hill, the nearest sanctified ground to Mkushi.

Surprisingly, a church did not materialise in Mkushi for some years. There was a mission at Fiwila, about fifty miles away along often impassable tracks, which during our time in Mkushi was taken over by the Franciscan fathers. It had been founded as a leper colony, housing nearly two hundred badly maimed natives whose leprosy, thanks largely to the advances in medications for this afflicting disease, was now burnt out. There was a church there built by the missionaries in a lovely setting at the base of a hill. This hill was the source of the Fiwila River, from which the mission derived its name. Once a month, one of the three Franciscan fathers would arrive in his four-wheeled-drive Land Rover at one of the farms in Mkushi, where we would assemble on a Sunday morning, dressed in our best suits, for a simple Christian service. We took it in turns to hold the service on our farms, usually accommodating the preacher for the Saturday night as well. We appreciated his visits, which would be extended to Christenings and remembrance services, as in the case of David. The Father was rewarded with good meals, which were always well received, before his departure back to his demanding task at the mission station.

Father Stephen was the best known to us of those who visited in this way. A kind, gentle man in his late sixties, he had spent much of his life in New Guinea amongst rather more menacing natives than were found at Fiwila. He would regularly drive a jeep or ten-ton lorry to town for all sorts of supplies for his base, returning late at night and finding himself the only one available to off-load everything. On one occasion when he decided to leave the unloading until next morning, he discovered much had disappeared during the night. He had a hard life, with very little help or thanks from those he was caring for. He never complained except when his arthritic hip gave him torment. He left eventually with his small suitcase of worldly possessions and returned to New Guinea, where he spent the last few years of his life still soldiering away in the service of God and others.

The season progressed erratically, with spasmodic rains. In the early stages, I was worried that the crop was not going to grow, but just enough rain came to keep it going. Eventually, after a very dry year, interspersed with a couple of torrential downpours which put the river in flood and my pump house several feet under water, the tobacco, maize, and groundnuts crops were excellent. Unfortunately, so were everybody else's. This meant a record crop of tobacco throughout both Zambia and Southern Rhodesia, which the auction floors could not handle without bringing in a quota system, to give every farmer a fair chance. It also resulted in lower prices being paid by the buyers, there being plenty of tobacco to go around.

The maize crop produced a glut, in a country which had very little in the way of storage silos, to keep the surplus from the good years. As a result, the following year's pre-planting or expected price for maize was greatly reduced to discourage farmers from growing it. It appeared the farmer could not win. His income was likely to be down in a bad year and not that much better in a good year. His best ploy was to try to keep costs down. This was not easy, as the new government had brought out a minimum wage payable to farm employees. It resulted in an increase of more than 40 per cent on the wages bill. It also resulted in a reduction in the number employed, hitting hardest at those who were least capable due to mental or physical handicaps. Yet surprisingly, it did not take long to get used to paying the increased rates, so gradually the handicapped returned to their places doing those jobs of which they were capable.

I had been more fortunate than most, with three very good years at the start of my farming career. I had been careful with my costs and was now about to reap the reward. With all the outstanding bills paid off, we proudly took possession of a brand-new Mercedes 180, a car we were assured would stand up to the rough roads of our area. Similarly, other farmers had found they did not let in the dust during the dry seasons. This was important, as we used to put the children to sleep in the back of the car whenever we went out socialising in the evenings. Mother-in-law had returned to England after an ever more difficult time trying to adjust herself to the life in the bush. Getting stuck in the mud on farm roads and having to wait for a tractor to pull the car out was not her cup of tea. Breakdowns in our Peugeot station wagon had not been infrequent, and the lack of compatriots in the same age group as herself contributed to her final decision to return to what was her home country – England. Thus it was just four of us who set off for a ten-day holiday in our new car. This time, we went to our old haunts near Umtali to look up old friends and see how the estate was managing since our departure. Now that I had actually done things for myself, I looked at the lands and buildings through different eyes. It was still fascinating, and we enjoyed our tour. The rock rabbits were still jumping around at the top of the Kopje near the old seedbeds; many of the staff were the same and remembered us with big smiles, very happy to see we had two piccanins of our own.

We spent a couple of days at the Troutbeck Inn, high up in the hills a few miles from Umtali and close to the border with Mozambique. The scenery around there was beautiful; the setting of the inn, alongside a stream which had been dammed to form a lake, was idyllic. It even had a golf course, which was one of the attractions for me. With well-kept fairways meandering along the side of a hill and the lake, it was a delight (even if a few balls were lost in the plantations of sweet-smelling pine trees bordering the course). Trout, of course, was the speciality of the inn, caught in the nearby streams. It was a fisherman's and golfer's paradise but too expensive to spend more than a couple of days there.

We made our way back to Salisbury, which we were beginning to know quite well. The wide streets lined with modern high-rise stores were always clean, the people brightly dressed and sun-tanned. Even the youngsters gathering outside a cinema for the Saturday morning films were smart, clean, and orderly, with well-kept hair and polished shoes. We remarked on how nice they all looked. There was not, of course, a black face amongst them – that was not allowed.

The residential areas of Salisbury were possibly some of the finest in the world. Lovely well-designed houses, standing in quite large plots of land, seemed to vie with each other as to which was the best.

After some shopping days, during which Wendy managed to stagger out of her first toy shop with a teddy bear almost as big as herself, we planned our return home via the Kariba Dam. So after breakfast next day, we set off northwards to see the dam and lake, about which we had been hearing stories over the last few years, how some of the dam wall had been damaged during construction by unusual flooding of the mighty Zambezi River; how native workers had fallen from the scaffolding into newly poured concrete, there to become entombed within the dam; and later how villagers and animals were having to be rescued from the ever growing, ever deepening lake which was rising behind the dam wall.

The dam was now finished with the road across the top linking the two countries. We were amazed at the size of the wall, getting that dizzy sensation of vertigo when we looked over at the tamed river several hundred feet below. On the other side stretched the lake, with numerous trees standing in the water along the edges, soon to die of drowning as the water level rose ever higher.

We did not give much thought to what had gone into achieving this great construction nor to what it meant in the way of electric power beyond comprehension to towns and villages hundreds of miles away. We just looked and marvelled, enjoying the sight of so much water in one place. Already several small hotels had sprung up to cater for those who either worked on the site or, like us, came to gaze at the dam wall and scenery. We spent the rest of the day in one such hotel, with much of that time whiled away with the children in the small swimming pool. Kariba was always hot, apparently, and it was expected that the lake would increase the area's humidity, leading eventually to bigger and better thunderstorms.

One of the topics for Sally and myself during our excursion was further development on the farm. The three new barns built the previous year had all been successful. Now Sally felt was the time for a brick house for her – one which meant that she did not have to go outside each time when going from sitting room to kitchen or bedroom to bathroom. She reinforced her argument by reminding me of the night she went to the kitchen to warm some milk for Ian's bottle. Returning by torch light, she found an aggressive cobra rearing up provocatively at the entrance to our bedroom. She was caught in the horns of a dilemma: not wanting to wake the sleeping children or annoy the snake, but wanting to arouse me to come to her aid without stepping straight out of the bedroom onto the snake! Somehow, she achieved her object: I was awakened and got the message. Armed with a hockey stick, dressed as nature intended, I was able to despatch the snake which Sally kept dimly illuminated in the torch light. She had remained remarkably calm throughout this episode, but it was now obvious she had been saving it up to use on a later occasion: "I want a proper house!"

Mother-in-law's house had been lying idle for some six months, except when visitors came, when it was very useful as a guest cottage. The trick was to build on to that in such a way that we had an interesting house, not just a long, straight monotony. Eventually, after much discussion and models made for designing the roof, we planned to build a similar wing to the first but at right angles to it, incorporating a bedroom for the children and one for ourselves, with a bathroom in between. The two wings would be joined by a main room whose front, angled at 45 degrees, would consist mainly of large glass doors and windows, while the rear walls of each wing continued to meet at right angles. An interior wall across this corner would give us a very interesting and efficient triangular kitchen. The stone-faced veranda could stretch from one end of the house to the other, and wide steps to the front doors would make an imposing entrance. Much of the roofing material, in the form of wooden trusses and asbestos sheets, would come from our present pole-and-dagga house; in that way we could keep the costs at an affordable level.

Once more, Alfred was called upon to start building. Enough bricks were available from a large kiln made the previous year, so work on brick laying was able to start very quickly. The tobacco crop that had been stored in bales for grading had, for a change, been despatched to a commercial grading company, who were to do that never-ending task for me at the cost of about four pence per pound.

All I had to worry about on the farm was the easy reaping and shelling of the maize and groundnuts, leaving adequate time and labour for the new house. "Adequate time" turned out to be "just enough," not because of a shortage of bricks, labourers, cement, reinforcing wire, roofing materials, or any such important commodity, but because two little children, in spite of dire threats, insisted on helping where they could. Besides, what an interesting playground it was for a three-and-a-half-year-old budding athlete, as slippery as an eel, with a younger brother in tow. Alfred was the one to suffer first. He had just completed the laying of the cement floor in the main room, putting the finishing touches to a job well done, when in through the doorway from the kitchen ran Wendy and Ian to depart through the front door, leaving two trails of footsteps about half an inch deep in the setting cement. Admonishments kept them clear of the area for the next few days, whilst I started on the roofing. They enjoyed bathing in the old bathroom, which had now shed its roof to the new house. Then I started to lose my hammer and other tools, only to find that they had been purloined by other young builders, knocking nails into the sand in the garden. They also found the hacksaw very useful for sawing lines on the top of brick walls. Later, when it came to putting glass in the window frames, it was the owners of very small fingers who were the first to test if the putty was hard, but they probably enjoyed the painting better. Sally had written to a paint producer for a colour scheme for the new house: ultra modern, light, and colourful. We stuck to this where we could, in spite of assistance from the rest of the family, who were not too concerned whether the colours were the same on each wall or mixed. All they knew was that if there was a tin of paint open, within reach, then it had to be spread on the walls and themselves, and they were very happy to spread it.

Wendy also tried her hand at redesigning the back of the Mercedes one trying day. Not wanting to take her morning rest when Mother wanted, and knowing that she always went to sleep easily in the back of the car, Sally put Wendy on her blanket and pillow to rest on the back seat. Soon after Mother's back was turned, Wendy must have realised her dreams had come true, and she could have a go at driving Daddy's new car. Fiddling about in the driver's seat, she managed to release the spring-loaded hand brake, and as the open garage was on a slight incline, the car began rolling down the open road and toward the nearest tree. Before it got there, Mother and the nanny, who had been busily ironing on the veranda, were both running to the scene. The impact did nothing to deter Wendy's enjoyment of the ride. Sally, of course, was very relieved that she had not been hurt in any way but a trifle concerned at what the Bwana was going to say about the new V-shaped back to his prized car. Thus to Wendy's exclamations of "Oh, look what Wendy's done," Sally could only say, "Come here, monkey, before you find out what your daddy can do!"

However, in spite of these few setbacks and thanks perhaps to the help from the young assistants, we just managed to move into our new house before the next rains arrived. Electric lights from the ceilings took the place of paraffin pressure lamps, flush doors replaced cheap batten doors, and the concrete floors had all been covered with a coloured rubber-based flooring product. All these things contributed to a very lovely, happy new home.

A tractor was brought down to demolish the shell of our pole-and-dagga house, which now stood forlorn after nearly four years of admirable service. Spare boys were given the task of carting it all away, so that very soon, the site of our former abode was cleared, levelled, and planted with grass. It was to become a badminton court.

In one year, we had been rewarded with a short holiday in a new Mercedes car and a new house to live in. Life was good; we were happy. I was still optimistic, in spite of some pessimism creeping in to some of those around me. We would continue hopefully and see what the next year would bring.

My first jet, the Meteor VII Trainer

Formation practise at 30,000 feet

Supermarine Attacker on the catapult

Attacker being serviced

Sea Hawk launching in rough seas

Sea Hawk deck landing

H.M.S. Eagle, *Fleet Carrier*

Vampires over the snowy mountains of Scotland

Vampire Trainers over Losssiemouth

The powerful supersonic Scimitar

The way to the Scimitar cockpit

Naval Guard of Honour at Watford

Wendy shows off the tobacco, ready for reaping

The cured golden leaf coming out of the barns

A good stand of maize in the land

Reaping the maize by hand

The tobacco barns and sheds

Our pole-and-dagga house, with the foundations of the new cottage being excavated

The new cottage for Mother-in-Law

Sowing the tobacco seed

The new house ready for a braaivleis

Our family of four in the garden

Charlie Romeo *with Rosa and the children*

Shelling maize into 200-pound bags

President Kaunda visits the farm

Feeding a bun to Zambezi a wild elephant

Air Malawi Hawker Siddeley 748

Last flight with Cyprus Airways BAC 1-11

Part of the extension at the Flamingos

Happy retirement:
Sally and the author

Winds of change over Mkushi

Once again, the gods smiled on me, and I was one of the lucky ones to get a good drenching of rain right at the start of my next crop. Partly as a result of the previous year's bumper crop and the consequent low prices paid by the buyers, I had decided to reduce my acreage of tobacco to thirty acres and endeavour to get a higher-than-average yield. As the maize yields in Mkushi were generally much higher than elsewhere in the country, I increased that crop to one hundred and sixty acres, expecting to make a fair profit in spite of the lower seasonal price quoted by the Grain Marketing Board. I had a slightly smaller team of workers for the tobacco, whilst the maize was put in by a mechanical planter, sowing four rows of seed at one time. The smaller, easier crop of tobacco meant that I was able to keep up with it, with time to spare. This served me well in two ways: Firstly, I was able to take my labourers during spare days to reap from tobacco on neighbouring farms, where with rapidly ripening crops, the farmers could not keep up. Secondly, as we were not under any pressure ourselves, the labourers were not overworked. When reaping on other farms, I had brought in an incentive bonus system so that we all profited by it, including the farmer who had grown the crop: He had half of the cured tobacco returned to him.

But with elections a thing of the past, the natives were wondering where all the improvements were in their way of life. Many were drifting from the farms to the towns, where changes were first to be seen, as black faces steadily replaced white ones in government offices, post offices, shops, and businesses. A lot of white people were leaving the country, moving south to where the whites continued in power; black faces appeared in their stead. But on each farm, there was only one family of white faces, and they were not going to leave easily. The labourers were very touchy, ready to take offence for the slightest reason. Many farmers found they had strikes on their hands, which sometimes required the newly appointed Labour officer to resolve – generally in favour of the labourers. By handling my work force very carefully, I survived the period and achieved the high yield-per-acre that I wanted.

Bulldozers were available each year for clearing the trees for new lands, instead of the normal hand stumping, and this year, I took advantage of them. With a massive chain strung some twenty-five yards between two of them, they would clank their preponderant bulks through the timbered bush, pulling down the trees in a wide sweep. For the bigger, more stubborn trees, a third bulldozer would move up and add its force to push it over from behind. It was mesmerising to watch the land being stumped in this way, the trees coming out of the wet ground, roots and all. Land which would have taken many weeks to stump with farm labour was done in a matter of hours.

The team of drivers knew what they were doing. It was a dangerous job, where a slight error could have trees falling onto the Caterpillar tractor. Large anthills impeded progress, forcing the machinery to manoeuvre around them. Occasionally, the chain would break, necessitating further manoeuvring and towing of the chain ends together for a new shackle to link them together again – not an easy job. But the biggest danger often came from nests of African bees, which until then had been happily producing honey high up in a hole in the tree. No doubt they were known about by one or two farm labourers, who would go searching for bees and their treasured combs of honey, and by the honey birds who helped those same people find them. The first the bulldozer drivers knew would be when they were attacked by angry bees, whose nests had been shattered in an earth-shaking way.

Some weeks later, when the ground was drier, the bulldozers returned to push all the trees into windrows, or lines about forty yards apart. This ensured all the land was clear, except that which was destined to become roads once the cords had been cut.

The same team of land clearers was utilised on the club site to clear trees for a nine-hole golf course. An old Afrikaner golfer, George van Niekerk from Broken Hill, had been approached with an aerial photograph of the club grounds and a request to help us make a golf course there. He did. He seemed to know exactly what he was about when some weeks later, Glehn and I walked over the area with him and were able to mark out the route for the bulldozers to follow. Both of us were literally lost but faithfully put in marker pegs or blazed trees under his direction. When the land was cleared later, we marvelled at what he had achieved. We had the makings of a very interesting course, with trees bordering all the holes and shaping the fairways into doglegs one way or the other. Two farmers were allocated to each hole to complete the clearing and cultivate and level the ground, ready for planting grass with the next rains. Others were delegated to prepare level areas for the tee off, while still other volunteers had the job of carting sand from the vleis for bunkers and the sand-greens. For the latter, the sand was to be mixed with old engine oil to produce a reasonably firm surface, so everyone was called on to save his old oil. There was a lot of work to be done but many willing hands there to assist. Eighteen months later, we had a course to play on.

Our golf course became very popular in Mkushi, with all sorts of unlikely people taking up the sport. A professional golfer, Terry Westbrook, started visiting us for two or three days once a month, giving lessons from dawn to dusk and selling all kinds of golf equipment and clothing. Competitions were held against other teams, who found a weekend in Mkushi was very relaxing and enjoyable, certainly very different from what they were used to. The Mkushi Invitation event became a highlight in the golfing calendar. The course steadily improved with the work put into it, particularly the fairways, which during the rainy season were mown twice a week with the club tractor and mower, which was otherwise employed keeping the cricket pitch in trim.

By now, many more young couples had taken up vacant land and were developing their farms. With the added facilities at the club, together with boating and fishing in the nearby Mita Hills Dam, we began to feel quite civilised, such that a journey to town for shopping or spares was rather a chore. Only occasionally was the fact brought home to us that we were a long way from anywhere.

Two visiting cricketers did just that. We had met them at the road services depot on the main road, where the home team had congregated to welcome the visiting team and assign them to their hosts for the weekend. Driving two of them towards our farm, one commented on our isolation and asked if we ever saw any animals around. To this, I replied that we had a herd of seven sable antelope roaming our area, the usual baboons that raided the maize crop when the cobs were fresh, the jackals that liked our chickens and ducks, and the usual small snakes that were common throughout the bush. He was nodding understandingly until I went on to say we had a leopard on the farm a couple of weeks ago. At that, he obviously thought I had gone too far and was trying to pull the wool over his eyes. However, about two minutes later, as we turned the last bend on our farm road, there was the leopard again, lying in the middle of the road. It moved immediately as we approached, walking into the adjacent land of tall maize. We went on the last few hundred yards to the farmhouse, where I quickly picked up my two shotguns and some cartridges, gave a gun each to the two cricketers, and put them in the back of the open vanette, in which we set off to try and find the leopard once more. Fortunately, it had vanished, but after that, they believed everything we told them. I'm sure they still tell the tale of leopard hunting in Mkushi.

With our strong and fast Mercedes back to its correct shape after Wendy's effort, we could easily get to Lusaka in three hours. We would leave for a day's shopping at 4.30 a.m., arriving to have a quick breakfast in town before the shops opened. After a hard day, we would depart at 5 p.m. for the long drive home, laden down as usual. Naturally, I used to make rapid progress until Sally, who was a bad passenger, put her foot down and decreed that I limit my speed to 60 mph on the dirt roads and 70 mph on the tarmac. This worked well until one evening, when Sally returned from a trip to Broken Hill. In the course of general conversation, she commented on the fast driving of another farmer's wife: "That Bernie is a terribly fast driver," she said. "She passed me as though I was standing still, and I was doing ninety!" Needless to say, questions were asked, but she was hoist with her own petard. Thereafter, she also had to stick to the agreed limits.

Returning at night a few weeks later, a bush-buck jumped out into the road, smack into our path. We had no chance of avoiding it. The result was a badly smashed front and a leaking radiator. Fortunately, we managed the last few miles home, the car again having to go by lorry to Lusaka for more repairs

The season progressed, with the emphasis now on reaping nearly two hundred acres of maize and delivering it the fifty miles to the depot at Kapiri Mposhi. Shadow Wilke, my neighbour five miles away, agreed to go halves on the purchase of a combine maize harvester and a seven-ton Bedford lorry. We would take weekly turns at either harvesting the maize or transporting it. The combine, towed behind a tractor which powered its mechanism, cut off each dry maize stalk at its base, churned the lot inside itself, selected the maize pips from the cobs, directing them into waiting sacks before spewing the chaff out at the back. It left a very tidy land behind it and was very efficient, especially where labour was concerned. One driver with two labourers could reap more in one day than ten with the old method of towing a high sided trailer into which the reapers threw the cobs. A few more collected the bags, adjusted them to the correct weight by topping them up where necessary, then completed the stitching along the top using large sacking needles and jute twine.

In previous years, the bags of maize had been transported by the Road Services lorries which, with a trailer on the back, could collect about two hundred and fifty bags at a time. Two such lorries in a day would leave the loaders exhausted, as it was no easy task lifting the two-hundred-pound sacks high up onto the ever mounting stack on the lorry. The uncertainty of when the lorries would arrive was also frustrating. Many a time, they arrived late in the evening, expecting to be loaded immediately in order that they could be at the depot when it opened next morning. It was the increase in their transport rates by 60 per cent that motivated Shadow and myself to purchase our lorry. Many other farmers did the same. Now it was possible to regulate the operation by leaving the farm with the first load at 6 a.m., getting early into the queue at the depot at 7.20 a.m., and being back on the farm for the second load by 9.30 a.m. I did all my own driving and would then leave the boss boy and his loading span to load up with eighty bags while I went for a quick breakfast. Three loads could comfortably be delivered each day, with the early morning load being stacked on the lorry by 6 p.m. the previous evening.

The system worked well, being especially popular with the labourers, who knew what their task was each day. Similarly, they were able to take it in turns for a ride to the stores at Kapiri Mposhi, not that they were anything to boast about, but different from the stores which were springing up on some of the farms. As is always the case, the goods in the shops elsewhere appeared to be better and cheaper than those nearby. It was a hard, uncomfortable ride along the well-used road with its holes, horrible corrugations, and always the dust. Trying to pass another vehicle with its trail of dust was always hazardous, but we did not think of that, only of getting the job completed.

At the depot, the maize was checked for quality, moisture content, and weight before being unloaded manually onto an escalator, which lifted it onto the ever-growing stacks or straight into railway trucks. If the labourers there were working with a will, the lorry could be emptied in a few minutes. If not, it seemed to take forever, and the lorries queued up impatiently.

The return journey with an empty vehicle was much more bouncy than the outward trip. Sally asked me to get a tray of eggs on one occasion, when our chickens had gone off lay. Knowing the conditions, I was a bit wary of carrying such fragile items. I had a tractor driver named Steam with me, who had the job of nursing these eggs on the return trip. Even then, I was very worried and would often turn my head to make sure they were being looked after. They were. I happened to glance at him at the same time as the front wheels hit a bigger-than-usual pot-hole; he was carefully holding the tray of eggs, but not a bit of him appeared to be touching the seat. It was as though he was suspended in midair. Luckily, he landed safely and the eggs all arrived home intact.

On Saturday mornings, I would do just one trip, after which the lorry would have its oil changed during a general service and clean-up before exchanging it with Shadow for the harvester. That was enough for the week; the weekend was now for our relaxation.

Before the season was over, many of us were inveigled into supporting our intensive conservation area's stand at the Lusaka Agricultural Show. Mkushi had not previously subscribed to the show, but as an ever-growing area, producing a wide variety of crops, the committee felt we should make our presence felt with a Mkushi stand, on which would be displayed every variety of produce emanating from our farms. When the big day came for judging the events, we won a cup for our surprising display. We showcased not only the main crops of tobacco, maize, and groundnuts but also products from the farms which had diversified into many varieties of seed, growing tomatoes and vegetables from those farms producing for the Copperbelt, plus chickens, eggs, and turkeys destined for the same market. Beef and pork were on offer from some of the older inhabitants, who ran herds of cattle or had pigsties, and a wide variety of fruit was shown from those farms at the eastern end of the Mkushi area.

The show itself was very interesting, with the usual cattle and horses competing for rosettes in the ring, which was surrounded by stalls with farm machinery, agricultural advisers, fertiliser representatives, and snack bars. Other stalls did their best to attract the wives into parting with money for new fridges, ovens, furniture, curtains, and other useful household goods, which according to the salesmen, we could not manage without.

There was a show ball in one of the leading Lusaka hotels that evening, giving the ladies a chance to compete with each other, which they did unashamedly. It was the highlight of the farming year, well supported by the leading farmers throughout the country. The food was excellent, the music very different from what we were used to at our club, and most noticeable were the surroundings, which were large, solidly constructed, and decorated by specialists who knew their job, a very pleasant change, which we greatly appreciated and which made the occasion so memorable.

One of the most sought-after cups at the show was the one which went to the producer of the best tobacco on display. This was won by Colin Clark, a skilled and knowledgeable tobacco grower who was one of the first settlers in Mkushi. Taller than most, with never an ounce of excess weight on his lanky frame, he was always very particular in everything he did. His buildings were exemplary and well planned, with a spacious, fully equipped workshop in which to maintain his machinery in top-notch condition. He had a delightful thatched house, kept spotless by his house staff under the direction of Cherry, his wife, who had a *Cordon Bleu* in cooking and produced superb meals when you were invited to dine. But with three young children to look after, such invites were infrequent.

Colin always did his utmost to keep up with research experiments which could improve the results of his crops. With his enquiring mind, he would also alert us to changes in legislation which could affect us. Being the Mkushi representative on the Government Lands Board, he received early warning that farmers were to be forced to provide permanent brick housing for all their labourers. This was an alarming thought. I was perhaps reasonably fortunate, with a relatively small labour force, but for some farmers, with sixty or seventy families on the property, it was to become a major source of worry. Representations were made to the government through the Farmers Association's head office to find out just what the plans were, but after many months, no clear-cut answer was received. It was left to the local labour officers and party members to endeavour to influence farmers as they thought fit. On my part, I had another kiln of bricks made and drew up plans to start building a number of houses each year, starting with those for my boss boy and tractor drivers.

Worries did appear to be increasing at this time, as Zambia was becoming more and more a political state seemingly more solicitous about the countries around it than about itself. The Organisation for African Unity (OAU) was having a great influence on President Kaunda to cut off all ties with the racialist white south: Rhodesia and South Africa. Rhodesia in turn, under Ian Smith, had decided that it was unfair for Northern Rhodesia and Nyasaland to have independence whilst the third party of the old federation should be left out. They therefore made a unilateral declaration of independence and stirred up the hornets' nest still further.

Some RAF Javelin aircraft were sent to Ndola on the Copperbelt to help protect Zambia from any aerial attacks from Rhodesia, but the request for troops to guard the Kariba Dam was turned down by British Prime Minister Harold Wilson. The propaganda war started, engendering a feeling of antipathy to those countries which were the main source of the vital commodities needed to keep Zambia operating. Our spare parts became more difficult to obtain, as white

Rhodesians in turn felt inclined to disregard orders from the black North. Petrol became scarce, as there were delays in fuel supplies due to late payments for previous deliveries.

In Rhodesia, the white people appeared to be fully behind Smith and his independence declaration. There was a tremendous feeling of confidence and security for the future, knowing that they had the support of the very strong Republic of South Africa behind them. There was a happier feeling throughout the country, now that the uncertainty was over and a decision made. But in the hearts of many of those same people must have been the knowledge that the writing was on the wall, that their life of bliss could not last. We in Mkushi could sense it, as our uncertainties increased and inefficiencies developed as more and more partly trained personnel took over the jobs from which skilled whites had departed. As farmers, we felt we would surely be secure in the future. In Mkushi, we were now producing nearly one-third of the country's maize requirement, together with much tobacco, which was a foreign currency earner, as well as all the other commodities we had displayed at the Lusaka Show.

In a letter to my parents at this time, my unease was evident in spite of determination to continue and manage somehow:

"The white man has built something in this country and is not likely to just give it up without a fight. Here on my farm for instance is a perfect example – I have struggled to build my way of life and naturally I will not give it up easily. Things need to be pretty bad before we would think of leaving our house and farm which is bringing us in a reasonable standard of living such as we would not find elsewhere. Instead I will be forever trying to find ways and means of getting around the obstacles which get in my way, for example mechanise the maize until I can almost run my farm with only four or five assistants if necessary. Generally we would all be only too happy to stay here, it is our home. If we did leave, where would we go to and what would we do – we cannot pack up a farm and take that with us! I do not attempt to find an answer to that question, the future is anybody's guess. In the meantime we will try and enjoy the present."

The winds of change were blowing over Mkushi, and by golly, we were worried about how they would affect us.

Burglary

Every farming season is different for the farmer, the weather being the major factor which can make it a good or a bad year. In 1966, there was virtually a drought from Mkushi to Cape Town. The tobacco plants struggled to grow, had their leaves scorched in the hot dry sun, failed to develop into their normal healthy maturity, and flowered early. The maize similarly battled against the elements and produced fewer and smaller cobs than usual.

With the worries produced by the abnormal weather came other worries about this year's tobacco sales. An auction floor for the tobacco had just about been completed in Lusaka, where it was expected some buyers would come to purchase the Zambian crop. The method of selling would be on the clock system, where buyers would need to keep their finger on a button until the price was reached, above which they were not prepared to pay. We farmers were perturbed both about the operating efficiency of the new auction floor and the new system of selling.

As it turned out, we need not have worried, as all went well. The size of the crop was not as big as in previous years, but the quality was good, as were the prices paid.

About this time, the Zambia government joined with the rest of the world in sanctions against Rhodesia, in an attempt to bring down the regime of Ian Smith and his hard-line supporters.

This gave rise to much discussion amongst us, as once again our world was being disrupted for reasons over which we had no control. Similarly, we had a lot of friends and relatives in Rhodesia who were going to be adversely affected. More to the point, we were going to suffer, as so many of our goods and essentials came from Rhodesia and South Africa – fuel, for example.

Soon, we learnt that petrol and diesel were being rationed, although farmers were exempt as essential users. Immediately, however, there were shortages while the government made alternative arrangements, that of bringing in the fuel from Dar es Salaam in Tanzania. The problem was a distinct shortage of suitable tankers in Zambia and, secondly, several hundred miles of dirt roads. It wasn't long before a large fleet of small lorries loaded with fuel drums was making its way as frequently as possible from the depot on the Copperbelt to the Tanzanian border to collect fuel. The Great North Road rapidly deteriorated even before the rainy season came. Crashes of lorries in the dusty conditions were a regular occurrence, breakdowns also a common feature so that more unlighted lorries on the side of the road at night added to the hazard of what became known as "the Hell Run." Joining the rat-race of lorries to Kapiri Mposhi's maize depot was very demanding, but by now there was a driver to do the work of Shadow Wilke and myself in our new ten-ton lorry. He had the patience to wait in line at the depot for endless hours until his turn came for unloading, which was getting slower by the day.

Since independence, many of the better labourers had been drifting away from the farming areas and obtaining jobs in the towns. Large shanty towns were springing up on the edges of the major towns, where they would live until fortune smiled on them, which was not often. They would stay there, assisted by other relatives who were in employment, if they were lucky; otherwise, they would be forced to beg, borrow, or steal – very often the latter, as was evidenced by the ever-increasing rate of crime in a hitherto crime-free society.

In the rural areas, we had to manage with fewer and less capable workers, who now had not only a minimum wage but also a Provident Fund. They could not be discharged by an employer without the agreement of the local labour officer, and two weeks leave each year was to be given with pay.

These changes came in gradually over the year, accepted by us with a fair amount of grumbling about the extra costs and work involved. In truth, they should have been in force years before but were not. Now we felt the black government was doing its best to exploit the White employers, as we ignored the fact that the regulations applied to all. We accepted the changes without too much protest, possibly as we thought untroubled relations would be good for our future. With a much-reduced maize crop in the country, in which the African growers' crop was disastrous, we felt the value of commercial farmers, as we were called, to the country was increased. With sanctions against Rhodesia, the politicians would not want to import maize from there and would try to prevent a shortfall in Zambia.

This year, I started growing maize for seed in response to a call for some farmers to start producing Zambian seed, thus avoiding having to import it from the south. SR52 was the variety of maize planted each season at that period, to give farmers a high yield. It was an hybrid seed bred from two different strains, which meant if seed was taken from the resultant crop, it could revert back to either parental strain and produce disappointing results.

The seed growers had to plant the two varieties of parent seed under rigorously controlled conditions, in such a way that two rows of the male variety pollinated from its tassels the six rows of the female variety on the silks of its cobs. This meant that the land for seed had to be well isolated from any other maize land, lest any cross-pollination occurred, and at the time of the tassels appearing at the top of each plant, those on the six female lines had to be removed before there was any chance of them fertilising their own silks. Hence, every day for at least a month, a span of labourers had to walk along every six lines over a ten-acre field, removing the flowering heads when first they budded forth. We had a seed inspector who came around without warning and who would search the field for any trace of a flowering head among the females. If he found one, it would mean destroying the plants within a five-yard radius. We found he could be ruthless and nicknamed him "Hitler" (but he was only doing his job).

When the crop matured, the two lines of male plants were cut down and removed from the land so there was no chance of mixing up those cobs with the required ones from the other plants.

Reaping the main crop of seed was not the end of the process, as each cob had to be checked for uniformity and freedom from disease. Not necessarily uniformity in size, which naturally varied, but each cob had to have the correct number of rows of pips. Hitler would be round to check, searching for failures, which could mean checking every cob once more. If the selection was satisfactory, a pass would mean progressing to the next stage of shelling the cobs, by hand to avoid breaking pips, prior to grading those pips into their varying sizes, large flats, medium rounds, smalls, and other grades.

If the grading was passed, the pips could then be treated with a mercurial dust well applied and bagged in 100-pound bags labelled with the variety, name of grower, and size of seed. These would bear the Seed Growers Association seal of approval, applied once again by the inspector.

It was a labour-intensive crop but with a fairly small acreage of tobacco, I found it dovetailed in well, while the end result made it worthwhile financially. Like so many aspects of farming, it needed good organisation to be successful and regular supervision of the labourers at every stage. Farming was hard work for all concerned. Anyone who thought he could farm from his armchair quickly found out differently, but there were few like that in Mkushi. We worked hard, and during slack periods, we played hard.

Television came to Lusaka and to the Copperbelt, seventy miles away from us as the crow flies. With a specially designed antenna and ideal conditions, it was hoped we could receive pictures in our area, thus relieving some of the monotony of long evenings. After much technical advice from Richard Street, a deep-thinking, well-respected farmer who was meticulous in all he did, we got our specially designed antenna mounted on steel pipes to the great height of 106 feet! Stay wires held it straight from four different points, with the antenna amazingly pointed in the right direction. As for the picture, it was far from perfect. Often snowy with disrupted sound, even when we thought conditions were ideal. We tried all sorts of things but never got a really satisfactory reception. The television was not as successful as the aerial deserved.

We therefore directed our energies elsewhere, Sally becoming chairlady of the W.I. (which we called Women's Interference), and me becoming chairman of the club.

The ladies seemed to enjoy their regular gatherings, which would be held at the club on Thursday afternoons. They had talks from visitors, saw demonstrations of craft work from some of their very skilled members, and discussed ways and means of helping the indigenous women who might have got a vote but appeared to have little else other than a new baby each year. The ladies sponsored a W.I. branch for them at the Mkushi Boma, helping them overcome teething problems and become established. They also organised a mannequin show one evening at the club, with a great selection of model gowns and clothes brought down to Mkushi by a large Copperbelt company. Most of the mannequins were wives of farmers, many of whom were exceptionally pretty with lovely figures. We were most fortunate to have such pretty, talented girls around us, and there was another about to join the community.

Murray Heron, our demon bowler, had found a beautiful young lady in South Africa and was determined to marry her. First, he needed a house for Erica, not just the temporary refuge suitable for a bachelor. This got his full attention when he wasn't in his car, heading back south to see his fiancée. His house was going to have all mod-cons: bath, wash basins, running water and, of course, flush toilets. In his haste to get everything in working order before going off to get married, Murray heard that a piece of meat in the septic tank would quickly get the biological degrading process off to a good start. Not having a suitable piece of meat, Murray went off and shot a baboon, which he put in the tank and then disappeared for wedding and honeymoon. Apparently, the smell from his septic tank spread far and wide, and Murray was fortunate that a very good neighbour saved his marriage by remedying the situation before his return with his lovely bride.

Wendy was now five years old and very ready for school. She would happily come around the farm with Ian and me in the vanette, but correspondence school with Mum was definitely not favoured by either. We therefore found time to drive down to Salisbury to enquire into boarding schools suitable for Wendy, with Ian to follow later. This was very easy, with a good selection of schools to choose from. We chose Chisipite School, where Wendy would start at the beginning of the year. School clothes were organised, fees discussed, together with arrangements of which friends could take her out at weekends.

Looking around Salisbury, we were amazed to find the shops full of commodities which we could not obtain in Zambia. The sanctions applied to Rhodesia were affecting Zambia far more. It was unsettling, as was the quiet confidence of the people that all would be well, now they had their independence. There was a certain amount of arrogance among the white population and some contempt directed at those with Zambian number plates on their cars. We felt a bit lost in the middle of two groups, white Rhodesians and black Zambians, none of which wanted us. We felt even more lost on our return to find our farm house had been thoroughly burgled. We had not locked anything, since we had not found that necessary at any time until then. Our cook had been left in charge, but we discovered later that he had departed elsewhere with a couple of fully laden suitcases as we left for Rhodesia.

Sally was the biggest loser, with her sentimental collection of jewellery all gone, as were most of her dresses, skirts, and blouses. My shirts, trousers, and jackets were also gone. Our bedding had been taken, as was the radio and all our cutlery. The two suitcases had obviously been packed with as much as could be carried, ready for resale in the shanty towns of the Copperbelt. It's a sickening, creepy feeling that you get when someone violates your house, going through all your personal items to select those suitable for market. Other items are just discarded and trampled underfoot. Whatever is left is looked on questioningly – why was that left? What's wrong with it? Everything seems dirty and defiled. It took us a long, long time to get over it, even though the insurance company made up our loss.

Worse things could (and did) happen. We heard that the vice president of the Commercial Farmers Bureau, who lived and farmed in Mkushi, had been forced to leave Zambia. Like some others, he had been pronounced a racialist and told that Zambia did not want him. A week later, he was gone.

Getting the next crop into the ground kept us all not only as busy as usual but isolated on our farms for several weeks, as we worked each day from dawn to dusk. Individually, we would churn over the events of the year, perhaps getting them into the right perspective, uninfluenced by alarmist remarks of neighbours made after a few beers in the club. Plans were made for a children's Christmas party at the club, in which Santa Claus would arrive by parachute onto our cricket field, this courtesy of someone's friend who was a parachutist at the Lusaka Flying Club. He duly arrived dressed in a red outfit and crash helmet and landed right in front of a large crowd of fascinated children and parents. His sack of toys quickly materialised in his vicinity as he discarded his parachute, whereupon his method of arrival was forgotten for better things.

For our New Year's Eve Ball, we had an army band from Ndola Barracks coming to play dance music for us. This was a great achievement, brought about by a new couple to the block, Berty and Sandra Bowes. Berty, a tall, bony man in his early thirties with a receding hairline, especially in the middle, and eyes which always seemed surprised at this, had been in the British Army on detachment to Zambia, helping to train the local army in Ndola. After twelve years' service, he left as a major to become farm assistant in Mkushi with Sandra, his newly married wife. She was another of the lovely wives of the area, with her slim figure and lovely, deep brown eyes. It was no wonder Berty had fallen for her. Using his influence on old friends, he had arranged for some of the Army Band to play for us at the New Year's Ball, thus ensuring that the very difficult year ended on a high note.

Chapter 6
Charlie Romeo

Olly Johansson came to my farm early one morning as I was supervising the hoeing of the tobacco.

"Dick," *he said (I was known as "Dick" to most people, "Richard" by Sally, who preferred the longer name),* "could you come over to Kangalati and have a look at my airstrip? I'd like to know what you think."

I looked at him, somewhat bewildered. I had not even heard that he was making an airstrip, but more to the point, what did I know about them? I agreed to go over to his farm, Kangalati, later that day thus gaining time to think about airstrips and aeroplanes which had been far from my thoughts in the last eight years.

Olly was a small, ginger-haired Swede with freckles and a peppery temper. Like many small men, he bustled around energetically, getting things done. If, as in this case, he thought he wanted an airstrip, then next morning, he would start to build an airstrip. His farm was conveniently situated close to the Great North Road, where he lived with his wife, Muriel, and two very young sons in their delightful thatched house. Muriel was a tall, strong, well-built woman with a magnificent head of long auburn hair. Like so many in Mkushi, they were very hospitable people, and being situated where they were, visitors were a regular feature of their lives. Notice of their arrival was given by Hector, their large Doberman. Hector feared no one but was scared of thunder, as Sally discovered one day when she was having a cup of tea with Muriel. There was a sudden clap of thunder, frightening Hector such that he came leaping over the bottom half of the stable door into the sitting room and with one further bound was on Sally's lap (she unknowingly had chosen his chair to sit in).

Later, I looked at Olly's planned airstrip. It consisted of about forty acres of gently sloping land. This had been levelled and rolled with a land-plane, which Olly had constructed from an old lorry chassis and disused grader blades, discarded from the graders which occasionally serviced our farm roads and Great North Road. I knew very little about the Cessna 172 aircraft he was thinking of purchasing but considered it should be able to easily get airborne in the length of two aircraft carriers (without the need for a catapult). Similarly, three carrier lengths without arrester wires should still give plenty of room for errors when landing. As Olly had room to park a couple of dozen fleet carriers, I was quite happy that he would have enough room for his Cessna and told him so accordingly.

So began another chapter in the life of Mkushi farmers, as a great number became interested in this new activity. A flying instructor from Ndola flew to Kangalati each weekend to give Olly flying lessons and give others some air experience. I tried it myself, flying around the airfield at speeds where in my previous fast aircraft, I would not have got airborne. I turned down the offer of a partnership in Olly's planned 172, as Sally and I felt it would be better to have our own plane if we were going to start flying rather than to share one.

Richard Street and Dennis Bourdillon were the next to learn, and together with Olly, they purchased a red and silver Cessna 172, which from then on was known as Charlie Sierra, named from the last two registration letters on the side of the plane.

With one aircraft in the area, talk of flying was a regular subject at the club and dinner parties. The advantages naturally had to exceed the disadvantages. The ease of getting from farm to Lusaka instead of risking life and limb along the well-nigh-impossible Hell Run was paramount, as was the time factor: one hour and a bit compared with well over three hours each way by car. Getting home before dark was also a benefit. Transport in Lusaka from airport and around town was soon overcome by the purchase of a small Renault, in which the three pilots had an equal share.

On occasional Saturdays, we had other pilots dropping in to Kangalati, generally salesmen who had Pipers, Cessnas, or Beechcraft aeroplanes on offer. By now, I had made a few flights and got my private pilot's licence, with an open rating for all light single-engined planes, so I was able to try out many of the types brought to Mkushi on demonstration. One came which I thought absolutely delightful: a two-seater Cessna 150 with silver wings from the natural metal skin and golden yellow fuselage, and white letters on the side 9J RCR or *Charlie Romeo.* I'm not sure who persuaded who that it would be a good idea to buy this little Cessna 150. With a large potential market of new pilots, I thought it would be an ideal plane to use to teach people to fly. Similarly, with a small bench seat in the back, as was possible, according to the salesman, Wendy and Ian could be accommodated and even taken to and from school in Salisbury. Sally obviously thought it was a good idea to keep up with the other leading wives, as she offered to put up the money she had received from the insurance after the theft of her jewellery. That clinched matters, and the following weekend, *Charlie Romeo* came to its new owners, with whom it stayed very happily for the next six years.

It had been an exceptionally wet season, with almost continuous rain and a rapidly ripening tobacco crop to keep up with. But my relatively small acreage gave me few problems, and again I reaped the reward later. The roads were in a terrible state as Sally drove off to Salisbury five hundred miles away to put Wendy back to school for her second term. She appeared to be quite happy there, in spite of a few tears as Sally left her. The wrench was more with us, not having her around the farm and getting into mischief with her growing brother.

We determined that all being well, we would fly down to her at half term and spend the few days with her. With this in mind, I got my instructors licence renewed, started making an airstrip on my farm, and commenced a flying course for Colin and Cherry Clark and Shadow Wilke. These were the first of nearly thirty farmers and farmer's wives who in the next few years learnt to fly with *Charlie Romeo* (some learned in a plane that they had previously purchased). Generally, after forty hours, they had their private pilot's licence and then went away to see which plane would best suit their requirements. The Clarks, with a large family, bought a Cherokee 6, Naoumoffs a Beech Musketeer, Dendy-Youngs a sporty executive Mooney with retractable undercarriage, Terry Payne a Cessna 182, and others various Piper or Cessna models. They became invaluable to us as a quick, easy way of travel not only to town, but around the farming area, where airstrips sprang up and planes were housed. Also around Zambia, where we sometimes flew to the various game reserves for weekend holidays, and of course to Salisbury, where we took an ever-increasing number of schoolchildren. I found *Charlie Romeo* very useful for surveying the farm, checking on threatening bush fires, watching for maize theft, and later locating missing cattle.

Mfuwe, about one hundred and fifty miles away, in the Luangwa Valley, became a favourite place to go for a special long weekend before the main heat of the summer started. In loose formation with *Charlie Sierra*, we flew there to view the animals only a few months after Richard and Olly had gained their licences. Accommodated in thatched cottages, we set off in open jeeps early each morning and late each afternoon to view the wide variety of game in the area. Springbok, bush buck, and water buck we saw in their hundreds, grazing peacefully on the river plain. The elegant eland took more finding, as their coats melded in with the thickets where they would be browsing. Sables would also be in a group, apart with their curved horns bending high above their heads, similar in every respect to *ours* on the farm. Standing tall above them all were the many giraffes browsing from the highest trees. Buffaloes we normally saw in great herds numbering upwards of four hundred and which made off in a thunderous cloud of dust if we approached too close. The lumbering great elephants we saw in large numbers, about thirty in any one group. Young ones were numerous, as were solitary bulls with their long, heavy tusks. We often saw the elephants crossing the Luangwa River with a water mark halfway up their bodies as they climbed out. With the game ranger always in attendance, we got very close to many of these animals and were able to study them carefully. One hippo taking his morning constitutional did not like a jeep in his path back to the river and gave it a solid disgruntled nudge with his backside on passing! We felt he must have been out the night before with a similarly cross rhinoceros, which made a serious charge at us a short while later. The driver being ready, we made a rapid retreat.

On the river banks and in the river, apart from the large families of noisy hippos, were many large, menacing crocodiles. Although we were close to them, easily viewing the cleaning actions of the egrets on their backs, we could not judge their length. We would have come off the worse in the event we inadvertently met one on the river bank, just as we would have had we met the King of Beasts alone in the open. Most of the lions we saw were sleeping in the shade of some trees and looked just like big cuddly cats. They had no fear of us and were obviously used to being on show. Two appeared to be on guard duty, but we stopped a safe distance away, quietly taking our photographs, watching them watching us.

Early next morning, we visited a lion on his kill. There was very little left of the animal he was eating. Around him were gathered at least a hundred vultures waiting to clear up the crumbs from his table.

The only large beast of prey I failed to see in many trips to Luangwa Valley was the leopard. There were many around but generally only seen at night.

During the day, we relaxed on the edge of a lagoon in front of the camp buildings, watching the delightful bird life with a cool drink in our hands and sheltered from the hot sun. Monkeys roamed along the banks with their offspring holding tight on their mother's back. Occasionally, a hippo would make an appearance, walking slowly down to the water's edge and gently immersing himself in the cool water.

Our evenings after supper were often spent on the roof of the lodge with a drink in our hand, listening to the tales of the bush told by Norman Carr, who ran the camp. He had spent his life amongst the animals and had reared many, including Big Boy and Little Boy, two lion cubs which he was able to successfully return to the wild.

One story he did not tell concerned Sally and myself on one of our later sorties to Mfuwe. Three or four Mkushi planes had flown in for the weekend, and overnight, I became ill with a fever. There was a pool of water under the soaking wet mattress from my perspiration, I was so feverish. A French doctor there prescribed bed with aspirin and to get me home if possible. After some preparation, Sally and others got me into *Charlie Romeo,* whereupon Sally, who now also had her licence, flew me home to the farm and a doctor.

About twelve months later, at a dinner party in town with some distinguished guests, we learnt how "the pilot fell terribly ill at Mfuwe lodge, and his wife who had never flown in her life before climbed into the plane and flew him home!"

Sally used the small plane occasionally to keep in practise, and we took it in turns, flying to and from town. On one occasion when going up for an early morning flight, she asked Ian if he wanted to go with her. "Is Daddy coming too?" he asked and turned down the offer when he learned that I was not. That was the morning Sally decided to practise some stalls. She was over a friend's farm when she throttled back the engine. The garden boy, noticing the sudden loss of noise, rushed to "the Donna," as the lady of the house was often called, "Donna, Donna, the aeroplane," pointing upwards to where the plane had been. "It has no diesel!"

On another occasion, an agronomist, Mike Zyller, called at the house to see me, only to find Sally dressed for tennis and armed with a shotgun, with which she had just killed a cobra snake that had been terrorising the cook and the dog. Sally then locked the gun away, got a lift with Mike to the hangar, jumped into the plane with her tennis racquet, and took off to play tennis at a distant farm. Mike, who was later killed by some *irregular* soldiers, said he had dined out on that tale many a time.

Good news came that the Great North Road would be tarred. The bad news was that it would be two years before our stretch of fifty miles to Kapiri Mposhi would be done. It was now in such a shocking condition that Shadow and I decided against a lorry this year and negotiated with a contractor who had two seven-ton lorries to transport our maize for us. The vehicles were not in good shape, frequently breaking down and getting back late to the farm. One night, one failed to get back at all; it had crashed head-on into a petrol lorry, killing the driver and badly injuring his assistant. From then on, we reverted to the main transport company to finish our stockpile when it could.

Hank Faber, a Dutch man, farming between Tim Dooley and myself, decided he had seen enough of Mkushi. He had been a meticulous farmer, growing good crops, and had been prominent in building good, airy thatched houses for his labourers. It appeared he was going to run a scheme in Nigeria for a large tobacco company and had Berty lined up to manage his farm for a year, if I would keep my eye on him. He put this proposition to me one evening and at the same time asked me if I would like to buy his herd of cattle, just over one hundred of them. I could use his dip and facilities until I got my own organised, and he would be leaving in two weeks' time.

So while other farmers were leaving the county, I was still optimistic that we would be able to continue our farming way of life, to the benefit of the country and ourselves. We were now into cattle, one hundred of them.

My knowledge of cattle was almost limited to squirting milk from their teats, and most of these big beefy animals did not have teats. I had to learn fast. I found out about a cattle handling and artificial insemination course being held on a farm near Salisbury three weeks later and made arrangements to take it. Sally and Ian would join Lynn Street, who was going to a holiday hotel near Durban during that period.

The course was intensive, covering the breeding of cattle by inseminating them with semen through thin plastic tubes with a rubber bulb on the handheld end. The semen, previously collected from a prize bull, was sucked from a phial into the tube by means of the rubber bulb and then the tube inserted carefully into the cervix of the animal, which was in season, whereupon the semen was squirted into the right area by a quick squeeze of the bulb. Finding the appropriate parts of the anatomy was one of the things we practised each day, with our arms regularly disappearing up different cows' backsides!

The course also covered a lot of ailments of cattle and dealt with the recommended veterinary treatment to give as well as preventative measures, which were better. It covered de-horning of animals, in which the advantages of hornless (or polled) cattle were discussed. Breeding up the standard of the herd was discussed in depth and the ease with which it was possible, through the use of artificial insemination, whereby quality sperm from the best bulls could be kept on the farm in containers full of liquid nitrogen.

When I returned to my farm, I realised I still knew very little about cattle, but I did have a few ideas, some knowledge, and I had lost any fear of handling them, which I suspect I had previously. I viewed my herd through different eyes and realised that I needed to spend a day doing some castrating with the Burdizzas, which made me tremble with fear whenever I looked at them, and other than regular dipping, they should be fine until the end of the rainy season, which would keep them in good, lush green grass.

I could thus concentrate on getting the next crop into the ground and bring the books up to date, to ensure we were still a profitable enterprise, which we were.

On the debit side, we learnt of various people being put in detention in Lusaka, with only wild rumours about the reasons for this. Broken Hill was renamed Kabwe, after a chief who ruled that area many years before. Road names were also being changed to the names of Zambian martyrs or other revolutionary leaders. The fuel tanker came onto the farm and filled the petrol tank with diesel instead of petrol. The boss boy, who was not a tractor driver, thought he would be helpful one afternoon by driving the new tractor into the shed. Unfortunately, he crashed it into the wall, which cracked badly, at the same time a steering rod snapped on the tractor. But these were spaced-out events in which the first was forgotten by the time the next happened, so we were not depressed by them for long. Christmas came round again, with all the schoolchildren home to be spoilt by their parents, with parties and presents galore. The time was fast approaching for Ian to go to school too. He had a toy machine gun in his Christmas stocking, which not only awakened us at some unearthly hour before it was light, but also disrupted our Christmas Day church service. The noisy gunning mechanism did not blend with our carol singing, nor did the odd cry from him as Mother gently "gunned" his backside. We believed in discipline for our young children, generally reprimanding the two together, as we were well aware, that if Ian had done something wrong and Wendy was around, then she had probably put him up to it! But we loved them lots, bundles of fun and mischief that they were.

The New Year's Ball had a topical flying theme, with the club decorated with parachutes, aeroplanes, a control tower, and runway lights. As usual, it was a great success and still in full swing when Sally and I departed at 4 a.m. What a wonderful life we had!

Chapter 7
Cattle Farm

1968 started well, with all the crops looking good, as were my cattle. Berty and I were getting on well together, as he required very little supervision or advice from me. He and Sandra were happy in their house and even planned to go skiing at the end of the tobacco reaping, if that was at all possible. Sally had an idea that she would like a swimming pool and started nudging me to consider building one. She thought the best place would be in our present front garden, where she felt it would enhance the look of our lovely house.

Stalling somewhat, I told her that it would not be possible there due to too many rocks such as we had met when digging the foundations of the house. Sally was not convinced, and when one morning I went by car to Lusaka, she quickly had the garden boy organised, digging a large hole in the driveway, just a few yards from the garage. There, after a few feet in several directions, he came up against large rocks. Disappointed, Sally got him to fill in the hole and level off the road, as though it had not been touched. Unfortunately, an hour before I got home, the skies opened to a normal heavy shower of rain, saturating everything. Approaching the garage, I saw Sally at the front door, waving to me. As I waved back to her, the Mercedes suddenly sank up to its axles, as though the road had opened up to swallow it. I switched off, but as the door would not open, I had to climb out of the window to greet my dear wife, who was waiting, with some trepidation, to tell me a story.

Across the Munshiwemba River from us lived Jock and Beth Cameron, with their young family. They had a large farm of forty-five hundred acres, which was not part of the settlement scheme, as it had been going for some years previously. They were perhaps not quite as sociable as others, not being such regular club goers. Jock was more intellectual than many, preferring his books to small talk. He came across to me one morning to see if I would buy his farm from him and his cattle too.

Life seemed full of surprises, especially in the early morning! He had ten tobacco barns, sheds, a workshop, a house and even a butchery, two hundred acres of maize in the lands and a hundred and forty head of cattle with attendant paddocks, dip, and handling facilities. Jock had suddenly become depressed by the state of affairs in the country and decided to sell up and move to South Africa. He was anxious to leave right away, without reaping the maize or anything except for selling his machinery. As a result, he was asking a very low price to get a quick sale. I could not refuse.

I checked with my accountant and with the bank manager to ensure that I would be making a wise move with the facility of financial backing when necessary. Then Jock and I went together to Lusaka to a solicitor, where on payment of a large deposit, the wheels were put in motion for me to become the new owner of his farm, and he was able to depart for the south.

I was now fully committed: tobacco, maize on two farms, seed maize, and with new calves, I now had 275 head of cattle. *Charlie Romeo's* flying courses took three afternoons each week; as chairman of the club, I had some organisation to do; and as secretary of the Farmers Association, I had meetings to arrange and minutes to record. Provided that nothing extraordinary happened, I felt that with good organisation and the assistance of my boss boys and labourers, I would manage successfully. The pendulum was surely on an upswing; all would be well.

Then came the economic revolution in Zambia: the Mulungushi Reforms. White farmers were no longer permitted to have bank overdrafts, all loans for farming were to go through the government's land bank, Farmers Co-operative Society cheques were no longer honoured, and all cheques for the purchase of fertiliser had to be bank certified.

These were far-reaching alarming reforms, which hit me immediately when the bank loan I had arranged to purchase Cameron's farm was refused at the last minute. The rest of the money had to come from the tobacco and maize sales as the sales progressed. This put a big squeeze on me. I had hoped to do a lot of fencing on Cameron's farm as well as constructing better handling facilities. All I could do was repair the setup which he had made some years before, until more money was available.

I had previously arranged an overdraft with the bank each season, an arrangement agreed with the bank manager after a short discussion of my plans at the start of each crop. Now I was forced to go to the land bank run by the government, whose funds were largely directed at the indigenous farmers. Commercial farmers, having completed the long application forms, often found loans refused for technical reasons so that they had to apply again or found they had been given much less than they had requested. It was disconcerting, as were the bank certified cheques for fertiliser. No longer did we have agronomists or fertiliser salesmen coming to the farm, as all fertiliser was now imported and sold by a government body. So having decided ourselves what we wanted, it was then necessary to calculate the cost of each lorry load, obtain bank cheques for each consignment, and then try to get it from the depot. All went well with me for four of the loads. On the fifth trip, the lorry returned empty. The driver complained the depot would not supply as my cheque was out of date; it was dated August, now it was 1 September. A phone call to the depot manager brought an apology but the increased time spent trying to obtain necessary farm inputs, together with the increased cost and frustration, was starting to have a detrimental effect on commercial farmers and their crops.

We hoped our Commercial Farmers Bureau, to which we all belonged via our Farmers Association, would take up these problems urgently with the government minister concerned. Surely, we thought, they would not want to import the staple crop from the other side of the border from the "racist" South.

One organisation where I was able to get financial assistance was from the Cold Storage Commission in Lusaka. Their representative visited my farm, where he counted the different classes of cattle. He then branded a percentage of them with the CSC brand and arranged for a substantial cheque to be paid to my bank account. My agreement was to sell my steers through the Cold Storage abattoir in Lusaka, whereby they would steadily recover the loan.

I was amazed how easy this negotiation turned out to be, as well as how successful it was over the next three years. As a result, I was a great supporter of the commission, even touring their clean, efficiently run abattoir on one occasion. They certainly helped me out quickly and easily when I was getting only obstructions elsewhere.

I spent a lot of time with my cattle at this time, de-horning both the calves and many of the larger animals as well. While they were in the neck-clamp, I also de-wormed each one, castrated any new calves and finally tagged them with ear tags. It was hot, dusty, hard work but gave me great satisfaction when it was all completed. All the animals were now on Cameron's farm, where they were gently herded each day by two or three herdsmen and paddocked each evening, where I could view them. Although I had tried some artificial insemination on the cows I bought from Hank Faber, my facilities were not up to standard for such a project, and I soon dropped the idea. Instead, I went with the lorry to a farmer in Mazabaka, with whom I had negotiated the purchase of three good Afrikaner bulls. They were big animals and appeared to be very happy with their lot when they viewed the many cows in my herd. They were carefully looked after to ensure they settled in with the others. But about two weeks after their arrival, my herdsman came to me to say that two of the bulls had sore feet. They were reluctant to walk. I was very worried and rushed across the log bridge over the river to see the ailing beasts. They had been herded into the handling pen, where they were both lying down and looking sorry for themselves, in spite of their great bulk. I was able to handle their feet without any objections from them. They were not swollen but were obviously tender. More expert knowledge than mine was necessary. Sally called the vet from Mkushi Boma for me, but as he only had a bicycle for transport, she told him to be at the airstrip at Mkushi in fifteen minutes' time.

As I wanted to speak to the commercial vet in Kabwe, I sent Sally off in *Charlie Romeo* to collect the African vet from Mkushi. He was not happy about getting into a small aeroplane, especially with a madam driving. Sally told him, "Get in or else," in her most diplomatic manner and rapidly brought him back to the farm. He was a small, middle-aged native obviously uncomfortable on a white man's farm with two enormous bulls, which he was expected to cure. Fortunately for all of us, the Kabwe vet made his entrance on the scene at almost the same time. He must have left his practise in Kabwe as soon as he had put the phone down after my call and driven fast in his Land Rover to arrive so quickly.

I had never met him before, so that when I first saw him, I wondered what the veterinary world was coming to. He was in his early thirties and had a fair wispy beard, which unusually blew in the wind. On his head, he wore an American-style Stetson hat. Round his neck, he had a shoelace tie held in position with a silver buckle. His fancy white embroidered shirt was most impressive when he removed his Harris tweed riding jacket, which he wore above his riding breeches and tooled leather shoes. He had some overalls and wellington boots in his Land Rover into which he changed, while he listened to what the African vet and I had to say. After carefully studying the beasts, investigating their feet, and even listening to their heartbeats through his stethoscope, he came up with his diagnosis: laminitis.

It sounded terrible. I had never heard of it before, nor, I fear, had the African vet. "They have probably had too much care and attention and have eaten too much maize," he said. "Keep them penned for a few days with just grass to eat and they should be fine."

At that time, I had been cutting out the male lines of the seed maize, feeding it to the cattle to save wastage. Obviously, the bulls had fancied this, getting more than their fair share. His diagnosis was right. An injection for each, and in two days, they were back to normal, and I was a very relieved farmer.

I came to know that vet quite well, although I only had to call him out on one other occasion. It most certainly went to show that looks can be deceptive. Meanwhile, what of the little African vet? As a storm was brewing when we finished with the bulls, I told Sally that I would return him to Mkushi. There was a bit of turbulence from the storm on the way. When he got out, he thanked me, and from his somewhat pale face, he said, "I'd rather fly with the Madam."

Some weeks later, the flying families, led by Richard Street, decided it was time to go on a long weekend outing to Kasaba Bay, on the southern shore of what used to be Lake Tanganyika. There we could all try our luck fishing for Nile perch, which were to be found in the lake. We now had five aeroplanes available, so twenty of us departed on this long cross-country trip, via Kasama, where we refuelled. The faster planes went ahead of *Charlie Sierra* and ourselves, Ollie kindly slowing down to stay near us. I was very happy with that, especially when flying past the Bengwuela swamps, which was a very extensive lake and marshy area. One cough from the engine as we cut across one corner could have given anyone a heart attack, as looking down it was possible to visualise the crocodile-infested, mosquito-ridden marsh land from which escape would be impossible.

Kasaba Bay was delightful, the fishing poor. Only the experts like Lynn and Richard caught anything, but it was lovely on the lake in the early morning, watching the light strengthen over the shoreline, then to smell the bacon and eggs frying for breakfast as we moored at the jetty on our return. Much of the day we spent swimming in the fresh water or sheltering from the heat under the large thatched sunshades on the sand. There were wild animals around like hippos, crocodiles, and Zambezi, a great elephant who regularly strolled through the camp, grazing around the huts. Colin Clark fed him with two bread rolls which he happily accepted, Colin little realising the danger of what he was doing. I met up with Zambezi a few years later, when I awoke one bright moonlight night wondering what the scratching was on the mosquito netting at my window. I was fearful that a thief was trying to get in. I quietly edged the curtain to one side to find this great elephant grazing on the grass around the border of the hut. Every time he lifted his trunk to his mouth, one tusk was rubbing against the netting! There was little I could do, so I trustingly got back into bed and went back to sleep. Regrettably, Zambezi became a bit of a menace to the visitors of the camp and had to be destroyed soon afterwards.

The flying section returned successfully to Mkushi, greatly heartened by their achievement in this long cross-country flight. As a result, more people enrolled on the list to learn the art of flying.

We were unusually fortunate in Mkushi to have more than our fair share of wives who were very pretty, and one such was Carol Dendy-Young. She was artistic, which showed up in her dress, her paintings, and her flower arranging. She was also a good mother to her three young sons, who absolutely adored her, as did John, her husband, who was athletic, intelligent, capable, and brimming over with both energy and enthusiasm. He ran his farm like clockwork, with large crops very well managed. He paid his labour above average wages, firmly believing that if he looked after them well, he would get good results, as he did.

John had already learnt to fly, as he and Terry Payne were early students of mine. With John's dynamic enthusiasm, I arranged a programme for them both whereby I would fly with them on Tuesday, Thursday, and Saturday afternoons, teaching them something new, while on the other three days, they could each come and do their solo flights. They both had their private pilot's licence in six weeks. John bought his Mooney a week later, onto which I converted him the following week. John did not waste time. Now he wanted me to teach Carol.

With her unflappable, even temperament, Carol took to the controls with ease – she was a natural pilot. I still tried to get from her the very highest standard that she could achieve and remember having her in tears shortly before she was due to take her flight test with an examiner from Lusaka. She was not the first to cry from my firm treatment, as Sally had done so previously when I had been forced to put pressure on her during her flying training. But Carol dried her eyes while being consoled by Sally telling her what a beast I was, and then she sailed through her flight test, as I knew she would. Carol would have made an excellent flying instructor, but with changing times and events, it was not to be.

About two years later, John and Carol left Mkushi to try farming in South Africa at Franschhoek. John's money failed to come out of Zambia, and he battled for several years, both of them working from dawn to dusk, trying to make ends meet and pay off the new farm and raise their family. John tried every money-making scheme he could, while Carol made and sold craft work in a local shop. They saw an opening for a high-class restaurant and for a bakery in addition to all the other work. It was a hard, long road for them both but ended up as a tremendous success. *La Petite Ferme* is now one of the leading restaurants in South Africa, one in which all three sons are involved in some way.

While our children were home on the farm for their summer holidays, their grandmother flew out from England on the VC 10 to spend three weeks with us. Imagine her surprise when after clearing customs with her suitcase, I then took her across the tarmac and helped her into *Charlie Romeo.* There was quite a difference between the VC 10 and the two-seater Cessna 150, but being the grand lady she was, she did not bat an eyelid.

1968 was also the year when the active Lusaka Flying Club organised a weekend event which was to be the Zambian National Flying Championships. There were to be joyrides, parachute jumps, bombing of drums with bags of flour, a pylon race, and a flight test with a judge involving some basic instrument flying, dead reckoning, and a glide landing on to a spot on the runway from one thousand feet. Mkushi were well represented among the many pilots from Lusaka and the Copperbelt. Pilots of all ranges of experience took part, from novices to professional charter pilots. John Dendy-Young came third in the pylon race with his speedy Mooney, Richard Street dropped his bomb right into the barrel to win the bombing event, while I won the flight test using Charlie Sierra (not having enough helpful instruments in Charlie Romeo) and became the Zambian National Flying Champion. I won a large trophy and an engraved beer tankard which I still have and of which I am justly proud. We enjoyed our weekend and our victories.

Stormy Weather

The weather in Zambia followed a pattern which was, in general, quite predictable. Spring came at the end of August, with the gradual awakening of the bush, green stalks pushing their way up through the dry, brittle grass. New leaves would appear on the trees as the old ones shed themselves after a final blaze of colour. The temperature would warm up steadily into October – the suicide month – when swimming pools were used at all times of the day in an effort to cool off. It would be a dry heat until just before the rains at the beginning of November, our summer rains, brought about by the convergence of the northeasterly and southeasterly prevailing winds which circle the globe, moving seasonally with the sun between the Tropics of Cancer and Capricorn.

Then the clouds would build up each morning, and we would hope for a welcome relief from the heat by a shower of rain that afternoon, before the clouds died away. Once the rains started, we could hope for a similar occurrence each day until March, when the convergence zone moved back to the north, away from us. We would then have dry, cooler days. The grass and shrubs would quickly lose all moisture and colour, the earth harden until it was brick hard, and the occasional frost would hit us at night, turning banana leaves black as well as killing off any other still-green leaf. Autumn was only distinguishable as being the end of the rains and the start of the cool, dry days of winter. Throughout the winter months, the sun would continue to shine on most days, so that a jersey was the only additional clothing necessary.

Occasionally during the summer, the main convergence zone would come to a stop over our area, and we had regular heavy downpours of rain from the large cumulo nimbus clouds, which towered up to fifty thousand feet over us. At night, it was exciting to watch the lightning flashing away in these powerhouses and just hope they were not too close to home. The damage they could do was tremendous, as I was to find out in 1969.

The season had started wet, so that the tobacco did not look as healthy and vigorous as usual, although it was fully grown and ready for reaping next day. I was over on Cameron's farm, which was now fully paid off and renamed "Dixie Ranch." There I was, dipping and de-worming the cattle, knowing I would be fully occupied with the tobacco reaping for the next few weeks. I saw a big storm approaching and hoped it would slide past me so that I could complete the job in hand. It by passed me but not the home farm, where the thunder and lightning hid the sound of the heavy hail which hit hard the tobacco, maize, and seed maize. A tree had been uprooted in our front garden, and the lands and roads were awash with running water. A message soon came over to me that hail had fallen on the tobacco, so finishing off quickly with the cattle, I went to investigate. Never had I seen such devastation of crops. Every tobacco leaf in the thirty-acre land had holes and tears in it. At least half were broken several times over and left hanging on the stalk of the plant, while hundreds of thousands littered the ground, where they had been hammered by the hail or blown by the squalls of wind. The crop was a write-off. I would be lucky to salvage anything. I was pleased that I had fully insured against hail damage; I would get paid out for a change.

The maize lands were equally devastated. Where the maize had stood with broad green leaves several feet high, much was now lying flat on the ground and the leaves shredded, as though they had been passed through a paper shredder. It was unbelievable and quite shattering. I thought of all the work and effort that had been put into growing the crop to that stage, all for nothing. Hail inspectors assessed the damage to the tobacco as 100 per cent when they inspected the stricken land next morning. The seed maize I withdrew as a seed crop and would hope simply to salvage something together with the commercial crop, or what was left of it.

When I recovered from the shock next morning, I wondered what I could do to minimise the tremendous loss. I was able to discharge some of my labourers to jobs on nearby farms, while with the remainder I still endeavoured to salvage something from the broken tobacco. Neighbouring farmers who had seen the storm soon heard of my trouble, and like the good neighbours they were, they asked me to reap for them those lands that they could not keep up with due to the rapid ripening season.

Three weeks later, another storm struck. I saw it coming, black and menacing with a solid white curtain of rain underneath it. Before reaching me, the wind got up blowing hard in towards the approaching fury, before being sucked upwards many thousands of feet. Leaves from the trees blew off and quickly disappeared as I took shelter in our house until the storm passed. Through the torrential downpour, we could see the vlei turn into a raging river as we looked out through the window of our sitting room. Once again, I feared the worst.

Roofs had been ripped off five of the tobacco barns, top vents stripped from four others, and the corrugated iron on a shed roof had been torn but remained on. The hangar roof had been taken off completely and was almost intact, fifty yards away. Fortunately, no damage was done to *Charlie Romeo,* even though a brick had landed flat on the wing. Many trees were down, the airfield windsock was leaning at a crazy angle, and the main pump house was under water from the flooded river. Further upstream near the club, the earthen approaches to the main road bridge had been washed away completely. It was impossible to cross the river that way, and it remained impassable for the next two months.

As I set about repairing the damage on the farm with my labourers, I hoped I would not get a further storm that season, knowing that sometimes these things happen in threes. I did, but this time it was quite minor, and the damage came from the electrical power of the storm. Lightning struck the top of our 106-foot-high TV mast. The electricity then took a path down the aerial wire, burning it out on the way, blew off a wall vent where the wire entered the house, crossed to the main electricity supply from our generator, where the wire touched the aerial wire (which fortunately was not plugged into the TV set), then blew the fuse box off the wall and continued to the generator plant, setting fire to the fuel pump and storage tank. Once again, I had my work cut out in repairing the damage and trying to get everything back to normal. It meant taking down the TV aerial after we had rectified the other major faults, and that was a hazardous undertaking, to say the least. Trying to gently lower a hundred feet of piping to the ground by means of a tractor and farm labourers without breaking the antenna, or collapsing the piping on top of the many assistants, took every bit of skill that I possessed. The rewiring only took a few minutes, and then the game began again, raising it back to the upright position. It got there, but I vowed never to attempt to do it again.

We had seventy inches of rain that season, about thirty more than we normally measured in our garden rain gauge. When I found I had five tractors stuck on the farm, and it was almost impossible to move around without bogging down, I utilised the whole of my labour force in getting the tractors out, sent home the three of my neighbours (which had come to rescue mine), and put mine into the shed. Next, I organised the boss boy and labourers for the coming ten days before getting Sally into the plane with a couple of small suitcases and flying off to Johannesburg to get away from it all.

It was a lovely break, with the added bonus of Mum and Dad being with Audrey and Bill at the time. We were able to talk about our disastrous year, making light of our misfortunes, as one does when away from the scene of action. We would have liked to have had Mum and Dad with us on the farm during their visit to Africa that year but did not think it was a good idea at that time, as events had proved. So we enjoyed our time in Johannesburg, taking our nephews and niece up for a ride over their home in *Charlie Romeo* (and being reported for low flying by one of Audrey's neighbours).

After ten days, it was back to the farm, where things were not as bad as they were on our departure. It was nice to be back and catch up on all the news. Maize was now being imported from South Africa or Rhodesia over the railway bridge at Livingstone, in the dark of the night so that nobody would know about it. Rumour had it that it was costing the country £3 per bag, while we were only being offered 32 shillings a bag. We could only hope for an increase next year. The Credit Organisation of Zambia – the new title of the government land bank – now had a shortage of funds, so commercial farmers had to return to the commercial banks for their loans. First, however, they must have the approval of Zambian Exchange Control – yet another body to deal with. The commercial bank that I had been dealing with since I started farming was happy to lend me what I wanted, but it took time before I was able to get a straight answer from the controlling body.

The cattle had done extremely well during the wet season, feasting on the lush green grass. I had over fifty calves looking fit and well, on the one hand, and fifty fat steers now ready for market. With a framework around the sides of the lorry made from steel piping, I could get eight steers onto the back and transport them to Lusaka Cold Storage in the cool of the night. Seven trips should get them all there easily. But it was never an easy job getting the beasts up the ramp onto the lorry, the first and last one always giving the most difficulty.

One large beast was adamant that he did not want a ride to town; nothing would persuade him. Eventually, I decided I would have to shoot him and sell the meat to the natives (after taking some to distribute among my labour force). Accordingly, I enquired among local farmers for a gun. Across the river was a Mr Stevenson, who happily offered to lend me a gun with a packet of bullets. When I went to collect them, I was a bit perturbed when he gave me a brass rod as well, to poke down the barrel to push out the empty cartridge case. The bullets were encased in a greasy box, and the gun looked as though it had come out of the Ark. However, it seemed like it could do the job. After thanking him, I set off to shoot the troublesome steer.

I loaded the gun very carefully with one round and sighted on the animal in a clear space near the airstrip. When I pulled the trigger, instead of the expected loud *bang*, there was just a *click*. I tried again and again, with the same result. Deciding the bullet was a dud, I very carefully pushed it out with the brass rod and then, after laying it safely to one side, loaded the next. Once again, I got a click instead of a bang. Next time, expecting a click, I got a bang, which made the animal and myself look up in surprise. So the gun did work, after all!

I repeated the procedure until, with the steer now a bit bored by the procedure and lying down, I got a bang when I had expected one and accomplished the job I had undertaken.

I returned the gun to Mr Stevenson, carefully dropping several dud bullets into the river as I crossed. Thanking him, I mentioned the problem I had encountered. He was not surprised. It transpired both gun and bullets had belonged to his father, Chirapula Stevenson, many years before. "*Chirapula*" was the name given by the natives to an Englishman who had come to Northern Rhodesia in the early years of the century, initially to work with the telegraph office and later as a district administration officer. He married an

English girl, but the African lifestyle he led was far from her liking, so she quickly returned to England. Undeterred, Chirapula roamed a large area of the country administering English justice, as directed by the district commissioner. When at home, he lived in a double-storey pole-and-dagga house situated just off the Great North Road. He had a number of African ladies as wives and a large number of mixed-blood children as a result. Mr Stevenson, who so kindly lent me the gun, was one.

During the Easter holidays, we swapped planes with a friend, Arthur Crossley, who was a doctor in Kitwe. His was a four-seater Cessna 170, which we took on holiday with Wendy and Ian to the island of Inhaca, just off the coast of Lourenco Marques, the capital of Mozambique. We refuelled in Fort Victoria and then flew low level to Lourenco Marques – low level so that we kept in sight of the ground, below the overcast clouds prevailing at the time. We were all amazed at the number of animals we saw, mainly large tusked elephants and long-necked giraffes, moving anxiously away from the noise of our engine a few hundred feet above their heads. It was very flat, uninteresting countryside, with hardly any villages or buildings until we got close to the capital city. There were very few rivers or features suitable for map reading our way, so I was very pleased to get in contact with the control tower when about twenty minutes from the airfield. There, we surprised several other private pilots who had been waiting for three days for the cloud to lift, as they wanted to return to Salisbury.

Inhaca was a paradise island with coconut palms, lovely sandy beaches, and generally pleasant surroundings. We saw natives climbing up the palm trees and dropping the coconuts to the ground, where they de-husked them and broke open the nuts for us. We made friends with a couple from Johannesburg who had sailed to Inhaca in their small yacht. We took them for a ride around the island in the plane in exchange for an afternoon's sail in the boat. It was a lovely but expensive place to stay; we even had to pay to use the table tennis bats. We left ahead of time to spend a few days in Johannesburg with Audrey and Bill once again. This unplanned move was the result of a damaged wing-tip on the plane. I had been unable to tie down the wings in the usual way, and a storm the night before our departure had tipped the plane onto one wing tip. We were forced to take it to Johannesburg for some repairs. Never again did I fail to carry the appropriate equipment for securing whatever plane I was flying.

How useful and kind relations can be! We landed on Audrey and Bill for three days, and they accepted us happily, without complaint. It probably took them until we left to get over the shock of our arrival. It was great fun for all the children to be together, Audrey and Bill now having three: Brian, Brenda, and Kevin. We had a happy time together until we bid farewell and flew back to the farm.

At about this time, there was a spate of robberies around Mkushi. We had our pantry raided on two occasions, the club was broken into, and several animals on various nearby farms as well as ours were slaughtered at night and most of the meat carried away. Then Sally's Singer sewing machine, which she had left on the veranda wall, disappeared overnight. This was too much! I told Boss Boy John that I offered a good reward to anyone finding the sewing machine or the person responsible. Two weeks later, when we had just about given up all hope of seeing it again, John came to me to say that a sewing machine was being used by Star, our previous house-boy. He was living on a farm about ten miles away. I contacted the farmer on the phone and took John with me to see Star and check his abode. Not only was the Singer sewing machine there but also some other items missing from our house and now put to good use by our former employee. The police were called and Star together with the sewing machine as evidence was taken off to the Boma.

The court case came up about a week later, and Sally, as owner of the machine, was called on to give evidence of ownership. This she did as well as possible, but not to the satisfaction of the judge. He found Star guilty of being in possession of stolen goods (not necessarily Sally's), and he was sentenced to three months in jail. Sally and I returned to our car, bemused by the law. Fortunately, the clerk of the court restored our faith when, with sewing machine in his arms, he came running after us, saying we could now have our machine back. We had not been able to prove it was ours, but everyone knew it was not Star's, so returned to us it was.

Three months later to the day, Sally was driving along our farm road and saw six-foot Star approaching. He stood in the middle of the road and held up his hand, like an English policeman, for Sally to stop. He then greeted Sally warmly, asked how was the Bwana, Missy Wendy, and Master Ian, all the time keeping his wide smile on his face. He had been caught out, done his time, and everything as far as he was concerned was back to normal. I think it was a good job he didn't ask Sally for his job back, or he may not have gone on his way quite so merrily.

I was not the only one bemused by the judiciary, as shortly afterwards, the president had considerable differences of opinion with the leading judges in Lusaka. The Central Committee was dismissed and a state of emergency proclaimed. We were not sure how this latest event would affect us. We were getting to the stage of hardly noticing the many upsets any longer, just expecting them to happen and blow past while the next event brewed up. We still felt we would only lose by uprooting ourselves. We were having some good times and still had faith in the future.

Sally's faith in the future was not as strong as mine. I was always the optimist and expected everything to turn out for the best; Sally was often more realistic and, with her good memory, would often put a strong case to me in opposition of my views. Hence we both were able to see the two sides of the picture and assess the best action to take. It made for some heated moments at times, as Sally had the fiery temperament of her father. I dreaded following into shops with her, as frequently she would let rip at inefficient salesmen. Little Tamara, our cook, often found himself at odds with Sally, who once threw a frozen loaf from the deep freeze at him. Fortunately for him, it missed. Unfortunately for Sally, it bounced back off the wall and struck her on the chest, winding her badly. Tamara, seeing her in agony, stood there wringing his hands together, saying, "Sorry, Madam, sorry Madam."

Tamara was from Nyasaland (or Malawi, as it was now known). He was a small man with a very wizened face which broke up into big smiles when you joked with him. He was with us as a cook for several years, being particularly a favourite with Ian, who on arrival home from school would run to Tamara and throw his arms around him. Tamara, in his brilliant white uniform and small red fez, would stand there patting Ian on his back with his face a wreath of smiles saying, "Welcome home, Master Ian, welcome home."

One holiday, Ian brought chicken pox home with him – just a few spots, which did not bother him much. As they disappeared, Wendy came out in them, all over her body. She was regularly plastered with lotion to try to stop her itching and scratching, and as she was able to run around wearing only a pair of shorts, she soon got over the ailment.

As they returned to school on the last day of possible infection, Sally came out in spots. She had not had chicken pox as a child and now came out in such a rash of spots as to be unrecognisable. From the soles of her feet to the crown of her head, she was covered. She stayed in bed in a darkened room, and I managed to get an American doctor from a new training college nearby to come and see her. As he entered the bedroom and saw Sally, he said, "My Gawd, what a sight! If your husband can love you, now he'll love you forever!"

Chapter 8

Presidential Visit

As the years passed after Zambian independence, we farmers found it progressively more difficult to get the necessities of farming. Money was not being allocated to purchase items from abroad which the government considered could be manufactured in Zambia. By the time they did become available, it was often too late, and the farmer had to make do with an inferior product. Tobacco paper and twine of a lower grade than that required meant a loss of tobacco. This in turn meant a loss of profit and fewer farmers growing the crop the following year. In 1970, the crop was very much reduced in size, such that few buyers were interested in it, and with less competition at the auctions, lower prices were paid. It was a vicious circle and made the Tobacco Growers Association lobby government ministers for a support price; it was, after all, a foreign exchange earner through the sale of the crop overseas.

Bags for the maize crop were normally imported from India in bales of three hundred. Our farm now had a requirement for about ten thousand bags each season, a full lorry load. Imagine my feeling when I sent the lorry the 180 miles to Lusaka for the grain bags one morning and found only one bale of three hundred bags in the lorry when it returned that evening. "They say you are rationed to one bale each day," said the driver. "You can have another one tomorrow."

A new factory had been built near Kabwe (Broken Hill) to make these jute bags; unfortunately, they had not got into production quickly enough. Nor had they found out which sides of the bags needed to be stitched up, some having all four sides sewn, others none and all combinations in between. It was frustrating to put a new bag on the combine harvester, only to find the maize pips pouring out of the bottom! The jute twine also became scarce, as did the needles required for stitching the tops of the bags.

As our costs of production increased, due to inefficiencies like these and the ever-increasing time involved in town, so also income tax was increased and a new tax applied to new vehicles and luxury goods. The squeeze was on, forcing more farmers to pack up and try their hand elsewhere. As they left, others came to take their place, having heard of the many good things about Mkushi and very little about the tribulations. Murray and Erica Heron had left for greener pastures in Johannesburg, their place being taken by Bill Pyle. Bill had been a tobacco manager on a farm in Rhodesia, but as was often the case in the tobacco world, an excuse was found for not giving him the expected tobacco bonus at the end of the season. He therefore moved to Mkushi to try his luck on his own. Bill was a very likeable, easygoing farmer with a ruddy complexion, surmounted by an untidy shock of black hair. He had a wry sense of humour with a loud guffaw of a laugh, which was never far from the surface. When he came to Mkushi, he was a bachelor but very much in love with a wonderful girl, Janet, who worked with a financial company in Salisbury. It was not long before they married and Janet came to add her sparkle and wit to Bill's.

New blood into our area each year kept our spirits up, what we now looked on as the spirit of Mkushi. We were like a large family, with nearly one hundred farms settled in the area, sharing each other's hopes and fears. We knew that if we had a car break down anywhere in the farming block, the nearest farmer would give assistance, repair the car if possible, and offer hospitality to whoever was in the vehicle with bed, phone, or food, as required. It gave us a wonderful feeling of security, which perhaps blinded us to some of the realities of life in the world outside of Mkushi.

Since the time that Sally had experimented with the garden boy on where to dig a swimming pool and nearly buried the car instead, she had kept quiet, but that, of course, did not mean that the idea had been forgotten. Just the opposite! Under Madam's supervision, Nmadzi the gardener was gradually digging away at a large area to one side of our house, an area which if I had not limited it in its early stage would have been big enough for the Olympics and which would have taken him a lifetime to dig. Once started, pressure was applied in the usual way to get spare labourers to help dig the hole, for plans to be made for building this new addition to our home, and to find out all that I could about water filtration plants. Fortunately, as usual, Sally had got her timing right; labourers were available, and soon we were all involved in getting the new project completed.

I carted many loads of crushed stone from a quarry near Kabwe, brought several loads of bricks from the latest kiln, and managed to borrow a cement mixer from a neighbour. Alfred was not available for this job, having accepted a major building contract elsewhere, but I had another builder standing by who was put to work squaring up the sides and adjusting the bottom levels before the casting of the base of the pool. This was done in two halves, with an expansion joint in the centre, where the pipe was laid for the water filter. It was a hard job, involving a lot of mixing of the concrete. But at last it was done and the easier task of building the sides was left to the builder and his assistants.

Once our swimming pool was well and truly finished in its large size, we celebrated by holding the annual swimming gala. Ninety-one parents and children attended, bringing with them chairs, cool boxes of food, wine, and beer. All had costumes and towels and were able to spread themselves around the garden and pool, while numerous light-hearted events took place. They were mainly events for the children, who loved it. They did not have any fear of the water it being the ideal place for cooling off, so most of them were good swimmers. Wendy was an excellent swimmer and had won the *Victrix Ludorum* cup at school for swimming and diving. Tanya Clark, her rival, was just as good, so there was much competition between them. Ian, being that much younger, was not able to keep up with them, but it wasn't for want of trying, as he splashed his way energetically from one end of the pool to the other.

Charlie Romeo was still fully utilised, and students who had learned to fly on the plane could borrow it, for a small fee. On the afternoon of the gala, John Barton used it to fly around the Mkushi farms with a friend, but he got a bit wary of an approaching storm and also felt that the engine was not giving the power that it should. He cleverly put the plane down safely in a field, where the maize was only a few inches high. No damage was done to the plane or crew. Next morning, my friendly engineer from Kitwe came and inspected the plane and its engine. With some assistance from willing helpers and the pull from the engine, we got the plane onto the district road, which ran past the maize land. There, after a final check, I took off back to the farm. The plane went for its annual check a few days later and had an engine overhaul at the same time. One of the piston rings had broken, giving the slight reduction in power that John had noticed. Considering the amount of work the plane had done since its purchase three years before, I thought it had performed excellently.

Most of the year, the cattle grazed over Dixie Ranch, while the crops were grown on the home farm. But after harvesting the maize, there was a lot of useful feeding for the cattle on the chaff residue, provided the many bush fires did not get there first. As it was difficult (and inconvenient) getting them across the river on a small temporary bridge between Dixie and Berty's farm, I decided to build a more permanent structure. There was one place between my two farms with an outcrop of rock in the centre of the river as well as on either side. Knowing how the river flooded, I got Alfred to build large streamlined stanchions about ten feet high, using a strong mixture of concrete. On top were secured some hefty gum poles, across which three-inch-thick timbers were affixed. The road was built up on either side, and we had a small opening ceremony as I drove the vanette across from one farm to the other. The total span of the bridge was about sixty feet and I was quite chuffed by the end result. From then on, we used it as a short cut to the club, while the cattle were herded across it to get to the grazing on the home farm when maize reaping was complete.

Fires were a continual menace for cattle farmers, as in just a few hours, they could destroy the brittle, dry grazing, which was the only bulk food available during the dry months of the year. I was continually on the lookout for smoke, utilising *Charlie Romeo* as an ideal way of assessing the danger from threatening fires. Wendy's dog Scamp, who was always around me on the farm, would happily jump onto his seat in the plane, just as though he was going around the farm in the vanette. Sometimes, I caught sight of the person lighting the fire and would fly very low over his head to scare him and try to recognise the culprit. More often, there was only the smoke and flame of disaster heading our way. We had nearly ten miles of boundary to the two farms, where we would burn fire breaks early in the year, but these were often insufficient if a strong wind was blowing.

After landing from such a recce, John would sound the fire warning if necessary and gather all hands on to the tractor and trailer, while others would get in the back of the vanette, and we would head for the trouble spot. It was always a hot, difficult job putting out fires, and burning back from roads or firebreaks was often the only way to beat them. Nor could you be certain a spark from a smouldering timber would not rekindle the blaze next day. Fires were an absolute headache, and I'm sure they were responsible for turning my hair prematurely white.

Someone else whose hair was turning prematurely white was the president of Zambia Kenneth Kaunda. Soon after I had been elected chairman of the Mkushi Farmers Association, we received a message that the president and a retinue of various government ministers would be visiting some farms by helicopter and wanted to meet the commercial farmers at a meeting in the afternoon. This was to take place some four days later. After discussion with my committee members, we drew up a plan to show them a selection of farms and for me to address the president at the meeting covering the major points which worried Mkushi farmers.

On the appointed day, two large helicopters landed on my farm, and the president in his safari suit, white handkerchief in his hand, disembarked with his followers. After greeting me and Sally, he met John and the two tractor drivers who were lined up to shake his hand. Then after waving to the crowd of labourers and their families, he moved down to the tobacco sheds, which had been spruced up for his visit. He was very interested in seeing the tobacco, which was stored in bales at the time, ready for grading.

A short visit to our house followed, for some refreshment of orange squash, and then he and I flew in the helicopter over much of the farming area, making the occasional stop en route to the Boma, where lunch was ready at the district governor's house.

The district governor was Hugh McEnery, an ex-Fleet Air Arm pilot, whose main claim to fame was that of shooting down a MIG jet fighter in Korea from a piston-engined Sea Fury. He had tried his hand rather unsuccessfully at farming in Mkushi, where his political ideas alienated him from the white community. He swung more and more towards helping the African politicians at the expense of his farm and had been rewarded after independence by being appointed district governor of Mkushi. He was the only white district governor in Zambia.

After lunch, we moved over to the hall, where many farmers and wives had collected to see and hear the president. On their behalf, I addressed him with the paper which had taken the previous three days to weld together. I spoke of our hopes and our fears. Of the valuable crops we were producing, not just for ourselves but for the country. Of the way we were being treated as outcasts and not wanted in the country. Of the insecurity we felt due to the lack of police action against thieves and criminals, and of the fact that squatters could take over a farm, as they could not legally be evicted.

A training camp for freedom fighters had been set up next door to a farm on the eastern side of the Mkushi Block, and the families were steadily encroaching onto the commercial farm.

The president listened and then spoke himself, without referring to any notes, for at least twenty minutes. He was reassuring in all that he said and congratulated us on all our achievements. I'm sure when he returned to Lusaka shortly afterwards, as we returned to our farms, he felt that it had been a good day, just as we felt. Honour was done on both sides, now we could forget the day and carry on as before. Nothing changed. Not for a couple of months, then we had a policeman on each farm that had an aeroplane. He was there to guard the plane and make sure we did not take off without an inspector from the Boma first coming to check who was flying in it. As the inspector rarely had transport, the policeman eventually had the job of checking. First, we had to find the policeman, who was invariably in the compound, having some food. Then he would come, check through our handbags or briefcases for we knew not what, and then let us take off. This farce went on for many months before we brought enough pressure to bear to have the police guard taken off.

We were then stopped from flying into the Lusaka City Airport on the edge of town. A new international airport had been built about fifteen miles out of town, and we were forced to fly there instead. The hassle of the extra half an hour into town, together with the difficulties of carting foodstuffs, spare parts, and the usual accoutrements of a day in town through the departure lounge of an international airport, across the wide tarmac parking area to our small aeroplanes, was excessively frustrating. At the City Airport, we had been able to drive our car fairly close to our plane and easily load from one to the other.

Life was not getting any easier, but still we pressed on. Sally became president of the Zambian Association of Women's Institutes and had her spare time filled with correspondence and journeys to other institutes and flower shows. Where possible, we would fly, but Sally occasionally drove there by herself. This was worrying, as there had been incidents following some car accidents, where both white males and females had been beaten up by the natives. Great care was necessary on the roads, and we were advised not to stop in the event of an accident but to drive straight to the nearest police station.

The Mkushi Country Club continued to be the centre of our leisure activities, with regular features to cater for everyone. A Maxi and Mini dance was a great success, those lovely minis being the fashion at that time. As master of ceremonies, I had the most enviable task of measuring the minis and had a lot of offers for MC at the next event! That turned out to be a variety evening in which the members of each telephone party line got together to produce about twenty minutes of enjoyable amusement in competition with the five other lines. The usual excellent buffet was available halfway through the show. It was another wonderful evening of colour, wit, and talent combining to give us all some superb entertainment. Our line put on G B Shaw's *Passion, Poison, and Petrifaction,* as organised and directed by John and Denny Kennedy. It was tremendous fun to do and brought the house down with laughter and applause.

John Kennedy had farmed for a number of years in Southern Rhodesia, where he also had a bad accident – falling from the top of a tobacco barn and almost breaking his back. He was also diabetic, which did not help his recovery. A big man with receding hair, he was often in pain from his back, which also restricted him. But he always had a smile on his face and a cheerful word for all he met. Denny, his wife, was a stunner and perhaps the best-dressed woman in Mkushi. She had a lovely, slim figure to show off her elegant clothes and had been one of the ENSA entertainers during the war. It was at Denny's instigation that we should put on this play, with her taking the part of the leading lady and me as the villain of the piece.

John and Denny both learnt to fly in *Charlie Romeo,* but John could not go solo, as his medical would not permit him a licence. But he did get that far with me, going up blindfolded for his theoretical solo. Denny, although not such a natural aviator as so many of the other girls I had taught, progressed to get her licence. She was the only one to return from her long cross-country flight well behind schedule. She had lost her way but calmly contacted the Ndola Control, who talked her in to Ndola. After refuelling, she then navigated herself back to base to a very relieved instructor (and even more relieved husband).

With the crops despatched, the new lands ready for the next season, and Wendy and Ian back at their schools after their holiday on the farm, it was time for Sally and I to spend the next ten days discussing our plans for the next year.

We set off early in *Charlie Romeo* with a couple of small suitcases and two half-sets of golf clubs in the back for Lusaka and Salisbury. It was still quite simple to fly across the border to

Rhodesia, after clearing customs at Lusaka. We visited both children for a short while before continuing on our way to the Golf Course Hotel near Durban. It was a long way to go in a little Cessna 150, map reading all the way, as we had no radio aids for our navigation, no artificial horizon, and only a small magnetic compass. But get there we did, for ten days of enjoyable golf and relaxation. Both Sally and I were regular golfers when we had time, so ten days on a nice trim course with proper greens instead of sand was sheer luxury. We made the most of it, playing each day with different residents of the hotel. After dinner in the evening, we discussed how the season had turned out and the plans for the next crops. We had formed our own company, Dixie Farms Ltd., in an attempt to limit the amount of income tax we would be paying as a result of the recent tax increases. We had been successful each year of our farming and had paid the Inland Revenue Department a regular income. Now they were trying to get more with no risk attached to their business. There was a lot of risk attached to mine.

We decided that all being well, we would take Wendy and Ian to England in the coming year, spending a month away in total, visiting our relations and old friends. It would be twelve years since we had left, and many old faces would not be there. We would also see at first-hand how good life was for the residents of England and compare it with our own lifestyle. Could it possibly be as good? We would have to wait and see. Meanwhile, we all had something to look forward to.

Trip to England

"I bet you I could run four miles in the time it takes you to run three." So said Neville Wright to me at the bar of the club one evening. Neville, about ten years younger than me, was often boasting of his physical prowess. He was fit and full of energy, always rushing around and doing things at full speed. He learnt to fly in Rhodesia and had bought himself a Cessna 182, a much faster plane than the usual Cessna 172. When he first came to Mkushi, Neville was a gay bachelor, who was wooing Marian, a widow with two children in Rhodesia. He did his best to go to Rhodesia as often as possible for as long as the farm could spare him, until at last, Marian consented to marry him and move to Mkushi. So yet another lovely lady added her attributes to our farming area and was a calming influence, at times, on Neville. But only at times, as it was impossible to repress Neville, who would burst out with rash challenges, such as he had made to me.

With a bottle of whisky at stake, I accepted his challenge for a race one month later, on the ground of his choosing. I then went into training myself, running every evening along my farm road. I started with a half-mile, which was just past the fuel tanks and back to the house. Then each day, I went farther by one telephone pole, which added two hundred yards more. I was also timing myself to make sure I was keeping up to a reasonable pace. When the big day came, we ran along a firm level road near Neville's farm. Neville was starting one mile behind me. Miles Cornhill as referee started us using a shotgun to give the signal. It was an easy run for me, after my training on my undulating sandy farm road. I got to the finish line and waited for my opponent to arrive. Three weeks later, we ran together over the four miles of my farm road. I won another bottle of whisky and a laurel wreath from Denny Kennedy, having completed the course in just over twenty-four minutes. Poor Neville had an operation for appendicitis a few weeks later, but by then, there was no whisky left to return.

We came across a surprisingly easy year, with good weather for the crops, the labourers working well, and little new on the political front to affect us on the farm. I was growing a new variety of seed maize, which was not a hybrid variety and therefore did not need the constant de-tasselling. Instead, I was able to plant some lands to grass on Dixie Ranch. One variety of grass – Star grass – was planted by chopping up grass runners into lengths about six inches long and planting them every three feet or so, with half of the length below ground and half above. It was a slow process, and I only completed a ten-acre land in this way. I also had some Rhodes grass seed and had the brilliant idea that I could get this seed spread over another land by scattering it from *Charlie Romeo.* A few days later, the weather conditions were ideal to sow, and as if in answer to a prayer, a young stranger appeared on the farm. To this day, I cannot remember who he was or what he wanted, but I was able to persuade him that he would be happy to come up with me in *Charlie Romeo* to scatter grass seeds out of his window.

I gave him some overalls to wear, strapped him in his seat, and surrounded him with bags of grass seed. As I flew low over the appropriate field, I kept urging him to empty these bags of seed out of the window. I think the airflow past the window blew more seed into the cockpit than ever landed on the soil below. We made numerous runs up and down the field, with the seed getting into our eyes and mouths, in our clothes through to our skin, and of course everywhere but everywhere in the plane. When we landed with the now-empty bags, we both looked like enormous seed-sticks, such as you would feed to a canary. He was not much better when he removed the overalls, but he shook out some of the unwanted seeds and went on his way. I wish I knew what it was he came for. He never came back.

We bought a film projector for the farm with which we showed films to our farm families every few weeks. Each time we went into Lusaka, we hired a suitable film which we would show on the following Saturday. I would put up the screen (a large sheet at the entrance of the tobacco sheds), with the projector and viewers sitting inside or outside, depending on the weather. It was the only source of entertainment for our labourers, other than the beer parties which they held themselves.

On return from town one day, I told John – now a foreman, no longer a boss boy – that I had a film for the following evening called *Robin Hood*. With this, he gleefully clapped his hands together and with a big smile on his face aired his knowledge on the subject: "Ah, Robin Hood," he said, "a very good man! He's dead now, of course!"

Needless to say, that film was a great success, as were most of them. Westerns with lots of fist fights were always popular, raising loud cheers of support when the hero won his fight, but the scene which got the loudest cheers, surprisingly, was when some twenty British commandos were shown abseiling down ropes from three large helicopters. They thought that was really the greatest.

Another time the film show was popular was at birthday parties, which there seemed to be plenty of. For Ian's birthday, we had a film which showed a lot of animals. This quite upset Scamp, the dog, who jumped at the wall where the animals were parading, barking his head off yet happily making the party a success by his surprise antics.

After we sold the tobacco crop, which now had a support price, we made our plans for our holiday in the U.K. The tobacco prices were better than usual, as the Rhodesian crop was not so accessible due to sanctions imposed on the country. We were now getting up to seventy ngwee per pound for the best quality tobacco. Yes, the currency had changed from pounds, shillings, and pence to kwachas and ngwee, one hundred of the latter to the kwacha.

The maize was being harvested and transported along the now-completed tarmac road to the Kapiri Mposhi Depot, and we were being paid a respectable price for it. The cattle were thriving, with 110 calves growing steadily, leaving only the seed maize to sort out before we departed.

Wendy and Ian were thrilled at the news that we would be taking them on a big aeroplane to England. They had seen the large airliners many times at Lusaka Airport, where we regularly cleared customs for Salisbury. No doubt they had often compared them with our little Cessna but had not expected to fly in one. The big day came, and away we went in an Al-Italia Boeing 707, with high-backed, knee-crushing seats which made us wish we were back in the comfort of our little plane. Eight hours later, we landed in Athens, where we disembarked to have two days of sightseeing around the ancient town. There were not many tourists around, and the old monuments like the Acropolis were wide open for us to explore. We were amazed at what had been built by ancient civilisations. There was nothing like that in Zambia. We went on a coach trip to the Corinth canal, where fair-haired Ian and Wendy starred in the photographs of a group of Japanese tourists. Then on to a traditional Greek restaurant for lunch beside the sea. It was a hot day, so the two youngsters were soon cooling off in the sparkling clear water, with their panties as costumes. How we wished we could join them.

Our next stop was picturesque Venice, with its many canals, bridges, gondolas, and quaint narrow streets. We spent time at a water-side café, watching and filming the groups of tourists walking past. It was a long time since we had seen so many white faces or people who wore such a tremendous variety of clothing styles. In the main square, with all the pigeons, we nearly lost the children, who happily ran off exploring or chasing the birds. We rode the canals on a water taxi, ate delicious foreign ice creams, watched the lighted gondolas at night (with the occasional singer), and after two more days, got into a speedboat which took us to the airport. Next stop: London Heathrow.

When you return to the land of your birth after many years away, you may feel as I did: slightly overwhelmed and emotional that I had returned home again, even though home was in fact in Zambia. I looked on the towns and countryside from the plane with great affection, pleased that they appeared just the same as when Sally and I had left twelve years before. As we entered the arrival hall after passing through the green route of customs, I half-expected a clarion call of trumpets to announce to England that we were back. Not surprisingly, there was no such thing, just the very reserved English: "Hello, how are you? Did you have a nice flight?"

Sally's Uncle Stan was there to meet us and take us to his house at Slough, where Aunt Madge and Sally's mum were awaiting us with tea and cream cakes. They were as pleased to see us, especially the children, as we were to see them. In spite of the smallness of the house, they gave us a warm welcome and found beds for us for two nights, after which we were due to collect a small Bedford dormobile in which to live and travel around our relations and friends, taking Sally's mum with us. Once we had persuaded Stan and Madge that sun-downers, from the bottle of duty-free whisky we had brought them, were essential to sustain the lives of such as us, the ice was broken, and we all got on famously, swapping stories of life in Africa for those about life in Slough.

We set off in our fully equipped dormobile on schedule to see my Uncle Jack, Aunty Peggy, and cousin Carol at Berkhamsted, other friends nearby, and my sister Joan, now divorced and living with her two boys at Linslade.

We toured around the area for several days, getting warm welcomes everywhere, especially when it was realised that we had our beds with us and were not looking for accommodation. August Bank Holiday weekend, we were booked into a small hotel at Barton-on-Sea, where we spent the long weekend with my mum and dad. We had been fortunate to see them several times in Africa during their visits, and it was now our pleasure to see their delightful, comfortable two-bedroom apartment with a view from the window of the coast from the Needles of the Isle of Wight to Selsey Bill in the west. More whisky was consumed that night as we talked and talked and met some of their friendly neighbours. We slept each night in our dormobile at a camping site just up the road, after seeing Sally's mum ensconced in a bed-and-breakfast lodging nearby.

Next day, my mum cooked a magnificent meal of good English roast beef and Yorkshire pudding, with roast potatoes and vegetables. Knowing what it takes to cook such a meal for two, I know she must have been exhausted producing such a feast for seven of us. But that was family; we all loved it and sang Mum's praises and drank toasts to my sisters elsewhere.

We loved our time in England, finding it to be highly organised and labour efficient but very impersonal. People went about their business on their set tasks at regular times and appeared not to care about their neighbours. It was as though a set mechanism was working away which was not to be changed by anyone. After our many experiences, we thought people in England had everything going in their favour, except perhaps the weather, but they did not realise it nor consider how fortunate they were.

We took our little dormobile on to the Continent after dropping Sally's mum back at her small flat in Worthing. In France, we would drive for an hour or so before breakfast, stopping at the first village for croissants and fresh milk. In Switzerland, I took Wendy and Ian up to the top of a mountain on a cable car. Sally did not like heights, so she stayed in the Dormobile, writing postcards. The rest of us reached the top, where Wendy and Ian had the chance to touch snow for the first time. Dirty and slushy as it was, we had to take some back to Mum. Ian carried a double handful down the mountain in the hood of his anorak and proudly presented a pile of grubby slush to his mother.

We went to Lucerne to see the hotel where we had spent our honeymoon, ages before, and then bought rich chocolate and marzipan sweets that looked just like new conkers. We spent a night in a hotel by Lake Lucerne, where we luxuriated in hot baths and big, comfortable beds for a change.

All the while, time was flying by, and we had to get back for our channel ferry. Unfortunately, we had lost track of the days. A paper shop was not much help, as there were papers there showing two dates. Eventually, Sally plucked up courage and asked another couple in the caravan site if they could tell us what day it was.

"My," they said, "you must have been having a good holiday not to know the day of the week." We had one day left and made the most of it with the children, having races in dodgem cars on the beach at Le Touquet.

Then a week later, a reluctant and tearful farewell to our nearest and dearest before our flight back to Zambia, this time on a comfortable VC 10.

As after every holiday away, it is always nice to be back in your own comfortable home with your well-known bits and pieces around you, and your established routine to run, so it was with us; we were happy to be home, where all was well after our month away. The house was just as we left it, the labourers were happy to see us back again, the land preparation was up to schedule, the tractors still working, and the cattle in good condition. Yet something was wrong, something was different: me! I was restless. The holiday had unsettled me and Sally, to a lesser extent. Seeing our friends in England in their very stable way of life, with their children at nearby schools and their only worry was whether or not to take their raincoat with them, made us seriously consider whether we were living on cloud nine. Yes, we were doing some interesting, even fascinating, things; we lived in a nice house, had wonderful progressive dinner parties with exotic foods, flew our children to distant schools, and so on. But was it real? Could it last? Was it right in a developing third-world country with so much of the population impoverished? These thoughts and many others went round and round in my head as I picked up the threads of my farm work once again. Sally and I did not discuss the subject, but it was obviously at the back of our minds: Had we come to a turning point in our lives? I think subconsciously we had.

Enough of the non-hybrid seed had been grown that only hybrid seed was now required. I was not keen on the extra work involved on producing that again, so I withdrew from the Seed Producers Association and decided to concentrate on the tobacco and maize.

As soon as the maize was sown and showing through the soil, we had an aerial crop sprayer in the district to spray the lands with a weed killer. This was the second year an aircraft was available for this job, which generally ensured treatment of the lands at just the right time. Previously, a tractor and spray machine had to try to keep ahead of the fast-growing weeds at a time when all tractors were required to complete the planting. With our own airstrip so close to the lands of maize, it was a quick and efficient way of getting the weed killer onto the lands. It was very impressive to see the cloud of spray behind the plane settling onto a thirty-yard strip of land, the length of the field. A labourer would be standing by the next marker at each end of the field, to guide the pilot for each run. Safety precautions were virtually unknown and apart from wearing his bright yellow raincoat, which was for easy viewing by the pilot, no other precautions were taken by any of us. The spray covered everything, including Scamp the dog, who had great fun chasing after the low-flying bird.

I decided to sell the cattle. There were now nearly four hundred and fifty of them, in excellent condition, and the relief from the worry of bush fires, sickness, theft, and slaughtering by unseen persons in the middle of the night was profound. I'm sure that deep down another reason was there – that of starting to off-load the many facets of farming life and make it easier to leave. The future was in the balance. Christmas carols by candlelight at the club ended the year in a prosaic mood.

Weddings

The herd of cattle sold quickly at my asking price to David Moffat, a young cattleman who farmed a large ranch past the eastern boundary of the Mkushi Block. The Moffat family, who had connections through marriage to David Livingstone, had farmed the area for many years before the settlement scheme for Mkushi had been considered. Now David, a well-built, strong, fair-haired, and astute cattle farmer, assessed each animal as it passed through the spray race, calculated the figures, and quickly concluded the deal. His herdsmen came two days later and walked the herd to their new home, taking three days to get there.

I continued the hard work of reaping and curing the tobacco crop, which was better than normal, with ideal growing conditions favouring it, while the maize also looked superb. One of the joys of farming was to see crops at their maturity, standing tall and even, with a rich, dark green colour. The tobacco was shoulder high, so that the reapers were almost lost in the rows whilst picking the leaves, and alongside, the maize fields soared up to some twelve feet, where their tassels shed the dusty pollen on the cobs which had started to form about halfway down.

Training flights continued as usual, as did the flights to Salisbury at half-term to bring Wendy and Ian home from their schools. Being at different schools – Chisipite and Ruzawi – their terms and half-terms did not always match up, so frequently the planes or passengers were shuffled around. Sometimes, I would take Colin's Cherokee 6 and bring back a very full plane load of growing children; other times, it was just one in *Charlie Romeo.*

Both Wendy and Ian were doing well at their schools. Ian was perhaps the better academically, especially with his maths, while Wendy was outstanding at her sports and swimming. Ian enjoyed his cricket, in which he progressed to become a very useful slow left arm spinner, able to baffle both batsman and himself. He was also very capable of knocking up a few runs when his turn came with the bat.

Back on the farm, they both learnt to drive the vanette on the airstrip. After hitting a few rocks and walls on their first attempts on my little farm motor bike, they conquered it and found it very useful for playing hide-and-seek, with their similarly equipped friends, over many miles of the farm roads. The Mkushi children were always spoilt on their holidays, as we were all so pleased to have them back with us after the long weeks away, which were probably harder for us parents than it was for our offspring. Swimming galas, children's parties, and sports days at the club were just a few of the regular events planned during their holidays.

Other than that, they came with us wherever we went, such as to a Greek wedding on a farm on the south side of the Munshiwemba. A small group of Greeks had established farms there, not far from the Dendy-Youngs. They joined in the community supporting the club and Farmers Association, and one, Jimmy Karnesos, also learned to fly with me. As in the Greek tradition, if there is a wedding in the family, everyone gets invited to celebrate the occasion, so the whole of Mkushi seemed to attend the wedding of Nikki Papodoupolous. What an occasion it was! A Greek orthodox minister performed the unusual ceremony, with his unorthodox incantations. We kissed the bride, shook hands with the young groom, received our sugared almonds in delightful embroidered pouches, and were then free to tackle the laden tables of Greek speciality foods, which must have taken their small community at least a week to prepare. Extra plastic awnings were arranged on the sides of the farmhouse, and chairs had been borrowed from every farm around to cater to the large crowd. It was a marvellous day, only slightly dampened by a heavy rain shower which threatened to capsize some of the awnings, which now had enormous bulges of water sagging through the scanty supports, like cow's udders. A few dagger thrusts with a sharp knife soon relieved the burden, and the party continued.

We had several weddings in Mkushi, and rarely were they quite as expected. At an early one in Broken Hill, where Tim Dooley's daughter was getting married, the groom's brother raised an objection, claiming that the bridal couple had already been living together. Three of us managed to bundle him outside before any harm was done. It didn't stop the wedding, just added a bit of zest to it.

On another occasion, as the best man raised his glass after his speech to toast the bridal couple (as the father of the bride was in America), he said, "To the bride, the groom, and their five-day-old baby daughter." That was a secret which took nearly everyone by surprise!

At yet another wedding on a farm, we discovered people with glasses of beer in their hands as we arrived. This struck us as being very different, especially as the bride in her white dress was helping to serve people. "The wedding's off," someone whispered to us, "but the reception's still on." It transpired that the requisite licence to hold the wedding on the farm had not been obtained, so everything went ahead as planned, including the cutting of the cake, and the happy couple were married in town next day.

It is possible that at about this time, I was getting some pressure from Sally to decide what we were going to do in the future: stay or leave. If we left, what would I do and where? I had vaguely considered becoming a doctor but knew that would take many years of study. To find out more about it, I went for an interview with the dean of the Medical School at the University of Rhodesia. To gain entry there, I would need A levels in two subjects that I had not taken at school: chemistry and biology. Then seven years at the medical school; it was hardly feasible with a growing family and ever-increasing school fees.

We went on to Que Que, where our doctor friend from Kitwe, Arthur Crossley, was now in practice. He arranged for me to not only have a guided tour of the clinic and laboratory but also to be present during four operations in the theatre. It was fascinating, instructive, and enticing. I wish I could have found some way of spending nine years in qualifying as a doctor. Arthur was a dedicated doctor, thinking of little else. When he undressed to go to bed at night, he would leave a trail of his clothes on the way to his bed as he continued to think of his patients. Eventually, Dulcie, his wife, persuaded him that the laundry basket was the better place. That worked fine for three nights, then after the fourth, Dulcie found all his dirty clothes had been dropped into the wastepaper basket in the corner!

Before we left Arthur and Dulcie, Sally arranged to have a birth control injection from the clinic. Such things were not easily available in the Mkushi area, and possibly just as well. Within a few days of our return to the farm, Sally started to have fits of depression, for no apparent reason. Naturally, I thought it was due to the let-down on not leaving Zambia to start training as a doctor or due to the loneliness of living in the bush, with our children over five hundred miles away. It was some weeks later, after a very rough difficult time for us both, that another doctor diagnosed that the problem stemmed from the birth control injection. Whilst it was a relief to know the cause, it still took many more weeks before the effect wore off. When Sally was due to go to the Copperbelt for her annual W.I. conference, she encouraged me to go off for a week somewhere and get over the trying time we had both had.

With that in mind, I called at a travel agency in Lusaka on our next flight to town, enquiring about an all-inclusive break for a week. The only thing they could offer was eight days in Mauritius. Little thinking Sally would agree to that, I just took their card and left. Next morning, when Sally asked if I had found anywhere to go, I said, "No, they could only offer eight days in Mauritius."

"Well, why don't you go there then?" *was Sally's surprising reply.*

I phoned through to Lusaka that morning and made my reservation. The news spread like wildfire around Mkushi: "Dick Jenkins is going to Mauritius for a week by himself." Most of my men friends were very envious, their wives taken aback and unbelieving. What precedent was being started here?

Sally's conference was a great success, as was my holiday in lovely Mauritius. A small hotel, Le Morne Brabant, a few yards from the white coral sand, tucked away in the shade of the Casuarina trees with lots of lovely seafood and fresh fruit to eat; it was paradise. During the days, I swam, snorkelled, went deep sea fishing, or played golf. In the evenings, there was a delightful band outside by the little dance floor or a small casino inside, where you could try your luck with blackjack or roulette.

For a week, I luxuriated in the lovely atmosphere of this tropical island, forgetting everything except that I had a lovely family to return to. I vowed it would not be my only visit to the island; the rest of the family must also see it as soon as possible.

Back at work, I found myself vice president of the Commercial Farmers Bureau (CFB), in which we did our best to resolve the many problems besetting farmers throughout the country. We met with ministers and even the president, putting forward our views as forcibly and respectfully as possible. Sometimes we won; most times, it was a case of wait-and-see.

Ronnie Landless, a well-respected successful farmer who ran a large estate near Chisamba, was president of the CFB and planned a three-day trip by plane for the committee and secretary to visit farmers in the Choma, Kalomo, and Mazabuka districts. See some farms in each area and attend farmers meetings, getting first-hand news from them and giving them the latest news and views from their head office in return.

It was an eye-opener of a visit. If I had thought we were good farmers in the Mkushi District, I realised on visiting some of the old established farms in these other areas that we were only scratching the surface. Everything on these farms we visited spelled out farming of the highest quality. Yes, the farmers had been there for years; their children were now adults, either helping on the farm or working elsewhere. They certainly did not have the same worries as we in Mkushi. Their problems were more about pensions or getting money out of Zambia if they decided to retire in South Africa or England. As it was at present, such a possibility was very unlikely, and the way the economy of the country was going, it would become more unlikely in the future. Holiday allowances had just been reduced to two hundred kwachas each per year. Health facilities and doctors were also becoming a problem, as all the hospitals and clinics were being swamped by the hundreds of Africans clamouring for treatment. This was one of the consequences of the major drift to the towns of the rural natives. The towns had not the facilities to cope with such large numbers.

The three-day flight was a great success and influenced our cases to the various government departments with which we came in contact. The trip also illustrated the value of light aircraft in getting around such a large country.

To further the flying ability of many of my ex-students, I arranged to hire an aerobatic Cessna for a weekend and take up the many pilots and others in Mkushi who wanted to try their hand at doing a loop or barrel roll. Altogether eighteen people, mainly pilots, had a go for half an hour each: loops, rolls, stall turns, or hammer stalls (when the stall turn wasn't quite right). It was great, exhausting fun with an aerobatics display over the cricket field at the club as a grand finale.

It was to be the grand finale for quite a while, as soon after I had returned the Aerobat, there was a ban on all private flying. We could not get any information as to why or how long the ban was going to last. It appeared to have something to do with the approaching political changes in the constitution making Zambia a one-party state. There was nothing we could do about it except make our representations. It was another frustration in a long line of such. We could only hope it would soon go away.

We carried on hopefully as before and made a tennis court near the house, where our original pole-and-dagga house had been. We had turned the level piece of ground into a badminton court after demolishing the wood-and-mud buildings. Now we had extended it and laid layers of clay to form a hard court, with chicken wire netting around the sides.

It was finished in time for my fortieth birthday, for which we had invited Sandra and Berty to supper. We were all in the garden, inspecting the court, when we saw the lights of about a dozen cars approaching down the farm road to the house and heard the noise from their hooters disturbing the quiet of the night. With tales of terrorists and undisciplined army soldiers threatening innocent people, I was worried as they approached. But as they arrived in our front garden, it was clear they were all our friends, equipped with food, drink, and dance music to help me celebrate my birthday with this surprise party. There were about thirty of them from the farms around, led by Tim and Elaine Dooley. We had a great evening which went on into the early hours of next morning.

Sally now had a secretarial job to keep her occupied at the Mkushi copper mines. An Italian company was endeavouring to mine more copper from what had been a mine many years before. Sally went off early each morning in the Mercedes and returned at about three o'clock in the afternoon. For her birthday, I bought her a Honda motor car as her personal vehicle. She called it Goofy and took great pride in it. No one could drive it except Sally although I recollect Wendy being favoured with a try on one occasion. Goofy was ideal for the journey each day to the copper mine and left the Mercedes for me to drive to Salisbury to collect the children.

After so many easy flights to and from Salisbury, the car journey was distinctly harrowing, especially at the border post. I was treated with suspicion for wanting to go to Ian Smith's rebel country. The car was searched, as was my small overnight bag. I was asked numerous senseless questions and generally delayed. The Immigration and Customs were not the only ones doing the checking. The army presence was felt, as they too made checks and searches. When eventually I was cleared, I passed through the Rhodesian side authorities in a matter of minutes.

We went through similar searches and hold-ups on our return with the children's clothes, books, and toys being mauled over by inquisitive hands – hands with power! It was a job to keep calm and not lose one's temper. I'm sure they would have made the most of that.

We soon got home and put all that behind us, as Ian got a new chopper bicycle and Wendy a record player and some records for Christmas. The whole house did *Shake, Rattle, and Roll* each day until the end of those school holidays. Fortunately, it was built on good strong foundations.

Chapter 9

Border Closure

The ban on flying lasted until Easter of the following year; our little plane sat in the hangar, with a police guard nearby. Very occasionally, we managed to obtain a permit to fly to Lusaka and back on business, but the permits were difficult to obtain by phone, and news of one being granted was often received days after the flight was to have been made. Our lives were greatly affected, and we rued the extra hours it took us going everywhere by car. However, the flying ban was nothing compared to the next shock. The border between Zambia and Rhodesia was closed. Oh, how this upset us all. Our children in their schools in Rhodesia, us in Zambia, and apparently no way of getting to them. Naturally, we were all up in arms, mothers distraught, fathers depressed at this latest political upheaval.

The situation with Rhodesia had been getting progressively worse, with sanctions affecting the country to a certain extent, but a lot of assistance being readily available from the Republic of South Africa on the southern border of the rebel state. The Organisation of African Unity steadily applied political pressure, forcing other countries bordering Rhodesia to cut off all trade and business connections. It was easy for them to do so, as they were unaffected by whatever measures they thought fit to impose. "Close the border" they said, and the border was closed, never mind the white children or their parents. More and more camps training freedom fighters were being secretly set up with volunteers from Rhodesia, Tanzania, and other African countries, with instructors from Russia and China. Some of these were crossing the border into Rhodesia at night, making widespread terrorist attacks on a wide variety of targets. Land mines were laid on either side of the border as the army presence increased.

The Commercial Farmers Bureau used its influence to get the government to approve buses to collect the many children from Rhodesian buses at the border post; they were allowed through the shortest crossing, at Chisamba. This took some organising but was all in place for the Easter holidays for the children coming from school and returning there four weeks later. It was a great relief to all the parents involved, especially as the CFB had also managed to have the army moved back from the crossing at the critical time so that no unsought incident could occur. But most of us realised the situation could only get worse. Where else could we send our young scholars? We knew of no good schools in Zambia, Malawi, or Kenya. Getting to South Africa would be as difficult as Rhodesia, so only England was left. We were reluctant to consider that, as it was much farther away and the fares would just about double the school bill each year, and that was high enough as it was.

Yet again, our spirits rose as the children got home safely, and when the flying ban was lifted, we thought things were improving. Even the crop, which had started so badly in poor weather conditions, turned out to be excellent, one of my best. The only adverse event came during the curing of one of the final barns, when a stick full of dried tobacco fell on to the very hot flue pipe and caught fire, setting light to the whole barn. There was nothing we could do except plaster up the doors and windows with mud to try and limit the airflow into the blaze and wait for the fire to burn out, meanwhile monitoring that the fire did not spread to the barns on either side.

Naturally, there was nothing left when two hours later we were able to see the black mess inside. Of the tobacco, there was only ash. Of the tier poles and roof, there were only charred remains, while the large fifteen-inch-diameter beam across the centre of the barn still smouldered and needed a lot of water to extinguish it. It was my first and only barn fire, a fact for which I was thankful, as the mess and filthy smell of it lasted for many days. The insurance company made good my loss, but the extra work involved in refurbishing and reroofing the barn was something I would rather have done without.

On the lighter side, we had a croquet competition one Sunday at the Dendy-Youngs, where period costume was the outstanding rig of the day. Ladies in long dresses with aprons and bonnets, gentlemen in white trousers and striped blazers. Where they had all come from was a complete mystery. I do not, however, remember the croquet being played any less vigorously because of the standard of dress.

A Roman orgy was the next event at the club, which was decorated with white pillars made from tobacco flue pipes and plough discs on the top, holding flaming paraffin. They added authenticity to another excellent evening. I was able to spout Mark Antony's farewell speech to Caesar as written by Shakespeare and practised by me from the back of a tractor and trailer, which Sally was driving during an inspection of the farm.

Then I found a Cherokee 235 aeroplane for sale at a giveaway price. It had been neglected due to the long flying ban, and the owner had lost interest in it. So we became owners of a second plane, this time a fast four-seater which could take the family quite easily. *Charlie Romeo,* which had served us so wonderfully, was up for sale; *RAG* was taking its place. After a service, I flew it back to the farm, where I gave it a good wash and polish. Very soon *RAG* shone like new; it was a great little sports plane, much faster than our faithful Cessna, which had carried the whole family over so many miles.

I had promised to take the family to Mauritius after my solo trip there the previous year. At the end of May, during the children's short holiday, we all went off on a Zambia Airways all-inclusive holiday to the same hotel I had stayed in previously. The sun tanned us and the sand and sea relaxed us all. Wendy and Ian came deep-sea fishing with me one morning, and we saw a sight I'm sure we will all remember until our dying day. About fifty lovely dolphins swam alongside our boat, leaping out of the water in their graceful forms for at least twenty minutes. The water being so clear and calm, we were able to see every detail of them. It was difficult to know who enjoyed the episode more: the dolphins or us. We did not catch many fish; I think it was just four bonito, one of which we had for dinner that evening. It was a wonderful day, like all the others.

I tried my luck in the casino one evening, playing blackjack with moderate success. A South African building contractor was gambling in a big way and hit the jackpot on the roulette table. He stopped playing and bought champagne all round. We played golf together next day before he returned to his favourite sport in the casino. Coincidentally, the Dendy-Youngs were coming to the same hotel on the day before our departure, and I introduced this gambler to John. On his return to Mkushi, I asked John how the gambler had made out on his second week, only to learn that he had been forced to cable Johannesburg for some more money. Easy come, easy go! I had won a few pounds during my evening spell and left it on Sally's bedside table, which she saw with surprise and joy when she awoke next morning.

That was a very happy interlude, where yet again we forgot our troubles and expected everything to turn out right. We were sadly disillusioned on our return to find flying restrictions again in force. Special clearances could be obtained for business flights along certain routes. For farmers, this was later changed to monthly clearances, which needed to be requested two weeks in advance.

Problems had also arisen over the payment of school fees to Rhodesia. The Bank of Zambia would no longer approve them. But they would approve payment to a bank in Switzerland, which could, after taking their commission, settle the accounts for us in Rhodesia.

We had found a way through to Rhodesia by car, driving to Livingstone in the southwest corner of Zambia, crossing on the ferry into Botswana, and then crossing from there into Rhodesia near Victoria Falls. The route to Salisbury via Bulawayo was then open. The main difference was that it nearly doubled the previous five-hundred-mile one-way trip. Also, a deposit to the value of the car had to be made with the bank before clearance for the car could be given. This was to prevent the vehicle being left behind for the rebel Rhodesians to use.

I flew Sally and two other mothers to Livingstone early one morning, where our car was waiting for them, Henry McLeod having driven it there the previous day. They were then able to get away for an early start. Unfortunately, they missed the turning to the ferry, as they were so busy talking, and went nearly fifty miles in the wrong direction before realising their mistake. They got to Salisbury, where there still appeared to be little effect from the sanctions; there was still more in the shops there than in Zambia. They enjoyed being with the children and got back to the farm, exhausted, a week later. Tales of guards at the border were told with bitterness. They had to empty their handbags on to the roadside; take everything out of their suitcases, put it back, and then take it all out again; and answer insolent questions on why they were living in Zambia. All these things were wearing out the optimism that I still had for the future.

I relinquished the job of chairman of the Mkushi Farmers Association to Berty Bowes but maintained my position as vice president of the CFB. Ronnie Landless arranged another tour for us in the farming areas of Western Province, down to Livingstone. We tried to be optimistic about the future wherever we went in our two four-seater planes. It was not easy, and we came up against a lot of despondency.

Back in Lusaka, I dropped off two CFB representatives who had travelled with me and refuelled *RAG* for my flight back to the farm. Sally was expecting me by mid-day as we were due out to lunch at the Kennedys. Ten minutes after I got airborne from Lusaka City Airport, which had once again been opened to our use, I was told by the air traffic controller that I lacked army clearance for my flight and must therefore return to Lusaka City.

I argued, to no avail, that I had clearance for a month. He was adamant that it had been cancelled, and I must return. It would have been very unwise to continue, so back to Lusaka I went and secured *RAG* in my usual parking area. The question now was how to get back to Mkushi. I took a taxi to Ronnie Landless's farm, forty miles away, and borrowed a vanette from him to get me home, where I arrived at about five o'clock, much too late for lunch but in good time for a long lecture from Sally about the joys of living in Zambia.

The last straw came two days later: *RAG* had been run over by a ten-ton lorry. It was unbelievable. A loaded lorry had been parked by a hangar on the top of a gentle slope, the engine left ticking over and the brake left off, as it did not work. The driver took a box into the hangar, leaving the vibration from the engine to get the lorry moving, which it did at an ever-increasing speed down the slope. *RAG* happened to be in its way at the bottom, the first in a line of light planes.

The damage was considerable; it was suspected the main wing spar was broken. The insurance paid me out, as did an engineer to whom I sold the wreck. But the biggest damage in my opinion was that it made up my mind for me: I must give up my way of life, farming, and try my hand at something else. Zambia would, however, lose a farmer, lose an asset to the country, lose someone who had regularly produced good crops and given employment to some fifty people each year. It did not make sense.

Sally and I discussed the matter fully. We decided that on the farm that year, I would just plant four hundred acres of maize, lease Dixie Ranch to someone already interested in it with an option to buy, and take Wendy and Ian to England with us at Christmas, where we would find new schools for them. We would stay in England for a trial period of about four months before returning to reap the maize crop and decide where to go from there. It looked as though our days on the farm were now numbered, and we would be leaving, as many others had left before us.

Chapter 10

Leaving the farm

Making the decision was relatively, easy compared with the amount of work which had to be done to get everything organised by Christmas. The present crop had to be completed and transported off the farm, and the four hundred acres of land had to be prepared for the next crop. Fertiliser, seed, and aerial spraying had to be organised. Further afield, we were in need of names of suitable schools in England that could take the children in January. We planned to spend Christmas at the Red Lion Hotel in Henley, with Sally's mum and my parents joining us there, as well as Joan and her new husband, Roy, and Joan's two boys. Bookings had to be made in good time, as well as for the evening of our arrival. We had to consider transport and a place to live after Christmas, also what we should take with us for such a long period.

As the weeks progressed, so the various matters were resolved and others raised their heads. What to do in England for several months was a major consideration, as I did not fancy sitting around doing nothing. When I learnt of a two-months course studying for a UK commercial pilots licence, I thought that would be an ideal way of spending my time. I was accepted for the course, which was due to start near the end of January.

On schedule with the four hundred acres sown and aerial sprayed, directions for the care of the farm and crop carefully given to the foreman and tractor drivers, we departed on 19 December in the VC 10 for London. Ian's chopper bicycle and Wendy's record player were among the pieces of luggage in the hold.

Christmas was most enjoyable. It was very much a family affair with aunts, grandmothers, sisters, and cousins all happily mixed together for three days of festivity. Even the weather came up trumps, as on Christmas morning, Wendy and Ian looked out of the window to see little bits of white fluff descending. It was their first experience of a snowfall. After lots of delicious food, plenty of wine, wonderful Christmas presents all round, excellent TV programmes, and nonstop talk, the time came to disperse and get ourselves organised for the next stage. After perusal of the local paper, I found an old Mercedes in good going order and elsewhere a large eighteen-foot caravan, with a coal stove inside. In spite of the holiday period, we had them licensed and insured with a towing hitch on the Mercedes by the end of the year and were off to New Milton, with the caravan in tow, to look at a school for Ian. Durlston Court had been recommended to us, and as it was very close to Mum and Dad, we thought it would be ideal, as indeed it was. Ian did well there, becoming head boy in due course.

We booked Wendy into Upper Chine, an expensive girls school on the Isle of Wight. She enjoyed it there as much as any child can enjoy school, although it became inconvenient having to go by ferry to get to the school. It was from the ferry the girls would see how far they could skim their expensive boaters when they left the school ("Sorry, Dad, I lost it!").

At the start of their terms, we saw them into their new schools before setting off for Kidlington near Oxford, where I was due to start my course. We were lucky to find a small caravan site at the back of a pub, only half a mile from where the course was being held, which meant I could walk to my class each morning. Sally tried the labour exchange to see if there was any suitable work for her in the area and succeeded in getting one in the stores department at Beas Helicopter, on the airfield. The sixteen pounds a week she received was a great boost to our morale and kept the wolf from the caravan door for the three months we spent at Kidlington. Once each month, we had to move away for one night, as the caravan park's licence only allowed us to stay for twenty-eight consecutive days. We would hitch up and drive round the corner to the Rugby Club, returning the next day.

Going back to school at the age of forty-two was a culture shock of the first order, especially as the other fourteen in the class were at least twenty years younger than me. I had several incentives to ensure I did well. Firstly, I was not prepared to waste time and money without achieving my target: a commercial pilots licence. Secondly, just as I had Wendy and Ian on the mat to discuss their end-of-term school reports, I knew that I, also, would be on the mat in front of them if I failed. I would lose much credibility in their eyes. Thirdly, I was determined not to let a class of young whipper-snappers get the better of an old codger like me. I selected the one I thought was the brightest and set myself to attain or surpass his results, feeling sure he would pass the exams and effectively pull me through with him.

The instructors were excellent in all ways. I could not sing their praise too highly. The classes ran to time in a clean, warm building, with good facilities available as aids to the learning process. We started at nine o'clock each morning, had a coffee break at ten thirty, an hour for lunch, then continued until four o'clock in the afternoon. Then, like school, we had homework to do. It was tedious for Sally, as after a quick cup of tea and cream cake on my arrival home to the caravan, I took out my books for another two hours of study. During this time, Sally cooked our supper. We could then relax and watch some television on our battery-operated TV set. The nights got very cold, and we were happy that we had the coal fire to warm us. One night, we woke up to the sound of crackling and flickering lights; some newspapers left alongside the fire were burning away merrily and would undoubtedly have spread, had we not heard the crackle when we did. I put out the fire and we got rid of the smoke after ten minutes. It was a harrowing experience, which made us much more careful in the future.

At the end of the eight weeks, with daylight lasting much longer each day, our course ended, as we sat the exams with an adjudicator from the Civil Aviation Authority. Two weeks later, the results were published, and I was up there with the *bright boy.* I had passed, as had all but three. By this time, I had also taken my general flying tests and done my night flying circuits, so I had completed all the requirements for the issue of my licence. No mat for me! I was thrilled to have successfully completed what was a difficult task, after so many years away in a very different environment. It was certainly a good reason to celebrate, which we did in the usual way.

For some reason, Margaret and Cyril had had enough of Australia at this time and returned to England to give the old country a try, like us. They were living in a stone cottage near Hereford, where Cyril's family came from. For Easter, after collecting the children, we towed our caravan down to their plot at Stone Cottage, where we were joined by Mum and Dad, Audrey from South Africa, and Joan and Roy. There were two important events about to take place, so the family gathered together in strength The first happy occasion was the Christening of David Powell at the nearby church. This was the first time that we had an opportunity to join in any of Margaret and Cyril's family milestones, so we made the most of it. Seeing little David in his mother's arms, none of us could have visualised what a great big man he was to become. With Cyril's family also in full strength, we all had a marvellous time, including the ladies who were distributing the many plates of food produced during the previous two days of cooking.

The second celebratory event was a family reunion dinner at a lovely restaurant in Weobley, it being Mum and Dad's forty-fifth wedding anniversary. The children had all been left behind in their beds, which was just as well, as some of the adults in our party let their hair down in such a way it might have been confusing in deciding who were the children! It was a memorable evening, the first time the Jenkins family had sat together at table for twenty-three years, and what experiences we had all had since then. Margaret to India, Africa, and Australia; Joan to Singapore; Audrey to South Africa; myself to Malta and Central Africa, while Mum and Dad had visited us all overseas (except Joan when she was in Singapore). Also, we all had our lovely children, three each for Audrey and Margaret, and two each for Joan and me.

At the end of May, it was time for me to return to the farm. John the foreman had been writing to me each month with news of how everything was going on the farm and how much rain had fallen each week, so I had a good idea of what to expect. I left Sally with the Mercedes car; she would tour around a bit with Audrey and return to Zambia with the children at the end of term a few weeks later. The caravan, which had served its purpose, was left with my father, who later sold it for me for a few pounds.

I was welcomed back at Lusaka Airport by my accountant friend, Duan Findlay-Cooper, in my Mercedes car. He took me to his home nearby for the night, treating me with the usual Zambian hospitality and listening with interest to all I had to say about life in England. He in his turn brought me up to date on the happenings in Zambia: There were more and more shortages, increased prices, increases in burglaries, and many more camps of freedom fighters.

I drove to the farm next morning, where I was very pleased with the way John and his few assistants had looked after everything in my absence. The house and garden looked lovely, a sisal plant on the rockery even shooting up its asparagus-looking seed stem as a welcome home. The sheds were as clean and tidy as I had left them, the tractors clean and in working order, firebreaks had been made around the lands, where the maize crop looked excellent. The small span of six were waiting to greet me with big smiles and shy handshakes, pleased that the Bwana was back, as I was pleased to be back too.

It was an easy week for me getting the farm into gear after my long absence. I was greatly assisted by two very good neighbours, Rosalie and Ian McLeod, who fed me and insisted I stay with them at their house each night, until I got organised. Good neighbours I call them, although we did not have any neighbours in Mkushi who were not good. Rose and Ian just typified the farming couples in the area. Ian was not really a farmer; the young-looking businessman was brother to Henry McLeod, who was farming on David Kaminer's old farm. After a long period of helping Henry during weekends and holidays, Ian decided to lease the farm next door to him and to open a fuel depot and sell spare parts for tractors and implements. His business rapidly expanded, such that he bought a Cessna 206 to bring spares into Mkushi from Lusaka every week. Henry concentrated on growing the crops on the two farms. The two brothers worked together as a very successful team. Both of them were even tempered, cheerful, and likeable characters whose generosity knew no bounds. Rosalie was a quiet, thoughtful, warm-hearted woman who supported Ian in everything he did. She kept all the farm and store books for him, made out the invoices, ordered fuel, listed spares required, ran the depot when Ian was in town, and ran her comfortable little home for husband and daughter. Henry was a bachelor for many years, until love struck him down and he married John Kennedy's most attractive sister, Mary Rose.

It was the weekend of the Mkushi Invitation Golf competition at the club, so I was able to assist in checking the scorecards at the same time I caught up on all the news. Everyone seemed pleased to see me back in Mkushi and very interested to hear what my plans were for the future – plans which at that time were vague, until the crop was harvested.

Although it was a happy, memorable event, my farming compatriots still faced fears for the future. While we were in England, some freedom fighters had barricaded the road from the club one Saturday evening and ambushed the first departing farmer. He was shot and killed for no other reason than that of being white. Who were now the racists? Nobody was ever caught or convicted of the crime; the police, as usual, did not have any transport at the time to investigate.

Neville and Marian Wright left the country early one morning, flying their two aeroplanes, the fast Cessna 182 and little *Charlie Romeo,* which Neville had bought from me just before we left for England. Many people thought Neville had put Marian at great risk, as she did not have a lot of experience and had been expected to fly quite low from Mkushi to the Rhodesian border in order to avoid any possible Zambian military action, continuing to Salisbury without any chance of refuelling. No doubt he had planned it carefully, as it was a long way for the plane to go nonstop. Both planes, loaded with their two children and other precious items, made it safely to Salisbury, where they were soon sold and Neville started farming again near Karoi. The police in Mkushi carried out a big enquiry into their sudden departure, but no one appeared to have known in advance about their intentions. It was a typical spur-of-the-moment action to which Neville was disposed.

As I started reaping the maize crop, I tried to resolve my feelings about England and Zambia. I quote from a letter to my parents at this time, one of the many letters my father kept in a box file and from which this book is largely compiled:

"I have been trying to resolve my feelings about England and Zambia, where to live and what to do and so forth. Well, coming back in the Jumbo jet I awoke at about 5.30 a.m. and looked out of the window to see the red glow of dawn in the sky to the East. Below the glow was darkest Africa. I may be wrong, sentimental or just mixed up, but that was Africa and could not have been anywhere else with a dawn like that. One hears of the call or pull of Africa and I must admit I felt it that morning.

To me Zambia for all its ignorance and squalor at times is an interesting and exciting place to live. It is rather like a youth trying to make his way in the world whilst a country, such as England, is like a middle aged person knowing everything, having everything and going along its own road somewhat blindly and unconcernedly. I think England must be one of the most beautiful of countries and has this place beaten by miles. But Africa has the call of the wild, wide open spaces, and in the world of today and tomorrow this is surely where the action and the focus of world events will be."

In Lusaka, I wrote an air law exam and got a Zambia commercial licence, on the strength of my British one. I had a quick conversion onto a Beechcraft Baron twin-engined plane and then spent two weeks flying it around the country for the pilot, who went on his annual leave. It gave me the chance to find out what flying jobs were available in Lusaka, as several interesting offers were made to me.

I pondered these offers as I progressed with the reaping of the maize crop, which gave me just over eleven thousand bags. I had some problems with the new polypropylene bags, which frequently disintegrated in the hot sun. I was told by the manufacturer I should keep them out of the sun, but that was not feasible in sunny Zambia.

When the children returned with Sally, they had their last holiday on the farm, driving the vanette and motor bike all over the place, swimming in the pool, and joining in all the activities at the club. Sally and I had made the final decision to lease the home farm for a year with an option to purchase, and we would move into Lusaka, where I would work as a charter pilot with Prestonair, the largest charter company in Zambia, with Beechcraft Barons, a Cessna 310, and a Beechcraft Duke coming in a few weeks' time.

I was to be chief pilot and to run the charter side of the business, while the owner was away in America for six weeks getting the new Beechcraft Duke. It was a good offer for a newly fledged commercial pilot, and I looked forward to the job with my usual enthusiasm. It would get me back into the world of aviation, where we could move if necessary without needing to carry a farm around with us, just a licence.

On 16 September 1974, we all took our last look around our two farms and bid farewell to John and the few labourers who had been with me for a number of years and who were being employed by the incoming farmer. Our household belongings had gone ahead of us, in the lorry, to a flat which was to be our home until we found a house we liked. Now we just looked on what we were leaving behind: our lovely farmhouse with its TV mast and swimming pool; the clay tennis court; the orange trees around the drive to the house; the barns and sheds which had taken so much time and effort to build, and the reservoir on the nearby anthill; the workshops and hangar, whose roof had been lifted off so cleanly during the great storm; the empty space where *Charlie Romeo* had rested for so many happy years.

We drove up the grassy airstrip, which had been planted with garden lawn grass by many mfazis several years before and kept in trim by the tractor driver with the mower. We passed our original lands, which had been bulldozed and windrowed, as part of the initial offer of the farm, over the vleis, where culverts had replaced the oil drums I had originally put in to make the farm accessible, and onto the top of the road to the place where we had got stuck in a large muddy puddle one rainy night after the long trip home from Salisbury. There were memories all the way, which filled us up emotionally and blurred our vision with the many happy recollections that came back to us. Mkushi and our farms had been very good to us, whatever frustrations we may have experienced. We would never regret taking up the challenge of starting up a farm in the bush. But the time had come to move on to a new challenge and a new way of life. We would have the true reward of Mkushi with us until our dying day – our friends and neighbours of the Mkushi Block, who would remain true friends wherever they may be.

Chapter 11

Interlude Charter Flying

The joy of flying must surely be in the blood of every pilot who takes to the air. Having an extra dimension to move about in, the height to see over hills and valleys, the speed to get to another panorama, the ease of control to sail around obstacles, and at the very back of your mind, keeping you alert, the knowledge that if something goes wrong, the aircraft and its occupants must go down, back to the earth's surface. All these factors and others contribute to making flying one of the most wonderful and pleasurable experiences life can offer. I had certainly found it so, whether it was in little *Charlie Romeo* or in the supersonic Scimitar of Navy days (now in the distant past). So flying light, twin-engined Barons and Cessna 310s around the country as a job was almost too good to be true. I loved it. The farms were leased, loose ends tidied up, the children back at school, Sally busy looking for a nice house for us. I was able to apply myself to learning the ropes of charter flying. I had to learn fast, as the owner of the small company was departing for America to collect the new Beechcraft Duke, leaving me to run the business for him.

Sally accepted the job of running the office and taking the bookings until he and his wife returned some six weeks later, so once again, the team was fully involved. Sally would get the first news of a charter by telephone, when a client would state that he wished to go to a certain place at a set time on a named day and return some hours later. If we had a pilot and plane available for that time, Sally would accept the charter, getting all the details to pass on to me on my return from whatever flight I may then be doing. Sometimes, people just wanted to reach the Copperbelt quickly, having arrived from a scheduled flight. They often wanted to go immediately. This could be done if there was a pilot around, as was often the case. Frequently, we did not know where we might end up each day. The planes would be kept fuelled up, ready to go. A pilot would be standing by for a flight which could depart within about forty minutes, giving just enough time for a flight plan to be calculated and filed with air traffic control.

Zambia is a very big country. Since its independence, it had been trying to develop the small towns in the rural areas by building schools, hospitals, government offices, and the general infrastructure associated with towns. Contractors of every sort needed to visit their development projects frequently, and flying there on a charter plane was the most efficient way of getting to the many remote places of the country. During the next three years, I flew to every corner of Zambia, finding out how vast and interesting the country was. I saw the source of the Zambezi River in the northwest corner, near Mwinilunga, the wide slow river and its enormous flood plains near Mongu in the Western Province, the spectacular Victoria Falls in full spate and during the dry winter months (when hardly any water flowed over the top), as well as the dam at Kariba, the holiday camp at Kasaba Bay, the old logging railway at Mwinilunga with its steam engines and wagons, Kasama the capital of the North, Lake Banguela and its vast swamps, and the enormous open cast pit at Kitwe.

I flew all sorts of people to these places: engineers, architects, ambassadors, fuel inspectors, surveyors, accountants, ministers, geologists, businessmen, tourists, the lot. Frequently, if they were going to be some hours before returning to Lusaka, they would take me with them to their project, be it an agricultural training school or an explosives factory. They would let me have a look around with somebody and leave me in whatever accommodation was available.

On other occasions, if there was a golf course nearby, I would decline invitations and make my way with my clubs to the course. When I was to spend a day near a river, I would be sure to take my collapsible fishing rod with me and some spinners. Once I caught a five-and-a-half-pound bream from the bank of the Zambezi in the Western Province. I proudly took it home and kept it in the deep freeze for many months, until everyone had seen it. But frequently, I would remain with the plane, on some remote little airstrip, with just a book and a packet of sandwiches. Some you win, some you lose!

Navigation around the country was a great challenge, particularly when the weather was bad with the convergence zone centred across the country, or conversely the hot smoke and dust haze which prevailed for many weeks of the year, making visibility exceptionally poor. There were very few radio navigational aids, just a few non-directional beacons (NDBs) centred near the major towns, with several at the new Lusaka International Airport. So map reading was generally the only way of finding your way around. My years of touring the country in the little Cessna 150 now paid dividends, and I never failed to find my destination (although I nearly did not find the small airstrip in the Luangwa Valley on several occasions).

Surprisingly, with business flying, we were not limited to flights within the country, nor did we require any permits. It was easier flying across borders than trying to cross them by car. As a result, we plied a regular course to Salisbury, Johannesburg, Botswana, Zaire, Tanzania, and occasionally Kenya. The Salisbury flight was the most popular with the pilots, so we had to take it in turns. If there was a spare seat, I would try to take Sally with me for the day. There we would take the opportunity to purchase some of those items which had disappeared from the shelves of the shops in Lusaka – things like soap powder, Bisto, pins, butter, golf balls, lamb chops. We could not buy much, as foreign currency was hard to come by.

The ease with which we were able to travel to Salisbury persuaded us that we should make the most of the opportunity by bringing Ian and Wendy back to school there. Paying the school fees was a problem, but as others were surmounting that problem, so could we. England was so far away, and we missed the children so much that we made the necessary arrangements – Wendy to go back to Chisipite and her sports activities, Ian to Peterhouse, where he would meet up with some of his old chums.

By now, we had found a dream house in the Roma area of Lusaka. It was a spacious four-bedroom building, sitting in an acre and a half of land, which included a lovely kidney-shaped swimming pool. The garden was mainly lawn, with a great variety of rose bushes. The gate opened onto a drive which led into a double garage, with servants quarters at the back.

The house was beautifully appointed inside, with parquet flooring throughout, quality light fittings on rheostat controls, a large American-style kitchen fitted out with cupboards all around, two lovely bathrooms (one of which was en suite with the master bedroom), and a small washroom for visitors off the entrance hall.

Sally was able to furnish it largely as she wished and looked after it with the assistance of our cook, Richmond, while I looked after the garden and pool with the help of Sebron, who I had brought down from the farm in Mkushi.

Once we had settled into the house, we were very happy there, making the most of it and enjoying the attractive pool. Sally was particularly happy to be close to a town again, where she could go for her shopping as and when she wished, even if there was not much to buy. We had lots of Mkushi friends dropping in on us, some of them spending the night, as we had a spare bedroom available. We made new friends in Lusaka, especially at the golf club, where we were now both members and played regularly, Sally with the ladies, me on Friday afternoons with a gathering of golfing farmers from around Lusaka.

I had always enjoyed my golf but rarely had the chance of playing regularly, on a good course with grass greens. Now I had the time and a good testing course at the Lusaka Golf Club. I made the most of it, usually playing twice a week. My handicap came down to eleven, where it remained, a comfortable handicap which allowed me to win my share of the monthly medals and the farmers Friday friendlies, where side bets were the order of the day.

Sally took her golf a stage further by getting the job of managing the club, and thus she spent a lot more time at the course than I did. When the children were home, it was an ideal place for them to go, spending hours on the fairways with their friends. Both of them learnt to play a very respectable game of golf, with easy unforced swings, so vital for good shots.

Two new friends we made through the golf were Paul and Koutsi Kos. Koutsi, with her nine handicap, used to play Sally, with her twelve handicap. She was a small, lithe, bespectacled woman you would think a strong wind might hamper. Never would you believe that she was extremely fit and strong, such that golfing and cross-country skiing were relaxation to her, the London Marathon and regular ten-mile runs just a little more testing. On top of that, she could speak half a dozen languages and was bringing up two healthy boys, Marc and Robert, who golfed with Ian and Wendy. Paul was a quiet, serious type who managed a shoe factory for Bata shoes. He must have been good at his job, as he had steadily progressed to the top job over a period of years. His golf handicap was also in single figures, but we spent more time fishing together than on the golf course. Paul had a small inflatable boat with an outboard engine, which we would take to the edge of the Kafue River, where we would assemble it. Armed with coffee, sandwiches, and rods, we would spend the day catching pike and bream along the reedy banks of the river. We seldom spoke very much, both concentrating on catching fish. It was Paul who taught me much of what I know about fishing. He also taught me the value of four-wheel-drive vehicles when a thunderstorm swamped the mud flats one afternoon while we were out. We had seven miles of muddy track to travel before we reached tarmac. I would never have believed it possible, but we made it, slipping and sliding at times but always getting through the many long sticky patches, which could so easily have trapped us for hours (or even days).

Due to shortages of equipment, we had to wait six months before we had a telephone at our new house. Then it took ten days to install! During that time, messages could be passed to us at the company. We were greatly saddened one evening as a message was delivered to us that my mother had died in the Lymington Hospital, following a stroke.

All had been going so well with our new way of life that when that happened, it was as though everything came to a sudden stop for a while. Suddenly, there was an empty space where previously there had been something of great value (although perhaps not valued greatly). Not until twenty years later, as I started writing these recollections, did I come to realise what a great part my mum had played in my life and what little thanks she received from me. I think and hope I gave her some joy and happiness, but I know the truth in the old adage:

"A daughter's a daughter all of her life, a son is a son 'til he takes him a wife."

I flew back to England next day, travelling first class, thanks to a concessionary ticket, on the superb weekly British Caledonian flight. My sisters and I comforted my father who, in spite of an uneasy relationship with my mother, was obviously going to miss her companionship dearly. Mum was cremated at the Christchurch crematorium two days later. We bid her farewell. She had not had an easy life; I think she had deserved better.

Around the club bar in Mkushi, some of us had discussed the possibility of flying a light aircraft to England. John Dendy-Young was one who was keen on the idea at one time and would have liked me to go with him in his Mooney. But for a light single-engined plane, it is a long way, fraught with difficulties of necessary clearances, airfields few and far between, as well as deserts and seas to cross. Attractive as it might have been, we realised the hazards and did not pursue the idea fully. Such a flight from Zambia was rare indeed, just speculated upon over a drink in the Flying Club bar. Wouldn't it be lovely?

When soon after my return from England, I was asked to take a Beech Baron to the Isle of Wight, I was surprised and delighted to have the opportunity to make this flight at someone else's expense, and with the backing of the Zambian government. The plane belonged to a government department and was used for insecticide spraying against the tsetse fly along the border of the fly area. They considered that their own pilot had insufficient experience to get the aircraft safely to the U.K. but would be happy to pay me, with plenty of travellers cheques to cover my expenses along the way. They also agreed that Sally could come with me as my navigator, when I explained that she had a pilot's licence. Then followed several days of planning the route and sending off telexes for clearance into the countries along the way. A week later, with just a small suitcase each, we set off on our first leg to Nairobi. All went well, and we spent the night at the comfortable old Norfolk Hotel, where I went over the route for the next day – to Addis Ababa for refuelling and then on to Khartoum. We were now in strange territory, with a very different slant to the English language, which made understanding the radio messages extremely difficult at times. The lush green hilly countryside of Ethiopia leading into the flat sands of the desert as we headed towards Khartoum kept our eyes and minds alert with interest.

Khartoum itself was hidden in a dust storm, but the airfield materialised at the end of an instrument approach. We thought we were going to have problems there, as they had not replied to our telex for clearance at the time we left Lusaka. Fortunately, it had been granted that day, and we were allowed into the country. We spent that night in a smelly hotel where moth balls were used in the drains to keep the cockroaches out. Perhaps it was the same in the time of General Gordon.

The third day's flight was to Cairo, but it was not possible to get there without refuelling. Eventually, we were given a clearance to route via Luxor, a military airfield, which would allow us to land there for refuelling purposes. Then followed a day of flying over sand and more sand. There was next to nothing in the way of communication, and it was extremely hot, with the sun beating down remorselessly. I would not have liked to make such a flight in a single-engined aeroplane. Sally kept me supplied with water and the biscuits we had with us, which were to see us through to Cairo.

The unchanging desert, with its black hills, lost interest after a few hours, so we were happy to see the River Nile and then Luxor come into view at the appointed time. Luxor to Cairo, with the great river in sight at times, was quite straightforward, and we landed at about eight o'clock in the dark at Cairo International Airport. We had a good meal that night at the airport restaurant, after showering and changing in the nearby airport hotel. We were celebrating our getting so far that we were now on the edge of civilisation. From now on, there would be facilities to assist us in the case of emergency and plenty of airfields available with radio aids as well as controllers.

We took the next morning off to have a look at some of the sites of the old civilisation of the pharaohs and visit the Sphinx and the great Pyramids of Giza. Cairo was not so full of tourists in those days as it is now, so we easily got a taxi, which took us to the site. We explored the outside and inside of the pyramids, marvelling at the close fitting of the enormous blocks of stone. A guide took us around, giving us all the details which were interesting at the time but quickly forgotten. He then took us around the Cairo Museum, showing us in our limited time some of the priceless treasures stored in that great building. Like so many, we were amazed at the quality of the discoveries from Tutankhamun's tomb. I wondered why a civilisation capable of producing such quality goods and building enormous pyramids some five thousand years before should have disappeared so completely from the face of the earth. Why wasn't modern Cairo and its people the leading nation in the world? History is a fascinating subject, full of riddles for us to puzzle over when we have time. Few of us have that time, like us; we looked, we listened with interest, and we moved on, this time across the Mediterranean Sea to Crete.

Iraklion was a nice little airstrip on the northern coast of the mountainous island. It was a balmy evening as we arrived, happy to have the major sea crossing behind us. There were no problems with customs or immigration, and we were soon settled into an agreeable little hotel not far away. We sent off postcards to Wendy and Ian, as we had done from each place where we had spent the night. While I went over the route for the next day, Sally went browsing around the nearby shops. There was a very friendly, relaxing atmosphere around Iraklion, which we enjoyed. Red tape or bureaucracy was not evident there.

Next day was the last full day's flying, taking us around the coast of Greece and across to southern Italy for refuelling at Bari. Then on past Mount Vesuvius, which we glimpsed through the broken clouds, and Naples with its wide bay, northwards along the western coast of Italy to the French Riviera and Nice. I'm sure Nice will be remembered by us as one of the highlights of the trip, as we were given a warm welcome by the smart lady receptionist at the airport, as though we were VIPs (which, of course, we were). Clearance was no problem, and we could park the Baron in an allocated parking place. Fuel would be available next morning when we wished. She then took us in her car to a large hotel nearby, not leaving us until we were booked in. That was not all. When we reached our bedroom, we had a lovely view from the window, looking out to the coastline and its many yacht moorings.

In the bathroom, Sally found special toothbrushes for visitors, along with other giveaway toiletries. She called to me with a cry of joy, wanting me to explore the bathroom. I refused, calling her to come to me instead. I had found a small fridge fully stocked with wines and spirits. Within a very short space of time, we were relaxed in easy chairs, looking at the panoramic view, enjoying our first glass of champagne. Tired though we were, we felt a celebration was quite in order; we really had reached civilisation.

Next day, after croissants and coffee, we flew the last leg of our journey across France, past the Channel Islands over the Channel to the coast of England. It was most noticeable that we were coming to English airspace when instead of having to battle to understand what the air traffic controller was saying to us, the man from the Channel Isles came through very loud and very clear, in a very Oxbridge accent. It was wonderful to hear, and we looked at each other and smiled; our difficulties were surely over.

I had warned Dad that we were coming his way, with an approximate arrival time. We flew over Barton-on-Sea, circling around his flat as he waved to us from his garden. Ten minutes later, we landed at Hurn Airport; our flight to the U.K., apart from the short trip to the Isle of Wight, was over.

After a few days recovering from the long flight with Dad's whisky, I flew back on Zambian Airways, leaving Sally to spend a few more days with her mother and sally forth around the shops.

Six weeks later, I did the flight in reverse, collecting the plane from Bembridge, where its spray equipment had been overhauled and modified. Then following a similar route, I flew back to Zambia, this time without Sally.

When I got to Luxor, I decided to visit the Valley of the Kings, which I had learnt of after talking to people about the pyramids in Cairo. I was able to get a taxi to see some of the tombs, including Tutankhamun's, the great temple at Karnak, and the beautiful-looking palace of Queen Hashepsowe, at the base of a high cliff of sandstone. It was all spectacular and thought provoking, well worth the visit. Unfortunately for the taxi driver, whose charge for the trip was double his initial estimate, my Egyptian shillings were exhausted and travellers cheques non-negotiable. I left him with a surprised look on his face and a pair of my old shoes in his hand, as I took off in the Baron, heading again for Khartoum and another night.

The following night, flying into Nairobi from the northwest was not fun. Because of the many high mountains, my safety height was up at twenty thousand feet, well above the level for oxygen. I knew the dangers both from lack of oxygen and from hitting the tops of hills, so I stayed up high until I was on a safe bearing from Nairobi Airport, when I quickly slipped down to a more comfortable level. After a good night's sleep at the Norfolk Hotel, I left early next morning on the last lap, arriving to a welcome reception party at Lusaka Airport at 4.30 in the afternoon. The fascinating and unusual trip was over, although the memories would last for a very long time.

The Baron was a great aircraft, one that I would happily take anywhere in the world. The Duke, onto which I converted on my arrival back in Lusaka, was even better, with its turbo prop engines and pressurised cabin. Twenty thousand feet was a normal cruising level for that plane, and it had an auto pilot (which I did not have in the Baron).

One of the perks of the flying world is the ability to get cheap rebate tickets and being upgraded to a better class if spare seats are available. Captains and pilots were often favoured in this way, as I had been on my U.K. flights. Wendy and Ian were very envious of this, since they had made a number of school flights to England, sometimes squeezed into the back of the plane. For their summer holidays, I booked a week back in Mauritius for us all, this time travelling club class in the new Zambian Airways 737. We kept it secret from the children until we got on board, when Sally and I sat down in two club class seats. Wendy and Ian, expecting us all to be somewhere in the back, were perturbed that we had made a mistake and said we had better get out quickly. It was a pleasure to see their faces when they learnt we were all travelling in the front. That holiday was paid for by the travellers cheques I had saved from my Baron flight from the Isle of Wight. Normal holiday allowances were now a thing of the past.

The situation in Rhodesia steadily deteriorated, with more and more freedom fighters (or *terrorists,* depending on which side you were on) infiltrating into that country. Killings and atrocities on both sides were heart-breaking as well as unnerving. Naturally, there were many repercussions in Zambia, whose propaganda against "the white racist regime of Ian Smith and his henchmen" was unceasing. There were "no terrorist camps in Zambia," according to the president. Occasional bomb blasts went off in Zambia, as the Selous Scouts of Rhodesia retaliated by terrorising the terrorists. Even the statue of *Freedom,* a sculpture of a strong native breaking the shackles of colonialism above his head, received a bomb blast (it did little damage). Sometime before, somebody had painted at the base of the statue "These kaffirs will break anything!" Tension and emotions erupted in different ways at different times, and some ugly incidents were the result.

There was a lot of stress, many shortages, numerous burglaries, and lots of inefficiencies. Vital commodities such as maize still came over the railway bridge at Livingstone in the middle of the night, so that nobody could see. The school buses were stopped and an Air Malawi aircraft chartered to fly the children to Rhodesia via Malawi. A boys school near Umtali suffered from a terrorist attack. Ian at his school, slightly out in the country and therefore vulnerable, practised drills regularly in case of a similar attack. Wendy was soon to take her O level exams, so we left her at school at Chisipite but moved Ian back to England to finish his schooling at Sherborne School in Dorset.

Next came the fear of a Rhodesian air raid to bomb Lusaka. The government decreed a black-out over all major towns and rigorously enforced it. To see the effectiveness after two weeks, I climbed onto the roof of our house one dark night. Yes, Lusaka was very much in the dark, except for the large square copper roof of the National Assembly Building, which was floodlit in its normal way. Oh, Zambia, how you frustrated us at times.

We spent a weekend in Mkushi with some friends, discussing the way things were going. It was depressing. We enjoyed the break but had no desire whatsoever to return. Negotiations for selling the farms had been completed; as to whether I would ever get any money out of the country, I would have to wait and see.

Prestonair decided to close down, as the owner and his wife had decided to return to South Africa and start a business down there. Over the years, he had managed to get quite a lot of money out of Zambia to that part of the world and so was able to move there and not be restricted by shortages of finance, in the way that would constrain others.

I managed another charter company for a while, having two Lear jets, superb, streamlined, fast twin jets. They were available for charters all over Africa and to anywhere in the world. Much of the time, the seats were removed so that they could carry boxes of day-old chicks from Swaziland to Lusaka. But even those days were numbered, as the flying ban came back with a vengeance. Army clearance was necessary for every flight, giving details of passengers and their business, wherever they were going. The phones were barely working, so one person was employed solely to travel to and from the army headquarters, attempting to get our required approvals in time for the flight. Clients wanting to use a Lear jet for an urgent meeting in Johannesburg might get clearance four days later, if they were lucky. Gradually, the ban was extended until the only route easily available was to the Copperbelt and back.

During much of the time of the war in Rhodesia, talks went on between various U.K. ministers and Ian Smith. Details were never forthcoming, but it was obvious that neither side was willing to budge. But in 1978, there were new talks and an apparent breakthrough, making a settlement look possible. On the strength of that, Sally and I went off to see what job prospects would be like in Rhodesia if there were a settlement. We had to fly via either Botswana or Malawi to South Africa and then on to Rhodesia. We went via Blantyre in Malawi, where the schedule broke down, and we had to be accommodated for the night. As the hotels were full, due to a conference, we were taken to a house near the airport, where beds were made up for us by a very friendly native. Next morning after breakfast, we sat on the balcony of Chileka Airport, reading our books. Our flight was due to depart at midday.

After a while, I decided to look up an engineer friend who worked for Air Malawi. Drinking coffee with him in his office in the hangar, he asked me what I was doing. I told him, whereupon he said, "But Air Malawi are looking for pilots, why don't you try them?" He picked up the phone and spoke to the operations manager.

I had an interview a few minutes later, followed by the offer of a job flying the Islander aircraft internally in Malawi on a three-year contract. I would be entitled to a free house, a gratuity after three years, free flights to and from London on the Air Malawi VC10 for the children while at school or college, and two free confirmed flights for Sally and myself each year. The salary was good, as were the future prospects onto other types of plane flown by the airline. When I got back to Sally and told her that I had the offer of a job with Air Malawi, she thought at first I was pulling her leg. I had only been away from her for an hour.

It gave us something new to consider as we flew to Johannesburg, to Audrey and Bill. I was now forty-six years old, too old (I thought) to join an airline, as I had no previous experience of that way of flying; in fact, I knew nothing at all about their methods. But I made many enquiries at Jan Smuts and Rand airports for possibilities of jobs with airlines or charter firms there, meeting with little success. Leaving Sally with Audrey, I went to Salisbury for two days, delighting again in the beauty of that city, with its perfect climate. I looked up Janet and Bill Pyle and Marian and Neville Wright, who now all lived there and with whom I used to spend occasional nights previously when I had flown to Salisbury on charter flights. I called on Air Rhodesia and the charter companies, to no avail. Until a definite settlement was forthcoming, they were not in a position to consider new pilots or expansion in any way. On the way back to Zambia, I happily put my completed application form into Air Malawi. The time had come to leave Zambia and move next door. One door was closing, one episode in our life almost finished. Another door was opening, new adventures, a new way of life in a new country. The old questions arose yet again: Were we doing the right thing? Would it turn out right? Only time would tell.

Chapter 12

Leaving Zambia

Our last few weeks in Zambia were not particularly easy. We had a lot to do and very little assistance from the authorities where we sought their help. Selling the house was quite simple, but the price was limited by a government housing authority, to which we had to apply before we could ask for the going price for such a house. That took time but eventually came through at the price we wanted.

I was at this time freelance flying a twin-jet Citation for Mines Air Services, doing only two or three trips to the Copperbelt each week. The rest of the time, I was teaching on my Cessna 172, which I had purchased cheaply the previous year. I was lucky on the sale of this, as the new owner, an expatriate, paid me in Sterling. That was the only real money we were able to get out of Zambia, and it did not amount to much. My bank informed me that if I emigrated, I would be allowed about five hundred Kwachas or two hundred pounds Sterling, my personal effects, and a car. With Ian's school fees alone totalling two thousand kwachas each term, I could not afford to emigrate, but got Sally to do so, allowing us at least her *Goofy* in Malawi. I applied to the Exchange Control for permission to take my Mercedes 200D with me for three years, the length of my contract with Air Malawi. I was prepared to leave the value of the car with the bank or customs, as required. This application was turned down.

Optimist to the last, I eventually obtained an interview with the head of exchange control in the Bank of Zambia and put my case to him, that of not having foreign currency in Malawi to purchase a new car and so forth. I was sure they would agree to my request.

"Mr Jenkins," said the financial controller for Zambia, "your car is now ten years old. In three years' time, it will be thirteen years old. It won't then be worth bringing back to Zambia; therefore, you cannot take it out to Malawi."

The logic of his argument floored me completely. No wonder my initial application had been turned down. For the first time in my life, I felt that the floor might as well open up and drop me the six storeys to the ground.

My Honda vanette, which had been so useful on the farm, was much in demand, as such vehicles were now hard to get. But not that hard to get, obviously, as before I had a chance to sell it, somebody stole it. A month later, the police were advertising for people to come and see if any of the stolen property which they had recovered was theirs. Vehicles were included. Sally went along to the police station and asked to see the recovered vehicles. On the way to them, she saw our vanette parked in the police car park!

"No, Madam, those are not the ones which have been stolen," said the constable. "Those belong to the police."

Sally, with the vehicle registration book in her hand, persuaded him otherwise, and we were able to get the vehicle back an hour later, only to have it stolen again before the month ended.

Thefts in Lusaka were getting worse by the day. Ladies walking down the main street had to keep their handbags tucked firmly under their armpits and could still expect some youth to have a go at snatching it. Groceries and shopping needed to be out of sight, in the boot of the car, to be reasonably safe. Your house needed a guard to protect it, both while you were out shopping and at night. Security lights, burglar bars, and dogs were not enough to deter the Lusaka burglars. Some would even wait for you to arrive and then hijack your car as you opened your gate. Guns were frequently used in these hold-ups, and the police if called would normally say that they had no transport. We were burgled one night for the fourth time, and the burglars actually took several things from our bedroom while we slept, prior to locking us in the bedroom. I would never have believed it possible. Fortunately, Dad was staying with us at the time and was a light sleeper. He got up to go to the toilet and obviously scared off the villains before they were able to take very much. He was also able to unlock our door for us.

On another occasion, another trick was attempted as heavy stones were thrown at our window in the middle of the night to see if anyone was at home. Awakened so rudely from my sleep, I loaded a shotgun, went to the front door, and blasted off two shots towards the gate. I heard the sound of feet running away and went back to bed to complete my dreams. Nobody ever enquired about gunshots in the middle of the night, it was becoming such a frequent occurrence. Definitely time to leave Zambia if you valued your health.

When my work permit for Malawi was at last approved, we were pleased to finalise everything and start packing. I hired a Baron from the charter company, loaded it up as much as I could with household items, which would be essential wherever we were, and flew it to Malawi without the Zambian customs even coming to have a look. Sometimes, you could count on inefficiency working in your favour.

Four days later, with both cars packed full of our clothes, bedding, valuables, dog, and children, we set off on the long drive to Fort Jameson and Lilongwe. I could take my Mercedes on a temporary basis, but would have to return it soon to Lusaka.

Apart from the complete lack of fuel stations on the long road between Lusaka and Fort Jameson, there was only one more incident to make us feel glad to be on our way out of Zambia. The road crossed the Luangwa River on a weakened bridge, which not only had a ten-miles-an-hour speed limit, but was also guarded by the Zambian military. Sally and Ian in *Goofy* were about half an hour ahead of Wendy and I, but we both got the same treatment from the many army representatives: "Go back, you were driving across the bridge too fast" was the order, even though we had both crossed at a slow walking pace, viewing the river on the way. Back and forth we both obediently went, satisfying their lust for power over the white man. They stopped us again to demand cigarettes and newspapers, but were unlucky as neither of us smoked, nor had we obtained a newspaper in our rush to get on our way. Fortunately, by keeping cool under trying conditions, we were allowed to proceed. We joined up at the border several hours later, and it was a very relieved and tired family that arrived at the Capital Hotel in Lilongwe, for our first night in the new country. We reached Blantyre next afternoon, ready and willing to start flying for the National Airline of Malawi.

Chapter 13
Malawi

Malawi was a small country with a large population ruled by a dictator – Dr Hastings Banda – who brooked no opposition in any form. Dr Banda's age was not generally known, but he was believed to be in his eighties. Although he looked very old, I was always amazed at his physical fitness. Regularly at any party gathering, or at the annual inspection of the country's crops, he would descend from his VIP dais to dance with each of the numerous groups of women. These were arranged in different coloured *chitenges,* bearing the president's head, fore and aft. He ruled with the assistance of Miss Kadzamira, the official hostess, and her uncle, Rupiah Banda, and woe betide anyone who stepped out of line. Expatriates were welcome in Malawi, provided they kept their noses out of political matters. So if you wanted to remain in the country, you never discussed politics.

Even the natives themselves seemed hesitant to discuss political matters, as any apparent opposition to the Malawi Congress Party would be rewarded by banishment to that person's village or by disappearing into Zomba Prison.

The natives were a very meek, friendly race, always smiling and happy in spite of the fact that they had nothing. Most houses were the small pole-and-dagga, thatched-roof type, except on the fringes of the main towns, where shanty towns had sprung up. There they used old corrugated iron, some bricks, some pieces of wood, and cardboard boxes. They seemed to spend their meagre earnings on clothes and were generally clean and well turned out in town or when visiting their friends on weekends. The women very often wore a length of coloured material, called a chitenge, wrapped around them, very often featuring the president's head on their bust and backside. Nobody was allowed to wear skirts which showed the knees, nor were ladies permitted to wear trousers. Men's hair had to be kept above the shoulder in length, so there was no possibility of mistaking the sex of a person.

Television did not exist in Malawi, as it was considered an unwanted source of propaganda and outside influence. As a result, the major pastime of the evening throughout the country resulted in thousands of children. Birth control was virtually unknown, so nearly every woman had a child on her back and several running alongside. After the age of five, they would go to the nearest school dressed in their blue or green uniform for girls, grey shorts and white shirts for the boys. Very often they walked miles each day to attend the classes, for which their parents had to pay. On special occasions when the president was visiting their area, they would line the route for miles, waiting patiently in the boiling sun, until eventually His Excellency and his retinue deigned to pass. They had a tough life, the Malawians, yet still they smiled. They were very likeable.

Malawi is a very pretty country, the long lake at the end of the Great Rift Valley its main feature, as well as its major source of food. It stretched some 365 miles in length and 52 miles across to the neighbouring countries of Tanzania and Mozambique. This freshwater lake holds over two hundred and fifty species of fish. Most of these are the small, exotically coloured, tropical fish which are caught and exported to aquaria all over the world. But the bulk of the fish caught are either the small *kapenta,* which are sun-dried on long racks alongside the lake, or the bream-like *chambo*, which are transported quickly to town for ever-ready markets.

The population of Malawi, nearly five million, was much the same as its neighbour Zambia but was squeezed into an area one-seventh the size. A large number lived along the lake shore in their small villages, getting their livelihood from the lake and a vegetable plot alongside their house. They thoroughly enjoyed the lake: washing, swimming, playing in it; cleaning their pots, pans, and clothes in it; watering their cattle there; and of course irrigating their gardens from it. They had their dugout canoes in which to go fishing and to pass on to one of their many sons when the time came to retire.

Apart from a few hundred thousand natives who had been fortunate enough to get a job in town, the rest of the population lived in the rural areas where subsistence farming was their lot in life. Malawi did not have the vast riches of a Copperbelt like Zambia. When President Banda came to power, he realised that it was not possible to employ everyone near towns and therefore directed and encouraged the majority to stay on the land.

The land regrettably was poor and undernourished, being cropped year after year with hardly any goodness being put back into the soil. Maize and beans were grown over any patch of soil that could be worked. A few government and private enterprise schemes did work very successfully, bringing hard currency into the country's coffers. Tea plantations between Blantyre and Mulanje, as well as a newer area near Mzuzu in the north, thrived well in the Malawian climate. But many of these had been thriving well before Malawi's independence. There were a few commercial tobacco farmers as well as training schemes for Malawians growing both flue-cured and Burley tobacco, a very different variety.

The government forestry department had planted a vast acreage of trees on the Viphya plateau in the northeast. It was a great supplier of straight wooden poles and softwood timber. I was given to understand that it was originally to be used for paper production, but the effluent from a pulp mill would likely have killed many of the fish in the lake, so fortunately, somebody stopped such a project in time.

Trees also grew on the magnificent Mount Mulanje. This soaring, ten-thousand-foot massif in the southeast grew many cedars on the large plateau near the top. Carefully controlled by the forestry department, the wood was available and generally sold in the form of cedar-wood boxes, carved and ready for the small number of tourists who visited the country each year.

There were two other areas of high ground in Malawi: Nyika Plateau in the north – a vast grassy plain some eight thousand feet high, on which roamed a few wild antelope – and Zomba Plateau, between Blantyre and Lilongwe. This was a favourite spot for residents of Blantyre during the hot months of the year, as a drive up the steep dirt road onto the plateau meant a drop in temperature of several degrees. A small inn at the top was excellent for beers and lunches, while the view from there was magnificent. The plateau was covered with pine trees in which several trout lakes were hidden away. It was also a favourite spot of Queen Elizabeth and the Duke of Edinburgh, who visited Malawi after the Lusaka Commonwealth Conference. They had the plateau to themselves, but on very few occasions when driving around this idyllic spot did you come across more than two or three other vehicles.

There were many such beauty spots in Malawi, especially along the lake side, with its rocky coves and sandy beaches. The one which surpassed all others was at Livingstonia between Mzuzu and Karonga, the northernmost town of the country.

Livingstonia was the home of the David Livingstone Mission, which had originally been sited near the southern end of the lake and where mosquitoes took a heavy toll of the missionaries. Now it is situated on a small plateau on the top of a twelve-hundred-foot escarpment, which drops sharply to a narrow plain by the lake shore. A river runs over the edge of the escarpment and drops in a sparkling display down the cliff side. It was possible to drive up to the mission from the road at the lake side, via a dirt road, with hairpin bends every few yards. It was a spectacular setting, with the high Nyika Plateau behind and the lake laid out below.

David Livingstone, the Scottish missionary explorer, was the first well-known white man to discover the area of Malawi during his many journeys through Africa. He approached the area travelling up the Shire River from its confluence with the Zambezi, until he came eventually to the great lake. How he managed to get his steamboat past the many rapids on the lower Shire River was a source of amazement to me; as for considering the Zambezi to be navigable on a commercial basis … There are so many things you can see from the air, getting a general view of the picture which might take days or weeks on the ground. I was lucky enough to fly all over Malawi, see all the beauty spots, follow the route of David Livingstone, watch the natives fishing in the lake, and still get home for supper. Mine was a privileged life.

Air Malawi gave us a fairly basic three-bedroom house - very small compared with the lovely mansion we had left behind in Zambia. But now I was just a first officer, the lowest grade of the company pilots, who did not merit a greeting from the operations manager's secretary! The best thing about our house was the attractive garden, which had been well laid out in the distant past and was stocked with shrubs and hardy perennials. A few days with a hose pipe soon brought new life to it, and as the garden blossomed, as did the delightful bird life.

We moved in the various goods and chattels we had transported from Zambia, which strangely enough included our burglar alarms. I set one – just in case – in the kitchen, where numerous boxes were waiting to be unpacked. Imagine our surprise that night to find someone had removed all the putty from around the glass of the kitchen door, then carefully removed the glass prior to making his entry. It must have taken him all of half an hour, only to be thwarted by the alarm shrilling off in his ear as he got inside! He got away with two or three dirty dishes instead of a good haul. Obviously, we were not going to get away from burglars.

Before I started work, I had to write a couple of exams and have various medical checks. By the time all that was finished, Wendy and Ian were both back in England, having flown there on the Air Malawi VC 10. Having finished her O levels, Wendy was now starting a secretarial course near Cheltenham. She was in the transition stage between child and adult, a difficult period for children but even more difficult for parents. At her college, she had a reasonable amount of freedom and ended the year being able to type and to play pool. Ian was next for his O levels. We did our best to encourage him and spur him to great efforts, but we all agreed that the person who invented exams should have been shot.

I had been given sufficient time to settle into our house and generally get myself organised before operating flights for Air Malawi. I had a couple of conversion flights on the Islander, a noisy, high-wing utility aeroplane with fixed undercarriage, which was easy enough to fly and gave a good view over its short, stubby nose. The Islander training captain checked me out along the routes I would be flying on the schedules, pointing out the landmarks and scenic spots along the way. The most difficult part of the job seemed to be keeping all the paperwork up to date. Most of the job was easier than charter flying, as the monthly schedules were published well in advance, permitting other activities like golf or social dinners to be planned days ahead. It was a simple matter to check the weather and the plane and be ready for the ground supervisor to bring you passengers and the load sheet a few minutes before the scheduled departure time. With only a controller at the destination airfields, there was no need to call anyone until approaching for landing. The route normally started from Lilongwe, where we spent two consecutive nights of duty, on to Mzuzu, and after thirty minutes there, we continued to Karonga. At Karonga, we would pass up to four hours on the ground before returning along the same route to Lilongwe. After the two duty days, we would have three or four days off whilst another pilot did his share of the work. What a life! In Karonga, I often got the fire wagon or ambulance to run me down to the lake side, where I would idle the time away swimming, sunbathing, and reading my book. The company provided a packed lunch each day as well as the overnight accommodation at the Capital Hotel in Lilongwe.

Air Malawi had a selection of aeroplanes: Islanders, Hawker Siddeley 748s, a Viscount, a BAC 1-11, and the VC 10. This meant a large number of pilots were required, most of them expatriates. It appeared that many of these were drifting away to bigger and better airlines in Europe, as the demand for experienced pilots was increasing. There was a chance of my moving up the ladder onto the HS 748, provided I could get my Airline Transport Pilots Licence (ATPL). As I had obtained a correspondence course on the subject from a friend in Lusaka when I returned the Mercedes there, I decided with the time I had available I should be able to complete the course and take the exams in London three months later. I carefully worked out my programme and stuck to it religiously, taking lessons with me on my flights for study at the stops along the route. It was an excellent course prepared by Avigation and included test papers after each lesson. These I would write as though under exam conditions and correct in red ink later from the answers in the appropriate section. Very occasionally, I wrote, "Do this again," on a section I did not understand, but in general, I enjoyed the work. It was a bit of a bore for Sally, as it took up so much time, but time was critical, as I had been accepted for the exams in London at the beginning of March. I did not get much support from other pilots who generally thought it almost impossible to pass the ATPL exams by just doing a correspondence course, especially where I did not have the benefit of the "corresponding." But by the time they made their views known, I was halfway through the course and determined to finish on schedule.

When I went for the exams, Sally and Wendy came too; Wendy had completed her secretarial course and decided she might like to try her hand at nursing. So as I went off to London, the other two went to the Luton and Dunstable Hospital for a general look around and an interview for Wendy. We were all relieved and happy that that was successful, Wendy being offered a place on the next nurses training course starting some six weeks later. We all met up again three days later at Dad's apartment at Barton-on-Sea, with my exams now behind me; the results would come about four weeks later.

Back in Malawi, we all had some time to relax for a change, and with Ian home for Easter holidays, golf was once again the sport for all four of us. We had joined the Limbe Country Club, as we considered that was the better course of the two available in the area, and made use of it at least twice a week.

When the letter arrived with the results of my exams, I had the children with me in the car to get some shopping for Sally. With a thrill, I saw that I had passed in each subject, with marks much higher than I could have hoped for. I casually threw the letter to the children as I passed the car on the way to a general store, saying, "Have a look at that." When I got back a few minutes later, they had both grasped the meaning of the results. We happily hastened back to Sally to give her the news of one of the greatest achievements of my life. We celebrated and spread the news far and wide.

Just two weeks later, I was studying again, this time for the technical exam on the Hawker Siddeley 748. The airline had decided to move me onto the bigger, heavier plane, together with another of the Islander pilots. We attended four days of lectures, wrote the examinations, and later went to Hyderabad, India, for training on the HS 748 simulator, which was situated there at the training establishment of Indian Airlines.

This was my first trip to India, as well as my first experience of an aircraft simulator. Neither then nor later did I come to like either of them. I was interested in seeing what I could of this new country, but we arrived at Bombay Airport in the heat of the day and then transferred in a dirty old bus to the domestic terminal, passing squatters' hovels and squatters squatting, finishing like wet fish at the other end, gasping for some fresh air.

As a welcome to a new land, I was not impressed by the sights or smells. Eventually, through the shambolic melee of the airport crowds, we got ourselves onto the next full plane to Hyderabad, hoping that would be better. My father had spent a few weeks in Hyderabad during the war on his way to Calcutta and Imphal, but had never said much about it. I was not surprised, as it did not appear to have any redeeming features as a town. It was just a motley collection of poorly constructed buildings which appeared to have gone up without any planning. The streets were vastly overcrowded, with poorly dressed people and vehicles, while oxen meandered where they wished or led cartloads of chattels through the cacophony. Vagrants, beggars, and blind men rapidly spotted us as tourists and vainly attempted to extract a levy on our passing. They had not reckoned on our being with our Indian Airlines representative, who scattered them with a few brusque words which were unintelligible to us (although the meaning was obvious). After ten minutes of them hooting, banging, and shouting, our vehicle drove into the haven of a smart-looking hotel where we were to stay for the next four days. It was clean and cool, and possessed a garden with a swimming pool. That was more than enough for us, both then and after four hours' training each day in the simulator.

The simulator was in a building on the far side of the airport, where we had arrived. There in an air-conditioned building were two Boeing 737 simulators and the one and only HS 748 simulator. Indian Airlines operated both types of aircraft and had equipped themselves with the appropriate training facilities, which could be hired out to other airlines when not required for their own pilots. Most airlines check their pilots every six months to ensure the standard of each remains as high as possible. The cost of checking anyone in an empty aircraft is exorbitant, as well as being far less safe when practising emergency drills. The simulator faithfully reproduced the cockpit of the appropriate aircraft, in which the crew could carry out every conceivable manoeuvre of which the aircraft was capable. Visual aids in the form of simulated runway lights ahead of the cockpit windscreen assisted the realism for takeoffs and landings, but in general, everything was done by reference to the instrument panel and the radio aids there displayed.

Our training captain took us through two hours of checks and procedures, after which we obtained a cup of tea before swapping over seats and continuing for a further two hours. With such intense training each day, we progressed rapidly, such that on the fourth day, we were able to handle the simulator through all the possible emergencies that might occur on the real plane. A normal flight from then on in the simulator was for an engine to fail just at the point of rotation and getting airborne, climbing up to the safety height in instrument flying conditions, homing to the appropriate beacon where it was necessary to hold for several minutes, with possibly another failure like the hydraulics no longer functioning to lower the wheels. Next would come an Instrument Landing System (ILS) approach which had to be aborted at the last minute so that a missed approach procedure would be called for and a further ILS approach in very marginal conditions for landing.

By regularly practising many combinations of unlikely occurrences, it was considered that a crew should be fully competent to cope with any normal emergency that might occur in flight. That, of course, is the reason flying with airlines is such a safe way of travelling. But the six-month training sessions in the simulator was something I never really enjoyed, even though it went on for the next fourteen years.

Back in Malawi, with my licence endorsed with the new aircraft, I had only one flight on it as a first officer before a return to

Hyderabad to do more simulator, this time in the left-hand captain's seat. Due to a sudden shortage of HS 748 captains and as my total flying experience was considered suitable, I was to start a command course immediately and was made up to captain shortly after my return from India and a few check flights in the plane with the training captain. Surprisingly, within twelve months of joining Air Malawi, I had risen from the lowest of the low on the little Islander, and had come of age as a captain on the HS 748. What is more, the operation manager's secretary would now bid me "Good morning" if she passed me. I had made it!

It only remained for me to complete my initial instrument rating in England and then collect my English ATPL. This I did later in the year, failing one simple part of the test, that of maintaining a back bearing on a Non-Directional Beacon (NDB); I did that bit again a few days later.

It had been a good year all round, with Ian doing well at Sherborne, where he had gained his necessary O levels and was about to start on two A levels. Wendy was established on her nursing career, which she appeared to be enjoying. She was busy emptying bedpans and giving enemas and such like: "Getting a good foundation," as I said to her, "working from the bottom upwards." Regrettably, she was not able to come home for Christmas, leaving just the three of us to spend the holiday together at the Ku Chawe Inn on the Zomba Plateau. We thought even Ian might not make it, as he missed the plane for Malawi due to a technical breakdown on the train to Heathrow. He was most fortunate to get on the flight next day, as all flights at the beginning and end of school holidays were packed full. So Christmas 1979 was a relaxing, enjoyable time for us in delightful surroundings and perfect weather. We toured the plateau, ate good meals, wined well, and golfed on the lush nine-hole course at the bottom of the hill.

Ian and I did some fishing in one of the dams. Only fly fishing was really permitted, and I had a fly rod with which I managed to catch numerous trees and bushes around me. Ian, initially unbeknown to me, borrowed my collapsible rod and a spinner, with which he rapidly caught ten nice-sized trout. We put them in the fridge of our Bedford dormobile and had a nice cup of tea. I explained to Ian that only fly fishing was allowed and that if a game warden were to arrive on the scene, he could be in trouble and was not to come anywhere near me.

Naturally, having had such success, he was keen to try his luck again, and just as naturally, a game warden pitched up. By this time, Ian had two more trout, which he brought over to show me while I was talking to the warden. He was permitted to keep the fish (fortunately not mentioning the ten already in the fridge) but was not allowed to fish again. Dad, meanwhile, had to suffer an hour of watching the warden try his luck at catching something with the fly.

Events in Rhodesia appeared to be taking a turn for the better, after blunt talks between Lords Carrington and Soames with the leaders of the warring factions. Rumours of a settlement deal in the offing were spreading hopefully.

Malawi had done its best to keep out of the political arguments against the Racist South, but with so few resources at its disposal, it needed to trade with South Africa in spite of pressure from surrounding friendly African states. The country was desperately short of petrol, with cars having to queue for days for a few litres of the scarce commodity. It could have been supplied from the Zambian fuel refinery on the Copperbelt, which was connected now with a pipeline from Tanzania, but the price of getting it from there apparently was far in excess of transporting it from the unfriendly republic to the south. Fuel and commodities used to come into Malawi from the east through Mozambique, but with a guerrilla war going on in that country too, the rail line from the coast was no longer viable.

South Africa was very good to Malawi, providing goods and services, and financing many of the country's projects. In return, it had one African president speaking out occasionally in its defence. It also got a steady supply of labour from Malawi for the gold mines. This in turn helped Malawi's employment problem as well as gaining the country sorely needed foreign exchange.

Air Malawi regularly flew plane loads of labourers to Johannesburg in the BAC 1-11, for six monthly periods of mine working. They went with small bundles of clothes, leaving their families behind. Six months later, they returned with bulging suitcases, blankets, and pockets full of Malawi kwachas, the earnings which the government had already exchanged for them. After a few weeks, many of them would reapply to return to South Africa for another spell. It was a highly organised operation in which the labourers were orderly and willing. Everyone except some politicians seemed happy with the scheme, but then you cannot please all the people all the time.

Not even Sally was happy all the time. Yes, she had her golf, which had taken her back to Lusaka to play in the Zambian Ladies Open competition with many of her old friends. Periodically, she had the children home for holidays. But unlike me, with a steady demand on my time flying aeroplanes, Sally had little to occupy her on a daily basis. Shopping for two did not take much time, nor did the supervision of our one assistant in the house and garden. She was getting bored, and with her boredom came a spate of migraines. We tried all sorts of remedies for these terrible headaches, including acupuncture from a Chinese man living in Lilongwe. She got only temporary relief, and even the acceptance of a job with the British Council in Blantyre did not alleviate her periodic suffering. It did get rid of the boredom, though.

I do not recollect ever having suffered from boredom, normally having a number of things I would like to do when time or circumstance permits. I had often felt I would like to paint pictures but knew nothing about the subject, since I was removed from the art class at school. Now with my vast experience of life, I thought it would be fun to try again. An American lady was offering art classes on a Tuesday morning each week, and after enrolment, I managed to get there most Tuesdays for many months. I don't recollect learning very much from her, except the essential basics of getting some paint on a brush and putting it on paper. It's the first and hardest step; the rest is easy. I did not paint a lot or very often. I was not very good at it but I enjoyed my masterpieces, had many of them framed, and even sold some in our local art club exhibitions. Years later, I considered that I had graduated to the level of some of the great masters when I too had one of my paintings stolen – and I was not even dead.

Generally, my life in Malawi was very pleasant with steady flying, regular golf, social events, painting, and occasional trips to the lake for some fishing. I was able to send some money out of the country each month to swell my slowly growing investments in real money, while Ian's schooldays and their attendant expenses were rapidly coming to an end.

Sally and I decided it would be a good time to have a last family holiday abroad, as job commitments might prevent such an event in the future. As I was able to get rebate tickets, we decided on a trip to America, to California. Mike Scott, my old school chum, with whom I used to go canoeing on the canal at Watford, was the British Airways manager at San Francisco Airport. He had often invited us to visit there by notes at the bottom of the regular Christmas cards with which we kept in touch. With assistance from him regarding hotel bookings and a hire-car reservation, we planned a three-week tour from San Francisco, south along the coast road to Los Angeles, eastwards to Las Vegas, then northwest to Yosemite Park and Lake Tahoe before ending up back in San Francisco. We ensured Wendy would be free to come, that my leave was granted, and that Sally could be spared for a month from her office. Ian would be finished at school, with his exams a thing of the past, so it was all systems go.

Holiday in America

We all made the rendezvous as planned in a hotel in Sloane Square, where we spent the night before our departure. A taxi next morning took us to the British Airways daylight flight to Seattle and San Francisco over the frozen polar route.

We had enjoyed some fabulous holidays together over the years: Malindi, Inhaca, South Africa, Mauritius, England, Switzerland, game reserves in Zambia, the eastern highlands of Rhodesia, and so on. America, however, topped them all. It was wonderful to be able to tour around with two lovely, adult children, a boy and a girl, our own flesh and blood, who were on the threshold of starting their own careers in life. They were now old enough, at seventeen and eighteen, to intelligently share in everything that was going on, discuss what we saw, help where help was required, joke when something went slightly amiss, and they were responsible enough to do things together without our having to worry about them all the time.

Travelling again in club class to San Francisco started us all off in a good mood. We viewed the polar ice cap and later Mount St. Helen's, which had recently erupted. Mike Scott met us at the airport and put us up for the next three nights in his delightful home just to the south of town. From there, he and Muriel, his wife, took time to show us the many sights of San Francisco, including Fisherman's Wharf, the giant redwood trees, Alcatraz, and of course the wonderful Golden Gate Bridge, which Sally and I walked across. We ate at a very American diner nearby, with their two sons of a similar age to Wendy and Ian, where the charming waitress "just loved my accent."

It was a warm, hospitable welcome to America. After we collected the big Cadillac in which we were to tour around, Mike and Muriel saw us onto the coastal road before returning to their home. We continued gently along the spectacular route south past Pebble Beach and Monterey, visited Hearst Castle, with its amazing display of artefacts, and drove on to Los Angeles. I had no desire to spend time in such a large city as LA, but it did have two places I thought we would all enjoy seeing: Universal Studios and Disneyland. According to plan, after settling into a hotel with a nice swimming pool, we spent a day at the film studios, seeing some of the tricks of the trade. Jaws leapt out of the water at us, a bridge almost collapsed under our little tour train, aliens from another planet attempted to hijack us, and a river parted its waves to allow us to cross. We saw houses on fire, stunt men falling off roofs, Frankenstein's monster coming to life, and many, many other clever gimmicks, which appeared so realistic on film. If we were impressed with that, then we were overwhelmed with Disneyland next day. Oh, what a riot of colour, music, and spectacle that was. I really do not know who enjoyed it the most. Between us, I think we saw or did just about everything possible, but still we could have gone back for more. Words cannot possibly describe the spectacle before us, taken from the many fantasies of Walt Disney. Characters from his films meandered around in their colourful costumes, encouraging adults and especially children to enjoy the world of make-believe. From Wild West saloons came jazz music, while on street corners we came across three or four black-faced minstrels, with their banjos, singing songs of the Deep South. In spite of ice creams and sodas available everywhere, the vast area was spotlessly clean. There was no sign of rowdiness, just pure enjoyment by the thousands of people on a wonderful day out.

Our next stop was Las Vegas, the spectacular city in the desert. Our eyes widened with amazement as we cruised slowly down the Strip, looking for the Circus Circus Hotel, where we were booked for three nights. Never before or since have I seen anything like the enormous illuminated signs and displays on extravagantly designed buildings, endeavouring to entice the newcomer to town to spend his or her money in that particular casino. Every hotel had its own casino full of slot machines, all promising to pay out a fortune. The hotel charges were low in the knowledge that once you were there, you were likely to spend at least twice as much trying to get your money back. Our hotel foyer was designed like an enormous Big Top of a circus and where circus acts went on almost continuously from midday to midnight. There was no charge to watch them, and not many did, as the one-armed bandits continued to claim the attention of most. The bedrooms were luxurious, as was the elegant pool at the back of the hotel. We relaxed there and later sauntered down the Strip to investigate some of the fabulous sights.

In my schooldays, I had been awed by the size of the Grand Canyon and of Mount Everest. The memory of that had remained with me as something I must see if I ever had the chance. Now my time had come, and I had booked a flight for the four of us for the next day from Las Vegas to the Grand Canyon, where we would land on the southern rim of the canyon and later fly back in the same plane. It was vast! Our Navaho flew us low along the floor of the canyon, where we were able to look up at the sides towering high above us, over isolated pinnacles of rock sculpted by the erosion of centuries, and along many miles of its great length. When we landed at a small airstrip, a coach awaited to take us on a drive to various scenic spots where particularly good views were obtained. The bottom of the canyon looked miles away with the cliffs descending in ever differing coloured layers of rocky strata. We spent time taking lots of photographs and visiting a small National Park museum in which the formation of the canyon was illustrated in pictures. Then it was back to the Navaho for our return to Las Vegas and a free lunch courtesy of the charter company.

Mike and Muriel Scott joined us that evening, having flown down from San Francisco. We all went to see an ice show, which included dinner, at one of the big hotels. The standard was so good I got tickets for another show the following night. It was the Follies Bergeres, a musical extravaganza featuring lots of beautiful girls in lovely costumes which showed their legs and breasts in the most delightful way possible. If no one else was enjoying our trip to America, I certainly was. In fact, we all were, and the Follies Bergeres was all performed with such flair and good taste, I would have been happy to take anyone to see the show.

Next stop, after a drive through Death Valley, was Yosemite Park, a natural scenic gorge with sparkling waterfalls and towering rocky buttresses. A lovely, relaxing area for a couple of days reached by a pass nine thousand feet high across the Sierra Nevada mountain range. When we reached Lake Tahoe a couple of days later, the weather changed overnight, and we finished our holiday driving back to Mike and Muriel's house through snow-covered forests and over roads where snow chains were advised.

What a superb holiday we had all experienced. Apart from the snow at Lake Tahoe, we had enjoyed perfect weather throughout the whole trip. We had found the Americans very friendly and helpful, and were impressed by the way everything and everyone worked so well. Waitresses served you efficiently with smiles on their faces, obviously meaning you to have a nice day when they bid you farewell. Street cleaners, such as those sweeping up droppings after horse-drawn carriages at Disneyland, would step out of the crowd with brush and pan, make a very clean sweep of the mess, and retire before the next float or dancing group came past. In other countries, the dancers would be expected to act as though there was nothing there; there certainly would not be a cleaner around. Who would stoop so low?

With our minds full of all our experiences, we bid farewell to our very good friends, who had helped make our visit so enjoyable, and flew back to take up our lives where we had left off a few weeks before. Wendy went back to her nursing course at Luton, and Ian went for interviews and aptitude tests for the Royal Air Force as well as for the Metropolitan Police Force. Sally went back to her office in Blantyre, while I resumed my flying as captain of the HS 748.

Air Malawi was changing with new management. The VC 10 flights were stopped as being uneconomical, the aircraft put up for sale. The Islanders were due to stop before long, their routes to be flown by the HS 748. The Viscount had already been sold to Rhodesia, where a settlement had at last been reached and the bitter fighting come to an end. The number of expatriate pilots had steadily declined, and more Malawian pilots were gaining experience as first officers on the HS 748 and BAC 1-11. Priority was now given to them, to build up their experience, until they could qualify as captains and eventually "Malawianise" the airline. On the Hawker Siddeley we had only four captains, which meant that when one was on leave, we were flying six days each week; it was a hard life.

Ian passed both his interviews, but as the RAF wanted him to wait for a further year before joining them, he decided to try the Metropolitan Police instead. After a farewell party he gave for his friends, which nearly wrecked our small house, I flew him to Lusaka, where he connected with the B-Cal flight to London and his new career.

The birds were flying the nest. We had given them both the best upbringing and schooling that we could. Only time would show whether we had been successful; meanwhile, their futures were in their capable hands. We had every confidence in them both and happily gave each of them twenty-first birthday parties in England in due course, attended by large gatherings of friends and relations. The key of the door was theirs.

So now we were two, just Sally and I, approaching the end of my three-year contract. When I was offered another with a much nicer house, we accepted. Our lifestyle was very pleasant; why should we change? Work progressed, and I became a training captain on the 748, teaching new cadets, testing first officers, making up new captains, and going regularly to Hyderabad to do instrument rating renewals and six-month checks on the 748 crews. I always had plenty to do but enjoyed doing it.

Both Sally and I played a lot of golf, Sally joining a group of ladies who went off to play in other countries' open competitions.

She played in Botswana, Kenya, India, and Zambia. While I joined in an annual Lucifer competition held at Sunningdale each year, with prizes and speeches at a superb dinner at the Savoy Hotel in London. Neither of us came away with any trophies, but playing on superb courses was reward enough.

We played on some excellent courses in South Africa during one of our holidays, touring from Durban to Cape Town along the Garden route. We had another Air Malawi couple touring with us and enjoyed the golf and shops during the day, bridge and dining at night. By now, with all my playing, I had got down to a single-figure handicap, keeping just ahead of Sally's. It's a lovely game. I thought once of becoming a professional golfer but decided I had better make my fortune first so that I could afford to be one. So far, I haven't made my fortune and am still very much an amateur golfer.

Golf was partly the reason we went to Sun City in Bophutaswana in 1983, for our silver wedding anniversary. Sally wanted to go somewhere special, and I knew that the golf course there was reputed to be one of the best in southern Africa. So we treated ourselves to a couple of nights at that unbelievable entertainment complex. It was the closest thing to Las Vegas that I have ever seen with its casinos, slot machines, and spectacular shows. Marty Caine was performing while we were there, a wonderful artiste who kept us all laughing in between her songs. The costumes of the supporting cast and the décor of the stage was lavish and most unexpected in such an out-of-the-way place.

Unexpected letter

More unexpected was the letter awaiting us on our return to Blantyre. Sally's mum, Rosa, had passed away about fifteen months previously. She had been taken ill in the residential home in which she had been living for the last few years and had died in hospital, worn out from her life of toil and crippling arthritis. The relationship between she and Sally had never been very close, neither of them discussing much of the years gone by. No secrets disclosed or confidences shared by either.

Imagine then our surprise and shock when a letter from Sally's cousin John, on the return from our silver wedding anniversary, disclosed that Sally had a half-brother and sister! Frank, her father, had been married with a family before suddenly departing for Cork, Ireland, with Rosa, a similarly highly qualified hairdresser who worked in the same salon. Sally and I sat down with a stiff drink each to assimilate and discuss this astounding piece of news. Apparently, all members of the family had been sworn to secrecy; they were not to reveal the news to Sally. John, for reasons known only to himself, had decided that the time had come for Sally to know and also to meet her half-brother and -sister, with whom he was in contact.

The way of life has changed tremendously over the years, and what was obviously a scandal of the first order in the early thirties is now a very normal occurrence. So Sally and I largely joked over the letter. It would not make any difference to us. But deep down, it was obvious that the news had shaken Sally more than she said. She had sometimes wondered about her parents, since as a child, she had found a photo of two small children, a boy and a girl, in her father's drawer. She had never disclosed that she had seen it, guiltily knowing that she should not have been looking in her father's things. Subconsciously, her suspicions were aroused by that and the fact that although both her parents were good hairdressers in a top salon, there was never any spare money available. When her father died, her mother was left almost destitute and was helped by us from Zambia. Only with the letter did her very vague suspicions materialise into fact.

The full story came out a few months later when we met the rest of the family. Frank had been a top-class hair stylist in a large salon in Birmingham, where Rosa also worked in a similar capacity. Frank was married to a forceful woman who was saving for him to have his own salon, his own business. They lived with the two young children in a comfortable house in which, as was the custom of the time, she was the faithful housewife.

Frank, on the other hand, started dating Rosa, and eventually they eloped together to Ireland, Frank taking the money from the savings with them and leaving just a letter of farewell on the mantle shelf.

In Cork, they lived together as man and wife, working in a salon in town. It appeared that Rosa's wages each month went to help support the first family, who naturally were very bitter and unforgiving that such a scandalous affair should affect them. Frank never was granted a divorce, so he and Rosa were never married. Rosa changed her surname to Cullen by deed poll, prior to her first visit to us in Zambia after Frank's death.

Sally came on the scene just over a year after the move to Cork. She was loved by her parents in a constrained way, as they were both at work each day and had a secret background which they could not disclose. Frank also had a violent temper and was a strict disciplinarian.

Fortunately, as Sally grew up, she was good at tennis and badminton, which took her out of the small home and into groups of children with whom she was able to compete and communicate. When she joined the Wrens, she was happy to be free and independent – a feature she has never relinquished.

The meeting with half-brother and -sister, although interesting, did nothing much for any of us. Bitterness was not far below the surface, even though Sally was in no way the cause. Curiosity about who, where, and when was partly satisfied. Family genes passed down from Frank in looks and temperament were remarked upon. But overall, no firm friendly relationships were made. It was a disturbing interlude which I'm sure we could all have done without.

Before my second contract was completed, I had been converted onto the Beech Kingair, a delightful light turbo-prop aircraft, one stage in advance of the Beech Duke. Air Malawi had got this plane and three Skyvans, theoretically to fly thousands of the Malawi Ladies league to meetings with the president. That had quickly proved to be logistically impracticable. They would therefore be used to supplement the Air Malawi schedules or even be utilised for charter work. Only two of us ever flew the Kingair, and we had some interesting flights, to unusual destinations. On one flight to Nampula, Mozambique, I was warned to take some food with me, as the town had been cut off by bandits for a considerable time. I was taking some Malawian government officials to discuss the possible reopening of the railway linking Malawi to the sea, and we expected to spend a night there.

There was plenty of bowing and scraping at the airport on our arrival. When we reached the hotel, it took the receptionist more than twenty minutes to find rooms which had light bulbs in them. They were unusually sparse, as was dinner that evening: banana soup, a greyish lukewarm slush, followed by banana stew, an even greyer thicker lukewarm slush! I was glad I had taken some sustenance with me. Before we left next morning, we went to the dining room for breakfast; this consisted of tea. No toast, no cereals, not even milk with the tea, just tea! I had explored around the town the previous day, noting the seedy look of the place, which had not seen any fresh paint since the Portuguese evacuated the country many years before. There was nothing in the shops, and it appeared that even currency was barely used any longer. The barter system was back in business.

A flight to Maputo a few weeks later counterbalanced the previous trip. Once again, it was government ministers who were the passengers, and they invited me to join them for lunch at the Maputo Flying Club, on the edge of the airfield. A bit dubious of what might be dished up, I met up with the big party as planned. How glad I was to have done so.

We were each served at least half a kilo of succulent prawns in batter, just as starters. Then followed prawn and octopus stew. It was delicious. I cannot remember if there was any sweet to follow. I would not have been interested, as I ate my fill of these excellent dishes. Lourenco Marques, or Maputo, as it was now called, had always been renowned for its prawns, but after the country became independent, rumour had it that they had been fished out by the Russians. Obviously, they had missed a few.

I signed a third contract with the company. They were keen to keep me, as pilots were short, especially those in the training role. With a good number of Malawians progressing steadily, it would not be long before all expatriates could be dispensed with. Meanwhile, I had a conversion course onto the BAC 1-11, of which Air Malawi now had two. The training course after the technical exam had been passed meant a return to a simulator, this time in Dublin's fair city, where I went with Harold Mukiwa and our training captain, Jerry Dunn. Mukiwa, a well-built Malawian with a slow, softly speaking voice, had flown with me a lot on the 748. He was a bright lad in his mid twenties who performed his duties efficiently and flew the plane well. Together, we were now put through our paces by Dunn, an ex-RAF pilot, who had been with Air Malawi with the VC 10. He was grey haired like myself and had an easygoing temperament, which did not detract from his efficiency when instructing or testing another pilot. When we finished our course in Dublin, both Harold and I knew a great deal about the handling of the BAC 1-11, thanks to his high standard of instruction.

Back in Blantyre, we were permitted to make a takeoff, a circuit with an overshoot, and a landing in the aircraft, after which it was on our licence; we were scheduled on flights as first officers from then on.

The BAC 1-11 was a great plane to fly. It would carry a hundred passengers in quiet comfort in the sturdily built airframe, whilst the noise from the unsilenced Rolls Royce Spey engines was left outside for everyone to hear. It was a smooth plane to fly, beating all the other types that I had flown with its powerful capabilities. I flew it in all sorts of weather conditions, from severe turbulence to smooth tranquil layers of air in cloud down to two hundred feet above ground. Never once did I have any qualms that the plane would let me down. When much later, I had to close down an engine before reaching Johannesburg with a full load of passengers, it appeared as though no one in the aircraft had noticed, although the safety services on the ground had been alerted. On that occasion, we were given priority routing to the Jan Smuts Airfield, where my single-engined landing was hardly felt. That was the only untoward incident in five thousand hours of flying in this superb plane.

It was eighteen months before there was a vacancy on the 1-11 for me as captain, during which time I was still training others on the HS 748 and doing charter flights in the Kingair. So my flying life was full of interest. Elsewhere, things in the country were not so good, and the Malawi kwacha had to be devalued. This meant that imported commodities were much more expensive, and the monthly remittance to my UK bank was reduced. Similarly, I could expect less real money from my gratuity at the end of my contract. This meant a lot to me, as apart from school fees and a few other minor amounts, I had not succeeded in getting my money out of Zambia.

A friend had persuaded me that he could move it out for me on the black currency market. It appeared at the time to be the only way possible even though I would lose out on the exchange rate. In fact, I lost the lot, as the person concerned used the money to purchase an aeroplane for charter work and was killed in it in a flying accident. So when we left Zambia, we effectively left with nothing and had to start saving all over again.

It was at this stage I started to interest myself in different investments in order to have my money working for me. Initially, I had everything invested in British government stock, which did me well and in my view continues to be one of the soundest of investments, particularly if you are not paying tax on the income. Later, I became interested in unit trusts and spent a lot of time each week charting the progress of some of them. I used to visit the many financial advisers who regularly toured the countries which employed expatriates. I even did a two-week course at Bristol so that I could represent an investment company in Malawi. It was all very interesting and made me some money, but not my fortune. I had to keep working, living for today while trying to put something to one side for tomorrow.

Having sisters spread around the world was quite useful to us; at least two of my three sisters were definitely in the right places, as far as we were concerned. Margaret and Cyril and their family were miles away in Australia, well beyond our normal range of travel. Joan and Roy were settled in Thame in Oxfordshire, where they had played a tremendous part in meeting our children during their journeys to and from their schools. They often visited them or had them for a few days at half-terms and were always on call should any emergency or problem arise with them. They had represented us when we could not be there with our children and never hesitated to change their plans if necessary to give Wendy and Ian preferential treatment. Not until they had both left school and were getting themselves established on their careers were we to see Joan in Africa. One of her sons, Bruce, had the family wanderlust in his veins and was established in a business in Johannesburg. He had met up with a delightful girl, Belinda, who was born in the country, and they were getting married at Constantia near Cape Town.

Joan and Roy were to be there, as were Audrey and Bill and ourselves. As the wedding was only a few days before Christmas, we decided to have the ten days together at an old Dutch-styled hotel near Stellenbosch, a small town surrounded by hills in the wine-growing area of the Cape Province. We celebrated the wedding in great style in a lovely little church full of flowers, which rivalled those in the gardens at the superb reception. It was a happy time for us all. A little later, Roy managed to get a game of cricket at Newlands, a hallowed South African ground, in spite of being badly sunburned the day before. He and Bill had many merry moments, trying to see whose capacity for beer was the greatest. There was not too much doubt that Roy, with his hollow sunburnt legs, was the winner of a competition in which I knew I would not have got past the starting post.

Before returning to England, Joan came to Malawi to spend a few days with us, which included New Year's Eve. Roy had returned to Thame to keep his business going, and we only had Joan, on whom we could lavish VIP treatment in an attempt to repay her for all that she had done for us and our children. It was a memorable occasion for her, regrettably not in the way that we had intended. She arrived suffering from a severe stomach upset, similar to one which had affected Roy during his last two days in Stellenbosch. Sally managed to doctor her, and we gave her a day to recover. At a special dinner on New Year's Eve, she was feeling a little better but unable to eat much or to drink her fair share.

That, however, was not all. We wanted to show her Zomba Plateau so went there the day before her departure in our Honda Civic. All went well until late in the afternoon; we stopped at the last viewpoint prior to starting our return journey back down the mountain. The car would not start again. Never before had it given a problem, but it appeared to be fuel starvation. I tried sucking the fuel through to the carburettor and as usual got my mouth half full of the foul-tasting fluid, which I spat out with a vengeance. Sally then switched on and tried the engine as I directed. It did not start, but a spark ignited some fuel on the engine on my arms and on my beard. It wasn't much, thank goodness. I was able to beat it out in a few seconds, but Joan was aghast at what was happening and must have wondered if she would ever get back to staid old England. We were in luck, as another car drove up a few minutes later, just as it was getting dark. The driver, a German tourist, offered to tow us to a garage about seven or eight miles away at the bottom of the plateau. I had a tow rope, so we were soon on our way.

I do not know if the German had ever towed another car before. It appeared not, as he set off over the uneven, winding, dirt track as though he was on a rally. His speed did not reduce as we went down the steep mountain slope with its hairpin bends. He did stop, though, when the towrope broke, which happened on a number of occasions, resulting in an ever-shortening distance between the two vehicles until, when we reached the garage, only a few knots separated us. Believe it or not, we never touched. The problem was soon solved under a bright light at the garage: a small hole in the petrol pipe to the carburettor. A new piece of rubber pipe, and we were serenely on our way back to Blantyre. Joan remembered her Malawi visit, and to ensure that we did not forget her coming, she sent us a framed piece of knotted blue rope, like our towrope, entitled "Zomba Plateau, 1st January 1987." We still have it.

Joan was not the first sister to visit us in Malawi, as Audrey and Bill had come a couple of years before, when we had the Dormobile. They were able to spend a week with us in Blantyre and then take the Dormobile off to the lake and tour around Malawi for a few days. We had called on Audrey and Bill a large number of times since we arrived in Africa, but had never been able to persuade them to come to our farm in Zambia. They had always been willing to accommodate us at short notice, whether it was for a holiday or for medical reasons. While charter flying in Zambia or flying the Kingair on charter for Air Malawi, they would meet me at the airport, take me home, and put me up for the night. It was wonderful being able to keep in touch that way and a great shame that they did not come our way more often. Of their three children, only Brenda, their lovely daughter, who also had the wanderlust in her blood and had travelled the world extensively with her backpack, came to Malawi with three of her nursing friends. I managed to borrow an old car for them, which was waiting at Lilongwe Airport as they arrived. For ten days, they then toured the country, using our house as their base. They were all a joy to have with us and obviously found Malawi and its people very friendly.

An unusually friendly and relaxed island that Sally and I found for a two-weeks holiday was Cyprus. A friend of ours had a flat at Paphos, with an old VW Beetle sitting outside. If we cared to pay her a nominal rent, it would be ours for two weeks. Wendy heard about it and, as she would have just finished her nursing exams, was determined to get in on the act. Ian had to continue at work, treading the beat, keeping the residents of London in order. We had a super time there with the sun, the sea, and the sand. We swam a lot, and I learnt to wind surf with the assistance of two young topless beauties (who were not really helping). We slept lots, ate the local dishes, and drank the local wines. We took the Beetle to the top of Mount Olympus during our exploration of part of the island, which we found to be full of delightful places and filled with people who were extremely helpful, spoke English, and were not out to thieve from us. Thieving and burglary was virtually nonexistent: an absolute boon after Blantyre. We visited a number of archaeological sites like the Tombs of the Kings, the Byzantine Castle, and the amazing Roman mosaic floors at the House of Daedalus. It was all so unspoilt that we vowed to return if we had the chance.

It was while Wendy and I were chatting one night that she asked for some advice from me. She was being pressured by one of the porters at the hospital to get engaged and to marry him. Although she did not love him, she thought that by getting engaged to him, she could stall him and put him off at a later time. She asked for my views. I was able to convince her that if she was not going to marry the man, it would be most unfair to take the relationship any further. As it also appeared that he had very little prospect of promotion or bettering himself, I also felt that Wendy would be hard pushed to enjoy herself in the future in the way she was doing at present, especially once she passed all her exams and became a state registered nurse, as we hoped. When it also transpired that the porter was divorced with a child, I told Wendy bluntly that her income would most surely go to bringing up that child. Three weeks later, the relationship was over, and Wendy was presented with the silver buckle which had belonged to her Aunt Audrey. The buckle being the badge of a state registered nurse. She had qualified in her chosen career.

A little more than a year later, when I had gone to England for my periodic simulator check, taking Sally with me, we met up by arrangement with the Kos family, which we had known so well in Zambia. Wendy had been seeing Marc and Robert occasionally, and as Paul and Koutsi were back in England after a spell in Indonesia, we were all meeting for dinner at the Strand Palace Hotel. Just before we went into the dining room, Wendy said that Marc wanted to ask me something. Sally and I were only mildly surprised when he asked for Wendy's hand in marriage. We were happy to have him as an addition to our family, but when I later got Wendy alone, I asked her:

"How come you never asked me my opinion first about whether you should marry Marc?"

Her reply, I remember very clearly, was, "Because I knew, Dad, I just knew!"

In the middle of January 1984, my dad passed away in a Southampton hospital from heart failure; he was eighty-four. He had spent more than his fair share of his retirement years in hospitals with hip replacements, knee operations, hernias, and the like. Yet he never complained (at least not to me). In fact, he never said very much about himself to me at any time, which brings me right back to square one with this story. Was I prepared to listen to what my father had to say? Was I interested enough to question him about his life and events? Was I not perhaps too taken up with my own life to find time for his? I wish now that I had a book telling me of his feelings, his activities, his life. Now in my retirement, perhaps I would have time to read it.

At least I did keep my mum and dad fully in the picture of what I was doing, as I found out to my surprise, when my sisters and I were sorting out Dad's effects. There was a large box file, full of letters and cards that I had sent to them from the day I joined the Navy. Some of these letters were over thirty pages long, with news and views of everything I was doing. It is from these letters that I have been able to review my life in this way, a review which I trust you will find as interesting as I have.

We bid farewell to my father at the Christchurch Crematorium, where Mother's name was displayed in the Book of Remembrance for the day of her cremation there some years before.

As I left Barton on Sea three days later for my return to Blantyre, I felt his presence outside his flat and above me where, with a deep, hearty, carefree laugh, he took his leave of me for the last time.

Scamp, our old faithful farm dog, had also died. It was I think thirteen years since we had got him from Denny Kennedy as a pedigree poodle, only to find as he grew up that there was also a lot of pedigree terrier in him as well. Although he had been the children's dog – officially Wendy's – he had always come around with me. He was a faithful scruff, always there, always the same, doing what he wanted to do. When he died on the operating table, as the vet attempted to remove a growth on a testicle, he was almost blind, having had several cobra snakes spit in his eyes over the years. He was very good at finding snakes in the garden, his barking at them alerting us all.

We had no intention of getting another dog, as too frequently we were both away from home. Even when Sally came back one day to say she had seen a litter of Rough Collie puppies, we were glad that we had not been persuaded to take one, especially as only a bitch was available. When a week later we got a phone call, saying the pick of the litter, a male, was not going to be taken as expected, we went along just to have a look. That was enough. We came away with Inca, a gorgeous bundle of fluffy fun. What a magnificent creature he turned out to be. Elegant, obedient, loving, faithful, intelligent are only a few adjectives to describe this dog. He loved being groomed and looked an absolute picture, just like Lassie of the films. He was so easy to train that it was a pleasure to teach him new tricks, like opening doors and closing them behind him. He was a great friend of our servant Enock, who would look after him if we were away, as we were for Wendy's wedding to Marc.

I had a vague idea that when children left school and started earning their keep, the financial drain on the family coffers would come to a stop. Then I thought it might end after their twenty-first birthday parties. I continue to revise my ideas. Our only daughter was to get married, and it was going to be a memorable occasion.

Organising it from Malawi was just one of those things; we would have to call on help from the family – from Joan and Roy. The wedding would take place in Thame from Joan and Roy's house, with the reception in a school hall not far away. Over a three-month period, Sally, Wendy, and Joan between them pulled the various strings together and got the wedding organised, so that when the big day arrived, all went off smoothly and happily for well over one hundred invited guests. Wendy, the bride, the apple of my eye, the one who has always been able to charm anything she wanted out of me, looked radiant. She and I waited for the antique Rolls Royce to return to collect us at Joan and Roy's house. It was the last chance for her to back out of the wedding if she wanted to, and I said as much to her as we stood in the hallway: "Are you sure you want to go ahead, Wendy?"

Two words were enough and brought tears to my eyes: "Yes, Dad."

I went to Roy's drinks trolley and poured us each a large sherry. "Here's to your future then, sweetheart," I said.

Walking down the aisle with Wendy on my arm amidst so many friends and relations made me feel so proud that I seemed ten feet tall. Marc was there waiting for her, and I knew she could not be marrying a nicer, kinder, gentler person.

The reception I remember mainly for its happy atmosphere, and then there were friends we had gathered over the years and relations whom we had rarely seen. It is a tragic fact of life that many loved relations are only seen at weddings and funerals. I am a great believer in calling on people if I happen to be in their area. If they are your friends, renewing or strengthening the ties is a pleasure for both parties, as it was at the wedding reception. We wined, we dined, we talked, we laughed, we listened to a couple of speeches, we saw the bride and groom cut the cake, and we toasted the happy couple. Finally, we saw them off in a well-decorated MG sports car for the first night of their honeymoon. We knew where that night was to be and also knew that because of nerves, they probably would have eaten very little at the reception, so we had organised some smoked salmon sandwiches and a bottle of champagne for them in their bedroom on arrival. For all of us, it had been a wonderful day.

For the next ten days, with Audrey accompanying us, we toured to the Lake District and on into Scotland, where at St Andrews we stayed for a couple of nights with an old Zambian friend, Eve Soulsby. A lecturer at the university, Eve showed us around the old town and took us to stay for a night with her mother, who lived in Braemar. We golfed on the Braemar course as well as on three of the St Andrews' courses. We watched the salmon leaping up the falls in the hills and lapped up the beauty of the Scottish Highlands on a fine day.

On the journey south, we visited some of the fine old English cathedrals and towns, and called on Berty and Sandra and their family, now living in England permanently. And so another wonderful holiday came to an end. Our life seemed to be full of happy events and interesting holidays. Long may it continue.

As had happened before and would happen again, a long spell in England had a disturbing effect on us. There was that stable environment where our children were now settled permanently, there were many of our other relatives and a growing number of friends who had returned there from Africa. There was security, law and order, routine, and yes, there was the English weather, which had played its part in our original decision to emigrate, but Malawi was changing for the worse, as less money was available for the purchase of commodities from outside the country. The currency was again devalued, so that in real terms, I was being paid less than in my previous contract, while doing far more work. My gratuity at the end of my third contract would be much less than the previous one. Burglaries were on the increase, getting to the stage of Zambia when we left there. Our house had a padlock on the gates, a security guard patrolling the garden (when he was not asleep), security lights around the house, burglar bars on the windows, burglar alarms inside. We locked the door of our bedroom and had a dog in the kitchen. Still the burglars had a go.

With the ever-increasing problems, the question remained where to go. For all its beauty on a fine summer's day, England and its cold wet weather, for much of the year, did not appeal to sun lovers like us. I searched for jobs as a pilot in various sunny climes like the British Virgin Islands, Portugal, and Cyprus, all to no avail, but as my third contract came to an end, and with only five expatriate pilots left with Air Malawi, the time had come to move on once more.

The company generously gave me a big farewell party and two carved African chiefs chairs as a memento of my nine years' service in the airline. I had no regrets. I had enjoyed all my flying, right from the start in the little Islander with its routes inside Malawi until I finished as BAC 1-11 captain on routes to Mauritius, Johannesburg, and Nairobi. I had taught a lot of the Malawian pilots to fly on the Hawker Siddeley 748 and sent two cadets solo in a Piper 140. I was confident that both parties to the contract were satisfied with the nine years.

We decided to move to Cyprus as a base, closer to England, still in the sun, where accommodation could be rented easily and where, with luck, I could write my book on Mkushi. In July 1987, we bid farewell to Malawi and our many friends left there. We were off for more new green pastures.

Chapter 14

Cyprus

Cyprus, the sun-drenched island at the eastern end of the Mediterranean, had left us with happy vibes since our holiday there with Wendy. Sally and I had also managed a few more days there en route to England on another occasion, at which time we looked closely into the possibility of living there. Unlike so many countries which require permits and a check of your grandmother's police record, Cyprus would allow you to stay for as long as you liked, provided you were not dependent on the country for support. Only selected aliens were allowed to work in the country on work permits, but for retirement, or holidays, open arms of welcome awaited you. There was plenty of accommodation available at a nominal rental, and everybody appeared friendly and able to speak English.

With all these advantages and others besides, it was not surprising that we chose to go there rather than back to England when we left Malawi. I had written to Cyprus Airways, hoping to get a job with them, but had the reply that they had enough pilots and were not looking for any more.

That did not deter us from our plans, and we ended up in our friend's flat in Paphos, with a number of suitcases while fifty-six boxes of our goods and chattels were due to follow on via Zambia (when there was room on a Zambian Airways plane). As we did not have a plentiful supply of money available, we had decided to take with us as much of our belongings as we could, rather than have the expense of having to purchase in Cyprus items such as we had discarded in Malawi. The cost of repatriating our personal effects being born by Air Malawi, it did not cost us anything to take extra with us.

It was hot in Paphos when we arrived there, an unusual heat wave being blamed as the cause. According to Sally, I was very unsettled, perhaps thinking of where we should start looking for a rented house to settle in, perhaps wondering what I was going to do in the future. Wondering also whether fifty-five years was too early for retirement and if our funds would last out as long as necessary. I had had a busy time packing all our boxes and suitcases before leaving Malawi, getting Inca into a kennel prior to his being flown to Cyprus with the appropriate papers, and getting the necessary tickets and bookings for the flight to Larnaca.

Now, in need of a rest, I was not on holiday. It was all rather confusing until Sally pressured me to contact Cyprus Airways again and to go and see the chief pilot face to face. We had by now purchased a new car, a Suzuki Swift, so we drove to Larnaca next morning specifically to enable me to call on the operations manager or chief pilot of Cyprus Airways at the airport.

In fact, I was put in touch with Captain Johnny Walker, the fleet captain of the BAC 1-11 aircraft.

Johnny was a small, dapper man of fifty-seven, with white wavy hair above an alert face with penetrating eyes. He left you in no doubt that he knew what he was talking about and what he was doing. He held a position of responsibility with the airline and was prepared to go to the limits to ensure that he did not miss golden opportunities when they were presented to him. In my case, I had not got the BAC 1-11 on my English licence, so he said, "Get it on your licence and come back and see me."

Next evening, I flew to England with my English and Malawian licences and current log books, had my English licence endorsed, and returned the following day. On my arrival at Larnaca, I left a photocopy of my licence on Captain Walker's desk with a contact phone number in Paphos. That was on the Saturday afternoon. On

Tuesday morning at ten o'clock, I had an interview with various representatives of Cyprus Airways. At one o'clock, I had a flight test in a BAC 1-11, and that evening I was back on an Airbus 310 for London to get my licence endorsed once again with the BAC 1-11, this time in Group 1, which authorises a pilot to fly in command of the aircraft. I now found myself unexpectedly employed in Cyprus with their national airline.

We soon found suitable accommodation in Larnaca, where Inca would be able to join us after his quarantine period in Nicosia, and where our fifty-six boxes could be stowed until they were unpacked. At the same time, I found my way along the many routes which the airline operated with the BAC 1-11: Dubai, Kuwait, Jeddah, Tel Aviv, Cairo, Athens, Thessaloniki, and many others. I found that I had arrived at Johnny Walker's office at just the right time, as two of his training captains had just left and two more were leaving in two weeks' time. Within a few weeks, I was made a line training captain, which meant I would be training pilots along the routes of the BAC 1-11.

Then started five of the most enjoyable years of flying that I could ever have hoped for. With the airline expanding with new Airbus 310s and 320s, many new pilots were needed. These were Cypriots joining the company as newly qualified commercial pilots, with a minimum amount of experience. They were entering as first officers onto the BAC 1-11, where Johnny led his team of four in training them until they were able to move up from the BAC 1-11 onto the bigger Airbuses. Johnny and Ernie Constable did the initial training on the simulator, followed by a few circuits in the aircraft, and then handed them onto Dick Plackett and myself for further training with passengers in the plane behind us. It was demanding, interesting flying, interspersed with command courses to upgrade senior first officers to captain or do periodic line checks on captains operating the BAC 1-11s. We all had a very happy working relationship, knowing that we could rely 100 percent on our compatriots doing their share of the job efficiently and well.

Our trainees, the Cypriots, were a joy to teach. What they lacked in ability at the start, they made up for in their keenness to learn. Any information that we could give them relating to flying was soaked up like a sponge. They were always prompt, cheerful, willing, and hard working, and what is more, a great many were excellent pilots. In the five years as a line training captain, sixty-five pilots passed through our hands, mostly from their initial conversion onto the plane. To do this, I found I flew some six hundred and fifty hours each year.

Once again, my instructional qualifications had got me into a job where I would otherwise have failed. I was able to remain in that job until my retirement at age sixty, by which time most of the expatriate pilots had left, their places being taken by-now-qualified Cypriot pilots. The Cypriots were very possessive of all jobs in the country, expecting to have two jobs each, and fought hard to exclude anyone from outside of the country. Internal battles to promote unqualified pilots as instructors were always fought by Johnny, who kept all the company political rows away from his team, leaving us free to concentrate on our training. As I did not have the final say on a trainee gaining his qualification as first officer, the final flight check being done by Johnny or Ernie after a recommendation from Dick or myself, I was able to be completely honest and forthright with the trainees. I had nothing to lose, and they knew it, so we all got on exceptionally well and made a great many enjoyable flights in all weathers, all around the sparkling Mediterranean.

During our first two years, we rented a lovely new house, with marble floors and a large undercover area, where our boxes were initially stored. Being a holiday island not too far from England, we had a large number of visitors who came to spend one or two weeks with us. While it may have been hard work, with some it was lovely having them and showing them the delights of the island. Paphos was always a favourite spot for a day trip, with the many places of interest in that pretty little town, the Byzantine Castle and the Roman mosaics always worth showing off to visitors. Kurion on the way there and the lovely scenery of the nearby coastline were ideal stopping places en route. Another day would be taken up visiting the mountain area of Troodos, which was lovely and cool during the hot summer months, or covered with snow during the winter. The wild flowers in the Spring are always a show throughout the island, and I have a photograph of my sister Margaret, from Australia, who spent a week with us, sitting in a field of yellow flowers, with the traditional olive tree in the background. Margaret enjoyed Cyprus with its many archaeological sites and more recent history, like the Kolossi Castle, which is in such good condition.

During the visits of our friends and relatives, I would continue with my work, if necessary swapping a flight with Dick if there was a clash of interests. It was a great pleasure working in such a friendly environment and, what is more, being paid real money at the same time.

The real money allowed us to purchase a dream of an apartment right on the beach by a small fishing harbour in Larnaca: only five minutes from the airfield and work. The lovely house we had been living in was too big for just the two of us, so we had spent a considerable time trying to find a smaller one in a place with a nice view. Unfortunately, all those we looked at were too small to live in. They would be fine for a few weeks' holiday but too cramped for permanent residency. Then we started considering places to purchase, thinking they might be bigger. Just before our wedding anniversary, I went to a new block of apartments which was still being constructed. I enquired the price and on being told was also informed that I could pay over seven years. I did not look at the apartments at that time but went home and worked out the figures, comparing those of buying an apartment against those of renting one. I did not say anything to Sally, as she had already had a mild dispute with the estate agent on a previous occasion, but I went back by myself later for a look at the flats on offer. The second one I looked at seemed to have all that we wanted: two bedrooms, large living room with open plan kitchen, one and a half bathrooms, and a veranda which looked over the gardens to the sand and the sea. Just to the left was the active fishing harbour. In the bay were large ships waiting to go into the port; in the distance was the coastline of Dhekelia, leading around to Cape Greco, and flying past about half a mile out to sea were the planes on their approach to the airport.

To me, it seemed perfect. I reserved the flat for a week and arranged to have the key available to show the apartment to Sally two days later, on our wedding anniversary (I did not want her to see the agent). When the day came, I led Sally to see the apartment, not telling her what it was she was about to see. After a couple of decoy stops, I led her to the proposed apartment, where after showing her around, I said we could afford to buy it if she thought it was what we wanted. It was so lovely and of course so unexpected that she was overwhelmed, and we were both in each other's arms in tears a few moments later.

Needless to say, we started moving our things into Castella Court a few weeks later. We had to slim down on many of our belongings, as not everything would fit in, but we ended up with a much more practical home for just the two of us. The biggest parting was with Inca, who spent some months with us in our new home and was as good as any dog could be. But as Wendy put it so well, he was like a walking wall! About this time, Sally got arthritis extremely badly, particularly in her hands. She felt that she could not safely manage Inca when I was away for the occasional night stop, so we were forced to look around for a good home for him. We were fortunate to find one with friends who lived on a large property in a small country village. Fond of dogs and birds, they welcomed Inca and gave him a loving home, where he was spoilt like a child. I missed him greatly, with his intelligence and lovely temperament. Even when I visited him several years later, he remembered me and spoke to me as though we had only just parted. Parting can be such sweet sorrow.

Living beside the sea with its ever-changing scenery was fascinating, with always something to look at, from busy little fishing boats going out of harbour into rough seas, to topless sun bathers soaking up the sun on the sand. I felt it essential to have a boat and learn to sail. Several other expatriate pilots were of a similar mind, and soon three of us had a partnership in a Stella cruiser, named *Orion*. A wooden craft just eight metres long, it was an ideal boat to learn to sail, and it gave me a lot of fun taking out friends and visitors into the Larnaca Bay for a couple of hours of gentle sailing. We were normally equipped with some beers or a bottle of wine and would be back in the marina before the wind got up too strongly, as it often did in the afternoons. Once, Sally and I had sailed across the bay to a restaurant beside a small fishing shelter. We had lunch there, and a strong wind was blowing into the harbour mouth as we left. It took two attempts to get out of the harbour as the under-powered engine could not make much headway against the wind and waves. Tacking back to the marina took us four hours in storm-tossed seas. The boat was terrific, but the conditions a bit much for novices like us. Right at the start, Sally was saying, "I'm never coming sailing with you again," to which I replied, "Don't give me pressure now, I've got enough to do!" It was a long, hard, bumpy ride home, and thereafter, I always headed upwind at the start of a sail to ensure an easy return.

A part-time resident of Castella Court who also had a boat was John Aston. He was a widower who had flown as a captain with British Airways for many years and later with Air Lanka. He became a great friend of ours, with his easygoing nature and friendly disposition. His boat was a forty-six-foot Mackintosh called *Waypoint Six,* which he and a partner had had built in Taiwan and then sailed to Cyprus. It was a magnificent boat with a powerful engine, air conditioning, fridges, roller reefing on the foresail, and hot or cold shower facilities at the top of the steps after a swim. It was sheer luxury and sailed like a dream. John would come out with me on *Orion*, but more frequently Sally and I would join John and half a dozen other good friends on his boat for a day's outing, which would include lunch, drinks, a siesta, and a swim.

With our life being one long holiday and trips to England for simulator checks every six months, we hardly needed to go away to anywhere else. But on the evening when Marc had asked to marry Wendy, he told me of a trip he had made in the Himalayas, trekking to the base of Mount Everest. My ears had pricked up immediately at information on such an excursion, and on the threat of not allowing him to marry my daughter, I made him promise to give me the opportunity of going with him if he ever considered doing the trip again. When he enquired whether I might be interested in joining Wendy and himself some six months later, I jumped at the chance. Plans were made, dates were fixed, leave was booked, and as much information as possible was obtained on likely conditions as well as the equipment necessary to make life bearable in the cold of altitudes up to eighteen thousand feet. Sally decided immediately that it was not the sort of thing she wanted to do and was happy to stay in the warm comfort of Cyprus.

I started a fitness course, walking for many miles each week. I used the stairs rather than the lifts to our third-floor home. Once a week, I walked up and down a nearby mountain, Stavrovouni, a good testing climb. With knapsack on my back weighted with a video camera, on loan to me from John Aston, and strong mountain boots on my feet, I could comfortably climb and descend the hill in an hour and a half. Before the day of departure, I could do it twice in three hours and felt fit enough to tackle Mount Everest itself.

The Himalayas

We all met up in Kathmandu in Nepal, where we spent two days looking around the various temples and markets of this unusual town. We walked just about everywhere, filming the interesting way of life, which was so foreign to us. Once we went in one of the three-wheeled taxis, and I was able to film some of the exciting ride as, with hooter honking, it threaded its way through the crowds, bicycles, cows, and water buffaloes, reminding me of Hyderabad.

We were in the hands of a travel group who briefed us on the trip we were making and introduced us to three other men, all Americans, who were the remaining part of our group. One was a correspondent for an American travel magazine, one a presidential doctor with a diamond-studded front tooth, and the other a seventy-two-year-old retired gentleman, who spent his time visiting interesting parts of the world.

Our trip started with a flight in a twin Otter into a tiny mountain strip at Lukla, eight thousand feet up, on the side of a mountain. There we disembarked with our kit bags and haversacks on a cold, cloudy morning, when not a lot could be seen. We were in fact lucky to get in there, as many trekkers were waiting to leave and had been waiting for several days.

We had the first of many glasses of hot sweet tea as our Sherpas loaded the various kit-bags on to our yaks, which had already been loaded with our tents, food, cooking utensils, and the numerous other articles essential for camping in the mountains. We walked only a few miles that day but did experience our first suspension bridge across the rapidly flowing Dudh Khosi River. About a hundred yards long, this flimsy-looking structure moved not only up and down as you crossed, but also from side to side. The handrail, if such it could be called, was at the height of your knees in places, so that a loss of balance could easily have you in the cold river fifty feet below. We came across many of these bridges in the next two weeks, each with a subtle variation to keep us alert. One useful lesson was to make sure a convoy of yaks were not about to come across in the opposite direction to you. They were very adept at crossing and uncaring that there was not room to pass trekkers coming in the opposite direction.

Camping under canvas in sleeping bags, in temperatures which went down to minus twenty degrees Celsius, took some getting used to. I had a tent to myself, while Wendy and Marc shared theirs. Even so, there was very little room. There was a knack to doing everything while sitting or lying down. In low temperatures, you learned quickly, as I did when trying to wash my feet in the small bowl of washing water which arrived morning and evening. If your foot caught the side of the bowl, you could be sure all the water would empty inside the tent, just where you did not want it. That of course was just a small part of the problem, because if you left your towel outside (or even inside) to dry, it would be as stiff as a board a little later. Drying one's face on a stiff frozen towel is very ineffective.

Each day took us up higher and higher into the mountains, with the grandeur of the greatest scenery on earth being gradually unveiled to us. The weather was excellent, so that Everest, Lhotse, and Nuptse were easily visible from Namche Bazaar just two days into our trek. We quite happily covered only the ground set by our leading Sherpa, as it was essential to acclimatise to the altitude as we ascended. Two German and one Japanese trekkers had died the previous week from the ever-threatening altitude sickness, which could attack you like the bends of a deep-sea diver, unless you gradually got used to the differing pressure and rarefied air.

We were happy not to travel long distances too, as the trail (besides being forever uphill) was narrow, rough, and rocky. On many occasions, when we thought we had completed a good climb, the track took us back down to the river, and we had to climb all over again on the other side. There was nothing smooth about the track, and when we stood to one side to allow yaks to come past, we could have easily dropped off the edge onto the rocky riverbed several hundred feet below. Under such conditions, as on the suspension bridges, one learns fast.

At midday, we would stop for an hour or so, relaxing on some nice comfortable rocks, where pats of yak dung were often spread around us, drying in the sun. Surprisingly, good food was served up to us by our cooks at midday and in the evening. Yak steaks, curry and rice, omelettes with tinned sausages, spam, and chips, all washed down with a plentiful supply of tea, coffee, or hot chocolate, were some of our many delights. Breakfast was generally porridge and biscuits, with the usual beverages.

Our tents were erected for us by our Sherpas, with a larger tent for our wicker table and stools, where we had our evening meals by the light of a pressure lamp (which had seen better years). We seldom stayed up late, as we were tired from the day's trek, and it was getting ever colder, the ice crystals glinting like stars on the inside of the tent. Similarly, our stools were not designed for relaxation. Were we missing the comforts of our normal way of life?

One comfort missed was that of a proper toilet. We had a little blue tent which surrounded a small hole in the ground, perhaps nine inches deep. That was our communal toilet, dug each day near our camping area. I was caught out on the first occasion by stooping down too low, so that I would hit the target. The problem then was trying to get up again without the aid of anything to pull on, with knees which had all but given up. Yes, I missed the comforts of home and have ever since appreciated a good comfortable toilet seat.

Ten days after leaving Lukla, we set off at five in the morning for Kala Pattar, our target destination at 18,300 feet, leaving our tents at Lobuche, whither we would return that night. It was to be the hardest day of our lives.

The first hour in the cold half-light took us gently up the side of the Khumbu glacier, of which we could only see the rocky sides reaching maybe one hundred feet above us. We crossed numerous frozen streams and then started climbing in earnest, up and down over the moraine of another glacier, up several hundred feet, along a rough, rugged trail strewn with boulders of all shapes and sizes, then up again. It seemed endless, and as we got to the top, it undulated up and down for what again seemed forever, until gradually the track changed; we had a bit of level ground and even some downhill. Continuing over very rugged terrain, it led us to Gorak Shep, an outpost of three small stone cottages, one of which went under the exalted name of the Hilton Tearoom. We stopped for welcome cups of hot sweet tea served in thick, chipped glasses and sat outside in the sun, getting our breath back while studying our final climb. The Hilton Hotel group might like to own an outpost on the Roof of the World, but I doubt they would ever be able to produce tea of the unique delicious flavour such as we tasted at Gorak Shep. It was unforgettably good after such an arduous climb, and there was still more climbing to come.

We were now at about seventeen thousand feet and had the final ascent in front of us. It started with a steep climb, eased off to a steady climb, and ended with the steepest bit yet. Boy, was it tough! Never have I experienced such a trial, and I did not realise until the last twenty yards – some two hours later – that I would make it.

Gasping for breath, with stops every five yards or so to gather breath, and looking down to place a foot in the best spot each time, I would say that the last forty-five minutes was done on sheer guts, coupled with persuasion from Marc. He had suffered from a headache right up to the last day but was now back to normal and quite rightly feeling on top of the world. Without his encouragement, Wendy and I might have stopped at a lower level. However, make it to the top we did, and we counted it a great achievement. Our reward was the magnificent all-round view of the greatest mountains on earth, interspersed with glaciers and ice packs. The whole panorama glistened in the snow as the sun shone down from an almost-clear-blue sky. It was fantastic, and the video camera I had humped all the way in my backpack worked a treat in recording the wonderful vista.

We ate our packed lunches and sipped some water to prevent dehydration, as we drank in the view and congratulated each other on getting there. Then after about half an hour, we reluctantly started down the slope and on the long slog back to Lobuche, where we arrived in the late afternoon, totally exhausted. What a day! Round our fire of burning yak dung that evening, we celebrated with a tot of whisky, which Marc had carefully carried with him for the occasion. Life was great, and as we started wending our way back towards Lukla, we started to think of meals and wines and hot baths which would once again be available to us when we got back to civilisation. Even though the downhill still appeared to have overmuch uphill in it, we made it back to our starting point eight days later, on my fifty-seventh birthday. Wendy arranged with the head Sherpa for a special supper for us: roast chicken and roast potatoes, followed by birthday cake. The thought was great but the chicken was so tough, we reckoned it must have run all the way from Kala Pattar. The cake too took some eating, but as a result, everyone got a piece. We were all back in one piece to where we started; that was the main thing.

There was a certain sadness about leaving the awesome region with its raw magnificent grandeur. We had learned a little about it, not least that if you venture into that area, you do so not on your own terms, but on the terms of the mountains. Fitness is not sufficient to survive, it has to be combined with that inner determination to keep going and conquer through thick and thin. Was it worth it? Most certainly yes, even though it half-killed me with the effort and the extreme cold. We had seen at first-hand the greatest mountains on this planet, in all their magnificence. The challenge of getting to Kala Pattar had been accepted and will ever be looked on as being one of the hardest things any of us will ever do in our lives.

While I shall always look back with pride on my achievement, I shall also feel very humble, as only one can who has faced up to the mountains and valleys of the Himalayas. Thereafter, I thought I would be more content to sit and perhaps write, rather than set out tilting at windmills.

A week later, I was back to earth in the simulator in London, striving to keep it airborne with a fire in one engine and my thoughts elsewhere.

Sally's arthritis quietened down or was brought under control about now by a Cypriot specialist in rheumatology. She got back the use of her hands, although never as strongly as before. She continues to have flare-ups for no apparent reason, which leave her hands and arms almost useless and in continual pain. As an occupation twice a week, Sally helped out in the thrift shop on the Sovereign Base Area at Dhekelia. The wives of the soldiers based there were able to sell unwanted items of clothing or children's toys, prams, and a variety of other items, which were then purchased by others. A small percentage of the price went to the Army Benevolent Fund or indirectly back to the families on the base.

Sally also started recycling Christmas and greetings cards, using selected used cards, from which the picture was cut out and pasted onto a new base card. Christmas greetings would already be printed inside the Christmas cards, but the greeting in the others would either be written by me calligraphically or copied by Sally from the original, using an illuminated frame. Several thousand cards have been made and sold each year, raising over three thousand pounds for her charity, Arthritis Research .

Although we were regular supporters of the Garrison Church of St George at Dhekelia, where Sally added her voice to the choir, as I led the congregation in opposition, much of my charity work was directed towards the Freemasons, which I had joined in Malawi. I had found the organisation to be well worthwhile, both as a source for good in this troubled world, and the Lodges were centres of friendship wherever one might find oneself on the earth's surface. Although much of what was given to our charities in the lodge was directed at Freemason families, it soon became obvious that it was not only wives and children of deceased Masons who were the beneficiaries, but also hundreds of other charities and worthwhile causes. For us to have a meeting once a month and to raise some money for others in that social way was to my mind beneficial to us all.

So with flying, boating, church, Freemasons meetings, and other social occasions, our lives were happily full. I did not think we had room for anything else until Tim and Sue Bolt came on the scene. Tim came to join Cyprus Airways from Dan Air, with whom he had been flying for fourteen years all over Europe. Like myself, he had learnt to fly in the Royal Navy, where he had spent twenty years of his life, ending up flying Sea Vixens as commanding officer of 893 Squadron. Strangely, our paths had not crossed, but we had other acquaintances in common. Now in his mid-fifties and losing a little of his hair, he was full of bounce, especially where parties were concerned. One of his favourite drinks was the Naval speciality of the Horse's Neck, consisting of brandy and ginger ale, although Tim was never too concerned about the latter.

Sue, his pretty wife, he had rescued from the Rock of Gibraltar in his youthful days. She quickly found her feet in Cyprus, getting herself fully involved in her painting of local scenes with the art group and playing bridge in earnest with several bridge schools. Tim and Sue found the social life in Larnaca very much to their liking, as were many of the local taverns, especially the Flamingos Restaurant at nearby Tekke, which was a favourite watering hole of a great many Larnaca residents. Between them, they added a lot of impetus to the social whirl and were always great fun to be with.

It was Tim who got me back to playing golf. The only course near Larnaca was on the Sovereign Base Area at Dhekelia, and it left a lot to be desired as a golf course. Oiled sand on concrete-hard bases and called "browns" in lieu of greens, stony fairways with sparse areas of grass, rubber mats to tee off instead of nicely trimmed grass tables, and pylons alongside fairways meant it was more of an obstacle course than a golf course. I had played there several times when I first arrived in Cyprus but decided the sea was more attractive. Now Tim, in need of a companion to play with, persuaded me to have another round or two at Dhekelia. I was pleased to find the course had improved a bit and that I had been missing my golf. Soon we had John Aston joining us, as it became a regular event, with some cut-throat matches and a lot of banter and gamesmanship. Fortunately, as the experienced golfer of the three of us, I was the one to set the handicaps and give away the strokes, which was always a hilariously contentious issue.

It wasn't gamesmanship in Kuwait, one of our regular destinations in the BAC 1-11, when Saddam Hussein of Iraq invaded the country. The threat of retaliation, together with the build-up of armed forces to push the invaders out of the oil-rich state, was ineffectual. The use of chemical and bacteriological weapons of war, threatened by Hussein, kept the forces at bay until the middle of January 1991, when the demons of all-out warfare were unleashed.

Cyprus was not over-far from the conflagration. The Sovereign Base Areas were used as staging posts, as well as information gatherers from the permanent listening posts installed there. Insurance companies named Cyprus as being in the war zone as far as tourists to the island were concerned, and as a result, Cyprus Airways was affected: Flights were reduced and other routes cancelled. Aircrew were encouraged to use up whatever leave was outstanding, as half the pilots could manage the remaining schedules comfortably.

Just at the critical time, we had an invitation to the wedding of Margaret and Cyril's eldest son Glenn, to be held near Adelaide in Australia on 16 March.

Australia is an awfully long way from Europe, and although we had thought of going there a number of times, we had been put off by the cost and the distance involved. Now, however, we had time available and passenger loads on flights were generally depressed due to the Gulf War, so that we would be assured of seats on rebate tickets. What is more, we now had a great incentive to go there, not having had the opportunity previously of going to our niece Joy's wedding.

After a little discussion, we decided we would go and see how they lived down under and represent the rest of the family at the wedding. Accordingly, on 1 March, we went by Lufthansa to Singapore, where we broke the long journey with a three-day stopover. The floral display of orchids which met us at the airport arrival hall will long remain in our memory, as will the cleanliness of this beautiful, green, flowery city. We visited as many of the tourist spots as we could in the time available and were impressed by everything. A Chinese art exhibition was displaying a vast selection of jade carvings, while farther afield were exotic gardens with pagodas and bridges such as you see on porcelain tea cups and dishes. At Newton Circus, the centre of hundreds of stalls of succulent foods, we were tempted to taste a wide variety of strange dishes We even had an oyster omelette, which I would never have dreamt to be possible.

We flew on to Melbourne, where after a few questions by the immigration authorities, they allowed us into the country. We found

Melbourne to be a warm, comfortable, old-fashioned town, giving off friendly vibes, as did Australia generally. We collected a hire car and set off slowly along the coastal route to Adelaide, stopping at every interesting spot along the way. Our previous conceptions of brash, beer-drinking, rude, unkempt Aussies, living in a litter-strewn country, without law or order, were changed overnight. We found everything to be immaculate, while the people could not have been more helpful or friendly. We were very quickly made to feel welcome and warmed to Australia more and more as the days went by. In many respects, the wide-open spaces reminded us of our years in Zambia. The challenges we had taken up in that country were the same as those being met by the Australians, and I would recommend Australia to any adventurous, industrious youngster looking for a different, uninhibited way of life.

We reached Adelaide and found Margaret and Cyril waiting for us at their homestead in Mount Barker. Margaret and later Glenn had both visited us in Cyprus a few years before, but Cyril we had not seen since our family reunion nearly fifteen years ago. A week with them was barely long enough to get past the stage of being strangers, renewing their acquaintance and progressing to family confidences and letting down one's hair. But chatter we did, until we knew more about each other's way of life: the good things and the bad, the hopes and fears of the past and the future. When we left for our return to Cyprus, it was like old times once more, and we were sad to part after this brief renewal of our family ties. Before that came about, we had all dressed in our finery for Glenn and Jeanette's lovely wedding. Any final impressions of uncouth Australians were dispelled at this joyous gathering of their friends and relatives from the local area. They were well dressed and well behaved, although we were puzzled by one incident. When the best man was making his speech, he mentioned that the bride, Jeanette, had lost her car keys, whereupon nearly every man present held up a rattling bunch of keys. Jeanette looked even more beautiful as she blushed.

We enjoyed the occasion to such an extent that we got hopelessly lost on our way back to the homestead from the reception, and Margaret and Cyril, who were leaving half an hour after us, got home first.

Before leaving Adelaide, we looked up Stan and Midge Borthwick, who had been our good friends at Lossiemouth in Navy days. Stan was just recovering from a heart by-pass operation and was looking rather weak as a result. Midge looked the same as ever, with her lovely, big brown eyes. We had kept in touch each year at Christmas and could not pass by without seeing them. One other face from the past was Alan Carter, who had been a friend of mine at junior school. By pure coincidence, Cyril had been filling up Alan's Rolls Royce one day at his garage and chatting away, as Cyril is wont to do. He asked Alan whereabouts in England he came from. When he discovered it was Northchurch near Berkhamsted, he asked if he knew of the Jenkins family. To Alan's affirmative reply, Cyril pointed to Margaret in the garage office and said that she was the youngest of the family. This had happened about a year previously. During our visit, we spoke face to face with each other after a forty-seven-year gap! Life is full of surprises.

We returned slowly to Melbourne for our return flight, spending our last day in the city. The morning was passed mainly around the shops and markets of the town as Sally feasted her eyes on the good things that shops always have on offer.

In the afternoon, I managed to get her away from the shops to the National Gallery, where I was able to feast my eyes on the great array of masterpieces by so many of the world's greatest artists. I was amazed at the tremendous collection housed in this gallery, which we had come across almost by accident. It certainly meant that our most enjoyable visit ended on a high note, as I have sung the praises of that gallery ever since.

A few days before we left Australia, the Gulf War ended, with all the oil wells afire, belching thick, black smoke into the atmosphere. If it had not started, I doubt if we would have gone to Australia. I'm very glad we did.

Back in England, Ian continued to enjoy his career in the Metropolitan Police. We tried to encourage him to study for the exams for promotion to sergeant, but to no avail. He assured us he knew what he was doing, so we respected his judgement. He became engaged to Kate, a delightful, slightly built nursing sister, who was loved and respected by the children in the wards in which she worked so efficiently. Kate and Ian had been living together for some time, as was the way amongst youngsters in this ever-changing world. There was no doubt that Kate adored Ian and was good for him, while he in turn cherished her.

They had an unusual amount of misfortune in their first few years together, starting with Kate's engagement ring. Bought at a jewellers in Hatton Garden, it was left with them to be altered to the correct size. On its return by post, it was lost or stolen, and it was many weeks before they were able to get a replacement from the shop, which in turn was waiting to be paid out by the insurance company. As the wedding day approached some months later, Ian's car broke down while he was busily rushing to make some arrangements for the big day. This necessitated some expensive repairs, yet the car broke down again soon afterwards.

Ian and Kate organised a superb wedding near Gloucester, where Kate's widowed mother, Frances, lived. Ian had planned that we meet her and her sons on the evening before the wedding, but last-minute arrangements meant that did not happen. We met up instead in the church vestry, where both bride and groom's mothers eyed their almost identical pink suits in the way that women do.

The day of the wedding was cold but bright and enjoyed by everybody. As usual, it went past in a haze of meeting people, listening to speeches, watching the cake being cut, and most importantly, toasting the happy couple. They departed in a car well decorated with balloons, tin cans, streamers, and "Just Married" placards, as a crowd of well-wishers waved them on their way. They were not leaving for their honeymoon until two or three days later, during which time Ian lost his platinum wedding ring and the boiler burst in Pendle Cottage, their lovely little home. A difficult start to their married life; it could only get better.

Kate later succeeded where we had failed to persuade Ian to do his sergeant's exams, as he did, and since then, he has passed all the necessary exams to become an inspector. They have turned Pendle Cottage into an immaculate home, where Alexander Richard came on the scene on 8 January 1994. What a wonderful little grandson he is. It is the pull from him and his two cousins that is responsible for our reconsidering our exile. Perhaps the time is coming for us to return from distant lands to that of our infant nurture.

Chapter 15

Retirement

There are some magical ages in life which appear to be very different from the rest. In airline flying, sixty was this special age beyond which you were not considered competent to command an airliner, although there was talk that this age limit would be raised. With me, my last flight as captain was to Thessalonika, Greece, on November 28, 1992. It was a thoroughly enjoyable flight past many of the delightful Greek islands, which at night look like jewels sparkling on a velvet background. I called farewell to some of the air traffic controllers who had kept me clear of other aircraft along the airways of the Mediterranean over the last five years, thanking them for doing their job so well. I knew they would appreciate a few words of thanks, as they control so many lives by their vigilance yet rarely meet or speak to any of the pilots except on business.

Many of my friends and compatriots were awaiting my return (on schedule) to Larnaca where I greased the BAC 1-11 onto the runway in my accustomed manner. I bid farewell to my passengers and my usual excellent cabin crew as I was wheeled away through the customs check in a wheelchair, with a placard which stated "Retiring." Tim Bolt recorded everything on his video. Inside the operations block, where I had briefed and debriefed my crews on so many occasions, sandwiches, farewell cake, champagne, and orange juice were available to celebrate my last flight.

Sally was there to hear the fleet manager, Bill MacDonald, say a few kind words about my service to Cyprus Airways, whilst I in turn said how enjoyable my time with the airline had been. It was one of those occasions where emotions are mixed.

I was happy, as always, to be among my friends and sad to think I was about to leave some of them for the last time. I shall always have great respect for crews of airliners, knowing the work that they do in all sorts of conditions. Their flight deck crew, in particular, are so well trained and disciplined that it is rare to find an unprofessional occurrence. The relationship with ground controllers was always respectful and polite, even under the most stressful of conditions, such as approaching Athens Airport during the busy summer season. A flight is judged by the passengers on the standard of the cabin crew, who are expected to be servants of all at all times. Dealing with people is probably the hardest job going, and to look after hundreds for hours on end can frustrate anybody, yet I never heard any complaints from my cabin staff. They also had to look after the two of us in the cockpit, ensuring we had different meals and did not suffer from food poisoning at the same time. Not that that was likely, as our meals were always excellent and plentiful. Occasionally, we could smell halloumi cheese and olives being grilled in the ovens. Some minutes later, we would be served with grilled cheese and sliced tomato on a fresh bread roll with hot, fat olives alongside (a Cypriot speciality which was not served to the passengers). My flying days were full of such incidents, which I will ever remember with happiness.

Sally and I drove home, where Ian and Kate and Wendy and Marc awaited us. They had all come over from England at Sally's instigation for my birthday, which was celebrated with a big party at the Flamingos Restaurant next evening. We had a theme of a "Shipwreck on a Desert Island," so that our sixty or so friends who came to join us that evening arrived in the clothes they were wearing when the ship went down. We have had many excellent parties over the years, but that one I shall always remember as being one of the best. The spread of food put on for us by Peter, the

Flamingos owner, was plentiful and delicious. Tim Bolt was busy with his video, recording the evening for us. The final great surprise came next day, when I went to settle the account, only to find there was nothing to pay. Sally, unbeknown to me, had already paid the bill from her savings account, thus making it an even nicer party for me to remember.

That same week, I was installed as Master of the Lord Kitchener Masonic Lodge, a position I held for the next two years. With the work involved in my Masonic activities as Master, I was well pleased that I had retired from my regular job first.

A week after the party, during which I completed my leaving routine with Cyprus Airways, Sally and I set off on our travels once again, this time back to South Africa. Our main object was to spend Christmas with Audrey and Bill at Sedgefield, a little village on the coast near George, where they were now retired.

Our plans took in visits to favourite places like Stellenbosch, where we spent over a week in a small friendly hotel, and of course to our many friends in the area. John and Margaret Fletcher, two ex-Malawi friends, had met us at the airport and taken us to their home for the first few days. John was a small, quiet man who was keen on his gardening, at which he was obviously as good as he was with figures, for he was financial controller of a group of hotels in and around Cape Town. Margaret was yet another of our friends with artistic talents; whether it was water colours, oils, or painting porcelain dishes, her flair was fantastic. To watch her paint was fascinating, as she was so relaxed and almost casual about her actions, which produced such professional results. They lived in a big house in the suburbs of Cape Town, where the drift of the rural African population towards the big cities was being felt by the increased number of burglaries. Alarms, burglar bars, locked doors were all much in evidence, a reminder of how fortunate we are at present in Cyprus.

At Stellenbosch, Bruce and Belinda visited us for tea with their two young sons (one of whom was tragically to die of a brain tumour about a year later). We drove to Franschoek to spend an evening with John and Carol Dendy-Young in their thatched house near their restaurant, La Petite Ferme. Glenn Curtis came from

Hermanus for a game of golf with me and invited us to stay with him and his new wife, Di, a few days later. Norma had been killed about two years previously, not far from Hermanus, when the plane in which she was flying to Johannesburg with her in-laws, her son Andrew, and his girlfriend crashed into the top of one of the hills, killing all on board. Andrew, our godson, had been the pilot.

While at Hermanus, apart from some more golf, we went fishing for crayfish. That was quite an exciting morning, dropping the nets in the sea area just where the waves curled over to break. The swell must have been all of fifteen feet high. The end result was delicious crayfish for each of us at supper that evening.

Other old friends we met up with from Mkushi days were Ruth and Dick Merryweather, one of the first to depart from the area, and Erica and Murray Herron. Talk of old times flourished over glasses of South African wine. We had all aged, experiencing other ways of life and both good and bad fortune since our last meetings. We had also received news of each other over the years from contact with other friends, so we were happy to meet again face to face.

Christmas was another happy event. Not only were we with Audrey and Bill, but their two sons, Brian and Kevin, and daughter Brenda, with her husband Pieter, were also there. Eight of us in one house for a week! Yet we all got on magnificently, with everyone doing their fair share of the necessary work, without any planning or direction. It was like being a member of a well-rehearsed team, like poetry in motion. Church on Christmas morning was packed at each of the three Communion services. Never before had we seen so many attending church; I wondered if it was due to apprehension of the white people in South Africa for their future. Apartheid was in the process of being dismantled, and African nationalism and black majority rule was about to take its place. The transition which we had experienced in Zambia some thirty years before had finally reached the Cape. We could only hope and pray it would not be too difficult a changeover. We were glad not to be going through it again ourselves.

Back in Cyprus, I became involved in all sorts of odd jobs, from plastering ceilings, painting wooden shutters, installing fan units, and covering car parks, to a major construction of extending the

Flamingos Restaurant for Peter. That involved roofing an area forty-five feet long and eighteen feet wide and putting in ceilings, doors, and side windows, plus an ornamental-tile-roof bar at one end. Most of that I did by myself, with some assistance, when necessary, from one of the waiters or from my golfing partners when it came to putting in the ceilings. It reminded me of my building days on the farm years before, which I never expected to experience again. It took me ten weeks to finish, and I was proud of my achievement; my old skills were still there.

In the last three years, Sally and I have continued our travels, with a tour of the Czech Republic, a cruise down the Dnieper River in the Ukraine to the Black Sea, and two tours in our motor home around England, Scotland, and northern France. We have continued to look up our relatives and friends whenever we have been in their area, and as a result, we have had many happy times together. At the wedding of Sandra and Berty's son Jamie, there was a large gathering of the Mkushi clan, which included Pamela Cornhill, the lady who gave lunch to the Dooleys and ourselves during our initial visit to Mkushi so many years before. She still resides on her farm there, although her husband died many years ago, and was able to tell us of present-day Mkushi and of our other friends who were still there. It was a memorable weekend; may we have many more.

Now in Lania, this little artists village situated halfway to the hills to the north of Limassol, I come to the end of my story. Tomorrow, Wendy and Marc arrive to spend two weeks with us, accompanied by their two lovely children, Matthew, who I know, and Emmeline, whom I have only seen in photos and on video. I am sure we will have a wonderful time together.

So let me conclude by just saying this: Life is never easy or free from fears and worries. Enjoy it whenever you can, but always value your relations and friends and be true to them, as you can help each other on your way through life. They are your greatest assets.

Finally, have faith in God, as with his help, anyone can do anything.

Printed in Great Britain
by Amazon